RACING POST
CHELTENHAM FESTIVAL GUIDE 2010

Edited by Nick Pulfor

Foreword by Edward Gillespi

Contributors

Gerald Delamere
Dave Edwards
Steffan Edwards
Paul Kealy
George Kimberley
Andrew King
Jessica Lamb
Steve Mason
Rodney Masters
Kevin Morley

Ben N......
Dave Orton
Rodney Pettinga
James Pyman
Ashley Rumney
Colin Russell
Alan Sweetman
Craig Thake
David Toft
Matt Williams

Designed by David Dew

Published in 2010 by Racing Post
Compton, Newbury, Berkshire, RG20 6NL

Copyright © Racing Post 2010

A catalogue record for this book is available from the British Library.

ISBN 978-1906820336

Printed by Acorn Web, Normanton, West Yorkshire

RACING POST
PRESENTS

POUND-FOR-POUND
CHAMPION
COLUMNISTS

PAUL 'SATURDAY' NICHOLLS **&** **WILLIE 'SUNDAY' MULLINS**

 In the build-up to the Cheltenham Festival get the **exclusive** insight from the champion trainers

RACING POST
CHELTENHAM FESTIVAL 2010 OFFICIAL MEDIA PARTNER

Foreword

FINDING a winner at the Cheltenham Festival is nowhere near as challenging as is often made out. The difficulty is resisting the other 25 races. Even the most strong-willed fail to apply the rule that has kept them in funds all winter, of not arriving more than an hour before the race that interests them and leaving directly it finishes, emotionally if not physically.

Having survived on a diet of even-money favourites against a handful of opponents, you are confronted by a succession of 24-runner races with bookmakers shouting 5-1 the field. An essential part of your weaponry is a guide that reminds you how previous festivals have panned out, which trainers prove hottest in March and what form to disregard as inconsequential. Hopefully, in these pages you might find a few clues.

If proof was needed of the anticipated outcome in the battle with the bookmakers, remember it is they with whom there have been discussions regarding cash security at the end of each day, not the punters. Upwards of £1m will be bet at the course on each race, so the potential is there to make this a life-changing experience, hopefully for the better.

I envy you the contest that lies ahead. Win or lose, have a wonderful week.

Edward Gillespie
Managing Director
Cheltenham Racecourse

Views from the specialists

The Racing Post's top tipsters and form experts offer invaluable advice on betting strategy and the horses to note, while bookmakers address the key issues in our Q & A

Timing is everything

Racing Post betting editor Paul Kealy says choosing
when and where to strike bets is vital to success

IN last year's inaugural edition of this guide we had a look back at the
previous year's festival races to see where the best value was and
reached the conclusion that taking a morning price was pretty crucial
to obtaining the best value. And a similar post-mortem for the 2009
festival shows that still holds true.

Of the 26 races at last year's festival, no fewer than 17 of the
winners were available at a better morning price than they returned
across any other platform, which includes the on-course SP, Tote
return and Betfair SP.

The Betfair SP returned second best, with seven top prices, though
regular exchange punters will be aware that, unlike on the Tote, you
can take a price on Betfair at any time and doing that would have
given you an excellent chance of beating the morning prices with the
bookies.

You probably wouldn't have beaten them all, though, because with
several layers offering individual prices the morning market is highly
competitive.

What you really should not be doing under any circumstances is
having a bet at SP. A high percentage of bets are settled at SP and this
is madness for punters, especially at Cheltenham as plenty of
bookmakers (the majority last year) will be offering 'best odds
guaranteed', which means if the SP beats the morning price, you get
that instead.

SP was not the best option for any of the 26 races and, while £1 on
every winner at the best morning odds would have yielded a return of
£323.65, you'd have got back just £255.86 at SP. That's some
difference.

Talking of difference, the Tote Exacta once again hugely
outperformed the bookmakers' equivalent, the CSF, just as predicted.
It was a little skewed thanks to two monster dividends on the final
day (a £1 exacta would have returned £3,600 more than the CSF
across all races) but ignoring those two you'd still be more than £800
better off across the other 24 and overall the exacta came out top 19
times.

▸▸Non-runner no bet

Just a quick word on the much-touted 'non-runner no bet' concession,
as I got a bit of stick over this last year. Yes, it is a good concession,
but on no account should you consider it carte blanche to eschew
bigger prices about whatever you fancy for the comfort of knowing
your stake is covered if something goes wrong.

17

No fewer than
17 of the 26
winners at last
year's festival
were available
at a better
morning price
than they
returned across
any other
platform

Festival info

Opening times Most betting shops open earlier during the festival, usually at 8.30-9am

Each-way Bookmakers often extend their place terms during the festival. In the big-field handicaps, it can pay to look for firms offering a quarter the odds for the first five places. The standard each-way terms are a quarter the odds for the first four places

Early prices Be quick if you want to take an advertised price on the morning of the race – most firms hold their prices for a maximum of 15 minutes when their shops open and some offer no guarantee

Best odds Several firms offer 'best odds guaranteed', which means they will match the SP if you have taken an early price and your selection wins at bigger odds

Free bets Many bookmakers offer free bets for new customers during the festival, which can boost your betting bank, but remember to check the terms and conditions. For a great range of free bets, go to racingpost.com/news/free_bets.sd

Specials A host of special bets – some weird, some wonderful – are available at the festival. Among the vast range of specials at last year's festival were top trainer and jockey, the number of Irish winners, which race would produce the biggest winning distance and even which day would be the windiest

WHERE THE BEST VALUE WAS AT THE 2009 FESTIVAL

	Best morning odds	SP	Tote SP	Betfair SP
Go Native	11-1	12-1	10.8-1	**17-1**
Forpadydeplasterer	**10-1**	8-1	7.3-1	7.84-1
Wichita Lineman	**7-1**	5-1	3.7-1	5.97-1
Punjabi	**28-1**	22-1	24.8-1	25.42-1
Garde Champetre	**4-1**	7-2	7-2	3.77-1
Quevega	**3-1**	2-1	2-1	9-4
Chapoturgeon	15-2	8-1	7.4-1	**10.86-1**
Kayf Aramis	**33-1**	16-1	20.2-1	19-1
Imperial Commander	13-2	6-1	**6.8-1**	6.58-1
Big Buck's	**13-2**	6-1	5.7-1	6.4-1
Something Wells	33-1	33-1	**48.7-1**	41-1
Character Building	20-1	16-1	**21.5-1**	20-1
Tricky Trickster	**20-1**	11-1	11.4-1	12.34-1
Mikael D'Haguenet	**4-1**	5-2	2.6-1	2.69-1
Cooldine	**9-2**	9-4	2.4-1	2.89-1
Master Minded	2-5	4-11	2-5	**0.41-1**
Ninetieth Minute	**18-1**	14-1	12.6-1	16.76-1
Silk Affair	**16-1**	11-1	12.2-1	**16-1**
Dunguib	**7-1**	9-2	4.3-1	5.03-1
Zaynar	11-2	11-2	5.3-1	**5.85-1**
American Trilogy	**25-1**	20-1	21.9-1	21.19-1
Weapon's Amnesty	**12-1**	8-1	9.2-1	8.88-1
Kauto Star	**9-4**	7-4	1.7-1	1.88-1
Cappa Bleu	11-2	11-2	5.1-1	**6-1**
Andytown	22-1	25-1	30.7-1	**37.07-1**
Oh Crick	**12-1**	7-1	8.1-1	7.8-1

Non-runner no bet normally starts at the earliest a fortnight before the festival, when the vast majority of horses' targets are well known. Yet when offering the concession the bookmakers tend to drastically squeeze their margins.

On March 1 last season, Bet365, offering non-runner no bet, were top price about only three horses from the top ten in the betting for the first day of the meeting, all in the Champion Hurdle (Osana, Crack Away Jack and Katchit).

And for 11 of the winners at the meeting, Bet365's odds were worse two weeks prior to the event than on the morning of the races, sometimes considerably so.

Fair play, however, to Bet365, who have always been first to offer the 'non-runner no bet' concession and have excelled themselves this year by also going 'best odds guaranteed', which means if you do take a shorter price and the SP is bigger, you'll get the SP. That is truly a terrific concession. ■

RACING POST
CHELTENHAM FESTIVAL 2010 OFFICIAL MEDIA PARTNER

Love a bet? You'll love the **best prices** on football

Profit from our Best Prices – FACT

If you want the best odds, there's only one place to go. When the Racing Post compared prices in domestic, cup and international football fixtures between 8th August 2009 and 2nd January 2010*, William Hill had more top team prices than any other leading bookmaker.

Don't settle for anything less.

POS	TEAM	BEST PRICES
C	William Hill	1651
2	Bet365	1016
3	Coral	887
4	Ladbrokes	869
5	Paddy Power	495

BEST PRICE TABLE 09/10*

Reading the market

James Pyman investigates recent festival gambles
to find out whether money really talks

FINDING winners at the Cheltenham Festival is not easy and
inevitably some punters look for short cuts. One is to follow the
money, based on the simple logic that it requires large sums of cash to
change hands for a horse to shorten at the festival and so a reduction
in odds can be taken as confirmation that a particular horse is strongly
fancied to win.

A significant source of eye-catching gambles is big-hitting punters
like influential owner JP McManus, who have enough bucks to single-
handedly drive runners down to shorter prices even in the festival's
highly robust day-of-race markets. Weighty tipsters such as the Racing
Post's Tom Segal (Pricewise) are able to spark Cheltenham punts too,
while some horses shorten dramatically simply as a by-product of a
significant number of people independently coming to the same
conclusion about their chances.

Following the money can yield success. Last year it would have led
you to RSA Chase winner Cooldine, who was backed down to 9-4
having been generally available at 4-1 when the betting shops opened
in the morning. But plenty of gambles go astray at the festival, as
those who jumped on board the punt on Alexander Severus last year
will testify. The Edward O'Grady-trained hurdler was sent off 5-2
favourite for the Fred Winter Juvenile Handicap Hurdle, having been
on offer with most firms at 5-1 in the morning, but he could manage
only fourth behind Silk Affair.

To judge how informative market moves have been at the
Cheltenham Festival in the past five seasons, I compared the starting
prices of all runners with the generally available morning odds in the
Pricewise boxes printed in the Racing Post of the day of the race.
Converting the prices into percentages and then subtracting the
morning-price percentage from the starting-price percentage gives us
an indication of the magnitude of the market move.

In the Cooldine example he was 4-1 in the morning, which equates
to a 20 per cent chance, but was sent off at 5-2 (the equivalent of a 31
per cent chance), so the market rated his chance of winning at start
time as 11 percentage points greater than when Racing Post readers
opened their papers at breakfast time.

▸The overall picture

Let's start with the basics by looking simply at whether market vibes
have had any significance. As you might expect, runners with positive
market moves outperformed those with negative vibes in the past five
seasons, as the record of runners who shortened was 57 wins from

> Of the horses
> that were 3-1
> or shorter in
> the morning,
> market drifters
> have fared
> better at the
> past five
> festivals than
> those who
> attracted
> support

Cooldine (left) was a big success for punters who followed the money on raceday when winning last year's RSA Chase

811 runs (seven per cent), although the drifters still accounted for plenty of the winners, with 45 wins from 973 runs (4.6 per cent).

Notably, the record of the more heavily backed horses – those who received sufficient market support to contract by five percentage points or more – was a modest five wins from 50 runs (ten per cent). Backing these horses blind at their starting prices would have resulted in a considerable level-stakes loss of £32.00, so it is clear that a punting policy of jumping on the back of big gambles would have fast-tracked you to the poorhouse.

It would have been a similar story if you had backed each of the big drifters to level stakes, as the record of horses whose price inflated by more than five percentage points was just two winners from 24 runners (8.3 per cent), resulting in a £16.75 loss to a £1 stake.

▸▸Bankers or blowouts?

One of the more fascinating findings of this research concerns the market moves of horses who were priced at 3-1 or shorter on the morning of the race. In contrast to the general pattern of horses who shortened outperforming those who lengthened, with horses that were strongly fancied in the morning (3-1 or shorter) the drifters fared better than those who attracted support.

Those who shortened posted 12 wins from 47 runs (25 per cent strike-rate) and you would have suffered a loss of £10.43 to a £1 stake by following them, but those in which the market had lost confidence boasted a better record with 15 wins from 46 runs (33 per cent strike-rate). You would have been rewarded handsomely by ignoring the negative market vibes on these runners, who accumulated a level-stakes profit of £21.32 to a £1 stake.

So why has it proved profitable to back these drifters? Well, the day-of-race market is both well informed and informative because it has been shaped by a number of factors, such as the key formlines from the months leading up to the race, bookmakers' ante-post

liabilities and the reputations of the horses involved. The day-of-race morning market therefore provides a fairly accurate and well-balanced overview of how well the runners are expected to perform.

It's a different story with the on-course market, which is heavily influenced by bookmakers without any ante-post liabilities who are looking to get the short-priced horses beat regardless of their form leading up to the festival. This general stance from on-course layers against short-priced horses could be why they have often made decent betting propositions when allowed to drift in the on-course market. These findings strongly suggest that if you fancy a horse at a short price, negative market vibes shouldn't put you off backing it.

▸▸Outsiders in handicaps

At every festival a number of the bigger-priced horses are gambled on in the handicaps, and recent festivals suggest it's often a positive sign when the money comes for a horse priced on the morning of the race at 12-1 or bigger in a handicap.

Oh Crick, winner of last year's Grand Annual Chase, was a good example of a springer who was able to justify market support. The Alan King-trained chaser was sent off at 7-1, having been generally available at 12-1 in the morning.

On the day of the race Oh Crick's price contracted by roughly five percentage points, and it's interesting to note that you would have made a level-stakes profit of £22.50 (six wins from 48 runs, 12.5 per cent strike-rate) if you had backed all runners at their starting prices in Cheltenham handicaps in the past five seasons that were priced at 12-1 or bigger in the Racing Post's priceboxes in the morning and then shortened by two percentage points or more before the start of their races. In stark contrast, the record of horses that were 12-1 or bigger in the morning and drifted by two percentage points or more is 0-20.

▸▸Reading the significance of market moves

Nicky Henderson sends an enviably strong squad to the festival, but market clues have often been misleading with his runners. At the last five festivals the record of his runners who started at shorter prices from those who were available in the morning is just two wins from 43 runs (4.7 per cent strike-rate), but the record of those who drifted to bigger prices by the off is a much better six wins from 51 runs (12 per cent). If you had taken starting price about Henderson's horses that fell into the drifter category, you would have trousered a £45.55 profit to a £1 stake.

Henderson seems to be an exception, however, because the market tends to be highly informative with many other big trainers. Take Willie Mullins for starters. Outside of the Champion Bumper, the record of Mullins-trained runners who shortened by greater than one percentage point reads 111583301. The finishing positions of Venetia Williams-trained runners whose prices contracted by more than two percentage points is 210012, Tom Taaffe is three winners from seven

runners with horses that were backed, and the record of Howard Johnson-trained runners who shortened by 1.5 percentage points or more is 3045111.

▸▸Jockeys to note when the money is down

Barry Geraghty has landed plenty of gambles at recent festivals, as the jockey's record on board runners that started at shorter prices than they were generally on offer at in the morning is five winners from 29 runners and £1 on each of these rides would have yielded a healthy profit of £24.50. Geraghty's record on drifters is a less impressive 2-29.

Ruby Walsh has been a man to follow when there has been a sizeable move for one of his mounts. Walsh is four wins from 12 rides on horses that shortened by four percentage points or more.

Tony McCoy's record is 5-45 on runners that shortened, which compares favourably with his 1-28 record on drifters. The time to catch the champion jockey has been when he has partnered a Jonjo O'Neill-trained horse carrying market confidence, as his record on board O'Neill runners that shortened reads F07F11513170.

▸▸The JP McManus factor

It is no secret that the powerful owner loves having winners at Cheltenham and the majority of festival runners in his famous green and gold hoops are trained to peak at the meeting. This could explain why it has been possible to profit by backing all JP McManus-owned horses whether they were cut or pushed out in the betting, though the big profit has come from going against the market moves. You would have just about broken even by following the money, as the McManus runners who shortened yielded a profit of £0.38, but backing drifters owned by McManus would have produced a substantial profit of £28.00. ∎

Wichita Lineman wins the William Hill Chase last year for the holy trinity of Tony McCoy, Jonjo O'Neill and JP McManus, three names to note when the money is down

Balancing the book

Matt Williams runs through his ante-post portfolio
and his views on this year's big-name 'bankers'

PRE-FESTIVAL preparation is vital for punters, with so much
form to digest, and I'm always thinking ahead to plan whether
to back or lay horses ante-post, wait until the day or strike a bet
in running. Making the right choice about when and how to bet
goes hand in hand with picking the right horses. My festival
portfolio is a mix of good chances and no-hopers and, although
I am looking at a loss in the Arkle Trophy, having taken an early
position about Copper Bleu and Medermit, I am still confident
of making a profit on my ante-post bets.

▸▸Go Native Champion Hurdle

Back-to-lay What is it with Noel Meade and bridle horses? He seems
to have trained a number of talented 'twicers' in his time, most
notably the legendary Harchibald, who should have won Meade at
least one Champion Hurdle. With his high cruising speed and
tendency to idle in front, it was inevitable Go Native would draw
comparisons with Harchibald, which seems a little unfair.

We are talking about a hurdler who has already proved himself on
the big occasion at Cheltenham, winning last season's Supreme
Novices, and it's difficult to crab the form of his last two starts. His
Fighting Fifth win was supposed to be a joke of a race, but I think
hindsight proves that not to be the case and his Christmas Hurdle win
was impressive. Granted, the form book says he struggled home to
beat Starluck, but he quickly put daylight between himself and his
rivals and we know he doesn't like being in front too long, so I am
blaming the jockey for not winning by further at Kempton.

The make-up of the Champion Hurdle suggests we are in for a treat,
with a strong pace more or less guaranteed. If I was limited to one
trade at the festival, it would be a back-to-lay of Go Native as I can
see him trading odds-on at some stage in the run. With this in mind,
exchange bettors can't go wrong backing him now at around 5.5 on
Betfair, with a view to laying off in-running at the cheapest possible
price. As always with this kind of advice, it's entirely a personal choice
at which point you jump ship (trade for a profit, covering more than
your initial stake), but I want to be aggressive with Go Native, going
for the jugular with a lay at 2 or shorter.

> If I was limited to one trade at the festival, it would be a back-to-lay of Go Native and I want to go for the jugular with a lay at 2 or shorter

▸▸Captain Cee Bee Arkle Trophy

Back-to-lay The 2008 Supreme Novices' Hurdle winner is unlucky
not to be heading for the Arkle Trophy with a 3-3 chase record, as he
was challenging Sizing Europe when falling at the final fence in a

Captain Cee Bee jumps fast and low, and there is plenty of mileage in a back-to-lay strategy on this strong traveller

Grade 1 novice chase at Leopardstown over Christmas. He got the show back on the road with a confidence-booster at Naas next time and it's scary to think he has looked so good in three chase starts despite not having his favoured good ground, with his two chase wins coming on heavy going.

Unless something comes out and does something spectacular, Captain Cee Bee will probably start favourite for the Arkle, but at around 7-2 or 3-1 there is still plenty of mileage in a back-to-lay strategy. He is similar to Go Native in many respects, and I can't find a stronger traveller in the Arkle line-up. He jumps fast and low, which makes for exciting and nervous viewing, but those qualities are a necessary evil in a top-notch 2m chaser.

▸▸Dunguib Supreme Novices' Hurdle

Banker I have seen a number of exciting novices over the years but nothing has caught the imagination like Philip Fenton's seven-year-old did when he romped home in the Grade 1 Deloitte Novice Hurdle at Leopardstown in February. His jumping lacked fluency, but the way he sauntered past the highly regarded Fionnegas was a sight to behold and, although there are concerns about his hurdling, I suspect he will be a lot better with a stronger pace. He proved himself at the festival by winning the Bumper last year, and this time racegoers are expecting a superstar to turn up. I am betting Dunguib will not disappoint and I can see connections of good horses looking for alternative races to avoid him. Punters who are on at odds-against have got themselves a hell of a bet and he is still value at odds-on.

▸▸Big Buck's World Hurdle

Banker He's got a similar feel about him as Dunguib and the lack of strength in his division serves to highlight his World Hurdle claims. Bookmakers are clutching at straws looking for something to beat him, as Karabak has already had a good view of his backside and pretenders like Tidal Bay are not in the same league as Paul Nicholls'

Williams' portfolio

Here are my bets so far (1 still have to back Captain Cee Bee and have more on Tavern Times), along with my expectations of how they'll fare.

Confident

Tavern Times 14-1 (Champion Bumper): I really fancy this one and, if he lines up, he could be my biggest position of the week

Go Native 6.8 (Champion Hurdle): a trading tool and I'll be looking to jump ship at odds-on

Dunguib 6-4 (Supreme Novices): I'll be going in again at odds-on, safe in the knowledge I will have the best part of four days to straighten the books if he fails to deliver

Celestial Halo 5.8 to be placed (Champion Hurdle): he always runs a race at Cheltenham and his odds to place are way too generous to resist

Hopeful

Celestial Halo 23 (Champion Hurdle): he is one of those horses who lets you down at skinny prices but goes and delivers a monster performance when you least expect it

Waste of money

Medermit (Arkle Trophy): took 20s, not even in the race now as he heads for the Champion Hurdle

Copper Bleu (Arkle Trophy): took 42 down to 26. Another who has been taken out of the race

Royal Charm (Neptune Novices' Hurdle): took prices around 13 and 12.5, but disappointed at Cheltenham and taken out of the entries

Joncol (Ryanair): backed him at 15 and got a bit giddy when connections said the Ryanair was his festival target. Then they decided against it. Gutted.

reigning champion. Heavy ground almost proved his undoing in the Long Walk at Newbury last time, but the way he quickened to get himself out of bother was impressive and there is no point trying to knock any part of his game, as conditions are likely to be ideal at Cheltenham. He can hit a flat spot in his races and some exchange punters might want to wait for a bigger price in the run, but too many knowledgeable backers are aware of this trait. If he wins, I don't expect his in-running odds to be huge.

▶Kauto Star Gold Cup

Banker The Gold Cup has been seen for most of the winter as a two-horse race – the defining clash between Kauto Star and Denman, with the Gold Cup score between the Paul Nicholls pair currently standing at one-all. All other things being equal, it seemed likely that punters would favour Kauto Star on good ground and Denman if it came up soft on Gold Cup day.

All things aren't equal, after Denman's problems in the Aon Chase. My faith in Kauto Star has never wavered and now he is a banker. Being fresh is everything to him and I don't believe the going is a huge issue. He just has more to his game than his rivals, Denman included.

▶Quevega David Nicholson Mares' Hurdle

Blowout The Willie Mullins-trained mare won the race last year in spectacular fashion, sprinting clear of her rivals to land plenty of big bets, but I don't think she's bombproof, as the opposition is going to be stronger this time. She has endured a troubled preparation this season, though it is worth noting she had just one run in February before last year's win. She enjoys a bit of give in the ground and we know the trip isn't a problem, but she jumped slowly early doors last year and punters should look for something to beat her.

▶Tavern Times Champion Bumper

Best each-way selection Thomas Mullins sent out Some Present to finish runner-up behind Dunguib in the Champion Bumper last year and Tavern Times is strongly fancied to go one better for owner Paul Duffin. At 14-1 ante-post, the six-year-old rates a great each-way bet. This son of Presenting was impressive on his racecourse debut at Fairyhouse in October, winning despite meeting severe trouble in running, owing to a poor ride. We haven't seen him since, but he is sure to warm up for Cheltenham by working at Leopardstown about ten days before his big target and, if he gets the green light, he will be a tough opponent. Willie Mullins doesn't appear to have a serious bumper horse this season and I fancy the best of the older brigade to be too strong for Dermot Weld's five-year-old Elegant Concorde, the ante-post favourite. ■

The specialist global insurer for bloodstock

MARKEL INTERNATIONAL
A Markel Company

www.markelintl.com

Festival Q & A

The bookmakers give their verdicts

	Who will win the Gold Cup?	**How do you see the Champion Hurdle?**
William Hill Jamie McBride	Kauto Star's Kempton effort was arguably his best ever and the path to a third win is clear. Cooldine looks next-best but it's hard to see him troubling the big two at their best	Solwhit is uncomplicated and sets the standard, but Go Native, Zaynar and Khyber Kim need things to fall right. Don't rule out Punjabi
Ladbrokes David Williams	Kauto Star looked every inch back to his best in the King George. Denman's fall at Newbury was less worrying than the manner in which he was (or wasn't) travelling	It's wide open. Solwhit and Go Native look the most solid. We didn't like Zaynar even before Kelso and he's a massive lay. Medermit is the pick of the bigger prices
Coral James Knight	Kauto Star looks pretty strong, but Denman looked unfit at Newbury and shouldn't be written off. If the Denman of two years ago turns up, he'll win	I'm very keen on Solwhit. I think he will be better at Cheltenham. A big field, strong pace and uphill finish will suit him down to the ground
Totesport George Primarolo	It's difficult to get away from Kauto Star. The others will have a chance only if conditions are testing, which is not beyond the realms of possibility given the recent weather	I couldn't understand why Go Native wasn't favourite after his success in the Christmas Hurdle but the market is right now. Medermit could be underestimated
Paddy Power Andrew Moore	Kauto Star will take all the beating but I'm going for Imperial Commander, who got close to him at Haydock and runs well fresh. The trip is his only question mark	Khyber Kim should be right there. Connections seem to have found the key to him this year and he is finally fulfilling his early promise
Betfred Alan Williams	Kauto Star looks as good as ever and Denman appeared to be struggling at Newbury. Imperial Commander should run a big race	Go Native looks the one to beat, but is he another Harchibald in that his run needs to be timed perfectly? Khyber Kim and Punjabi are best of the rest. We don't fancy Zaynar
Stan James Kelan McDonnell	Kauto Star looks as good as ever. Denman will need soft ground to have any chance. Calgary Bay has been well supported in our market without the big two	Solwhit and Go Native have the form in the book, but Khyber Kim looks to be improving at a rate of knots and there could be more to come
Boylesports Andrew Jones	Kauto Star all the way. It is hard to see anything troubling him	The ground is the key. Soft ground would make Solwhit hard to beat. On good ground Go Native can travel strongly and win in style

Can anything stop Master Minded?	Is Big Buck's a banker?	Which are your biggest losers?
He jumped (apart from the last) and travelled like a horse enjoying himself at Newbury and should be hard to beat. Golden Silver is my idea of the best each-way option	Yes, in my opinion he is the most talented horse in training. Tidal Bay could give him most to think about, but it will be disappointing if Big Buck's is beaten	Rite Of Passage, Alaivan and Kauto Star, but at the moment none is a significant loser
Only if his November problems return could we see Kalahari King giving him a race. Golden Silver makes the most each-way appeal	He has no chinks and we'd be dreaming of rather than expecting an upset. Tidal Bay has been heavily backed. Cousin Vinny is too big at 33-1 each-way	Dunguib and Rite Of Passage in their novice hurdles would be shocking. Captain Cee Bee would be a stinker and so would Day Of A Lifetime in the Bumper
Yes – the Game Spirit was a poor race. Twist Magic, Kalahari King and Big Zeb are all good-value each-way bets	Realistically he will get beaten only if he runs quite a bit below form. Tidal Bay has plenty of ability and looks clear best of the rest	Dunguib has been popular since last March and our Supreme book isn't looking too clever as a result. Nothing too disastrous in the other races
Master Minded looked back to his best in the Game Spirit and his injury problems would have to resurface for him to lose. Kalahari King could be best of the rest	Pretty much. The World Hurdle is a race the best come back to win time and time again	Cooldine is our biggest loser but we're worried about our position on Rite Of Passage in the Neptune. We've taken one or two lumpy bets on him at biggish prices
He is intimidating but not invincible. Kalahari King and Big Zeb were both impressive in their trials and could really serve it up to him	He is rock solid. Tidal Bay, Sentry Duty and Karabak have the potential to be contenders but it is hard to see anything finishing better than Big Buck's	Dunguib is a stinker for us and if he wins we will be starting the week on the back foot. Poquelin has been well supported in the Ryanair
No. His win at Newbury showed he is getting back to his best and he should come on for that run. Kalahari King looks the biggest danger.	He is a solid favourite. It was great to see Tidal Bay back on song last time but Karabak is our idea of the best each-way bet	The Thomas Barr-owned duo Osana and Alaivan in the Arkle and Triumph respectively. Alaivan worries us after his impressive win last time
We were taken with him in the Game Spirit and he looks a banker. Big Zeb goes well fresh but his jumping might not hold up. Kalahari King needs to improve	He hasn't been particularly impressive so far this season but he gets the job done. Powerstation has been well backed in the market without Big Buck's	Alaivan has a strong chance in the Triumph. Along with Poquelin, Master Minded and Big Buck's, he could make a most unlucky 15 for us
Should he be favourite? Yes. Should he be odds-on? No. Kalahari King, the rejuvenated Twist Magic and Big Zeb are viable each-way contenders	What can possibly beat this good thing? Trained by the best, ridden by the best, 100% record over course and distance. Superlatives simply flow off the tongue	Captain Cee Bee in the Arkle and, unfortunately, Big Buck's

Festival Q & A

The bookmakers give their verdicts

	Who are the ones to watch from Ireland?	The Supreme and Neptune: who'll win?
William Hill Jamie McBride	They look to have a strong hand and should have plenty of winners. Alaivan settled better last time, won impressively and can go close in the Triumph	It is not very original but Dunguib and Rite Of Passage have impressed and their festival experience will be a huge asset against fellow novices
Ladbrokes David Williams	Enough question marks surround Dunguib's jumping and inexperienced jockey to give us hope of laying the favourite. The Irish are stronger than ever in the Triumph	Get Me Out Of Here will serve it up to Dunguib in the Supreme, with a bit of luck. We're hoping Peddlers Cross will beat Rite Of Passage in the Neptune
Coral James Knight	We will be treading carefully with Willie Mullins' horses. His three winners last year made for easily the worst 24 hours I've endured in ten years at Coral	If Dunguib jumps, he wins, and I have been impressed with Peddlers Cross for the Neptune
Totesport George Primarolo	One to watch in the Bumper is Hidden Universe, who made a huge impression when winning at Leopardstown in January	It's difficult to get past Dunguib in the Supreme but Get Me Out Of Here could bustle him up. The Neptune looks at the mercy of Rite Of Passage
Paddy Power Andrew Moore	There are plenty of Irish favourites and the juveniles seem quite good, so I'll be having a strong look at the Irish contingent in the Fred Winter Hurdle	Dunguib and Rite Of Passage are all the rage, but Fionnegas in the Neptune and Get Me Out Of Here in the Supreme represent value
Betfred Alan Williams	We think Dunguib will win, we fancy Go Native, and Captain Cee Bee and Quevega could complete a big opening day. Dermot Weld is the man to follow in the Bumper	Dunguib seems to be Pegasus in disguise and Rite Of Passage looks like becoming top class. Blackstairmountain and Quantitativeeasing are our ante-post bogeys
Stan James Kelan McDonnell	Day Of A Lifetime has been the one for money in the Bumper following his debut win at Fairyhouse. Captain Cee Bee is too short at 7-2	The eight flights of hurdles look the only danger to Dunguib in the Supreme. We are sweet on Rite Of Passage in the Neptune. He is potentially top class
Boylesports Andrew Jones	Enterprise Park in the Albert Bartlett Novices' Hurdle	Dunguib's class will surely tell in the Supreme. If the ground comes up soft then Peddlers Cross would be my fancy for the Neptune

Who will win the Arkle and RSA?

Give us a value bet for the festival

What's your best bet of the festival?

Both races look pretty open. Somersby and Punchestowns are our worst results at the moment	Golden Silver was slightly disappointing last time but looked good before that and can outrun his big odds in the Queen Mother	Bensalem looks well treated off 143 and will surely go close in the William Hill Trophy
We'd like to get Captain Cee Bee beaten – Riverside Theatre is the one we like. Punchestowns would be lousy in the RSA and Long Run is our best hope of an upset	Medermit each-way in the Champion Hurdle still looks value and we'd be far from shocked if he won	Poquelin to win the Ryanair. Loves the course, will be fresh and, unlike many in the race, the trip will be absolutely perfect for him
Somersby looked good at Sandown and I hope he can win for Henrietta Knight. All the big names in the RSA have holes in them and we could get a shock	Each-way doubles on the Champion Chase and Ryanair – Kalahari King and Twist Magic on to Schindlers Hunt and Albertas Run	I've had one ante-post bet and that was Solwhit at 6-1 after he won the Irish Champion Hurdle
We were taken by Somersby at Sandown and have tried to keep him on side. Nicky Henderson holds the key to the RSA and we reckon Long Run is the one	Alan King to be top trainer in betting without Paul Nicholls. As well as a couple of live big-race contenders, he has a host of well-handicapped horses	Rite Of Passage in the Neptune Investment Novices' Hurdle
Somersby looks to have all the qualities you want in a chaser. If the pace is strong in the RSA nothing will be finishing better than Weapon's Amnesty	The progressive Candy Creek each-way in the Mares' Hurdle. She might not have the class of some of the others but has had a far better preparation	A drop in trip will suit Barbers Shop in the Ryanair. A replication of his run in last season's Paddy Power Gold Cup would make him hard to beat
Captain Cee Bee is a solid Arkle favourite. We hope Long Run can save us from a Punchestowns victory in the RSA	If Albertas Run goes for the Ryanair he would be a big each-way price at 25-1 given his form when dropping back in trip this season	Dunguib because he looks like a machine and has already won at the festival. Quevega for a repeat win in the Mares' Hurdle would be next best
We like Sports Line for the Arkle and Punchestowns for the RSA. Long Run doesn't jump well enough and Diamond Harry isn't as good as we thought	Schindlers Hunt has no Imperial Commander to beat in the Ryanair this year and was palpably the best horse in the Irish Hennessy last time until his stamina gave way	Khyber Kim to repel a strong Irish challenge in the Champion Hurdle. He was Listed class on the Flat and has a most progressive profile over hurdles
Riverside Theatre and Weapon's Amnesty. We badly need Captain Cee Bee beat in the Arkle	Sublimity in the Champion Hurdle. He had Solwhit off the bridle a long way out in the Irish Champion and on better ground 20-1 will look big	Ireland to win the Triumph Hurdle for the first time since Scolardy in 2002

The class of 2010

Racing Post Ratings expert Steve Mason runs
the rule over the major big-race contenders

»Gold Cup

Kauto Star regained his status as the best jumper in training when landing his second Gold Cup last season, his winning RPR of 185 just bettering the mark of 184 posted by Denman the previous year.

The 13-times Grade 1 winner has since raised the bar to new heights, his record-breaking fourth successive King George earning him a career-best figure of 192, more than a stone in excess of the average winning mark for the festival showpiece. After being written off on more than one occasion during his illustrious career, the ten-year-old is seemingly in the form of his life, having benefited from his trainer's decision to campaign him more sparingly.

Denman, who brushed a below-par Kauto Star aside in the 2008 Gold Cup, appeared to put his own problems firmly behind him when landing a second Hennessy at Newbury on his seasonal reappearance in November. That run under top weight of 11st 12lb was worth a RPR of 184 – on a par with his Gold Cup-winning performance – but even his biggest supporter must have doubts after his disastrous run in the Aon Chase. He still rates the biggest danger, but prospects of an epic struggle between the pair now look considerably less likely.

The big two apart, the field lacks strength. Imperial Commander and Cooldine, both winners at last year's festival, look the only decent options for those in search of an each-way alternative.

Denman still rates the biggest danger to Kauto Star but an epic struggle between the pair now looks less likely

▶Champion Hurdle

There doesn't appear to be a single outstanding candidate but, with seven horses rated within 3lb of each other, there is plenty of depth to this year's field and it appears highly likely that the winner will be forced to break the 170 barrier – a mark last achieved by Brave Inca (171) in 2006.

There is nothing to choose between Punjabi and Celestial Halo, last year's winner and runner-up, and both should run well. Punjabi warmed up with an easy win against weak opposition at Kempton and, although he disappointed in the Irish Champion Hurdle behind Solwhit, Celestial Halo still shares top rating and looks attractively priced.

However, it seems more likely that the winner will come from the up-and-coming quintet consisting of Zaynar, Go Native, Solwhit, Khyber Kim and Medermit.

Zaynar, a good winner of a vintage Triumph Hurdle at last year's festival, lost his unbeaten record at cramped odds at Kelso, but time may tell there was no disgrace in failing to give the talented Quwetwo 8lb in testing ground and he remains a serious player.

Solwhit shares an RPR of 169 with Celestial Halo and Zaynar and continues to progress. However, he is unproven at the track and would probably prefer the ground softer than is usual at the festival.

Go Native was an impressive winner of last season's Supreme Novices' Hurdle, though some would argue that neck runner-up Medermit was a shade unfortunate. I expect Noel Meade's strong-travelling seven-year-old to confirm superiority, though there would be no guarantee that either of the pair will finish in front of the dangerous Khyber Kim, who already has two verdicts over Medermit this season.

The Nigel Twiston-Davies-trained eight-year-old has belatedly found some consistency and could not have been more impressive in landing both his starts at Cheltenham this season. His current RPR of 167 falls a few pounds shy of what Rooster Booster had achieved in landing the same two races en route to success in the big race in 2003, but he has yet to be fully extended.

Punjabi has had a problematic winter but warmed up for his title defence with victory at Kempton last time

CHAMPION HURDLE

This year's top rated	RPR
Celestial Halo	169
Solwhit	169
Zaynar	169
Go Native	167
Khyber Kim	167
Punjabi	167
Medermit	166
Donnas Palm	165
Sublimity	165

How the last ten winners rated

Year	Winner	Win RPR	Pre-race RPR
2009	Punjabi	167	164
2008	Katchit	167	162
2007	Sublimity	167	148
2006	Brave Inca	171	170
2005	Hardy Eustace	168	170
2004	Hardy Eustace	170	156
2003	Rooster Booster	173	170
2002	Hors La Loi	166	166
2000	Istabraq	171	181
1999	Istabraq	170	176

10yr winning average RPR: 169

CHAMPION CHASE	
This year's top rated	RPR
Master Minded	181
Twist Magic	172
Kalahari King	169
Voy Por Ustedes	168
Big Zeb	167
Golden Silver	166
Petit Robin	164
Barker	163
Tranquil Sea	163
Well Chief	163

How the last ten winners rated

Year	Winner	Win RPR	Pre-race RPR
2009	Master Minded	169	186
2008	Master Minded	186	168
2007	Voy Por Ustedes	167	167
2006	Newmill	172	155
2005	Moscow Flyer	182	181
2004	Azertyuiop	176	179
2003	Moscow Flyer	174	168
2002	Flagship Uberalles	170	173
2000	Edredon Bleu	166	167
1999	Call Equiname	167	157

10yr winning average RPR: 173

▸Champion Chase

A RPR around the 170 mark is the benchmark for success in this race and, with a personal-best of 186 and a couple of other 180+ figures on his record, it will be a major surprise if dual winner Master Minded fails to complete his hat-trick.

It looked as though his best days might already be behind him when a downward spiral of winning RPRs culminated in shock defeat on his Cheltenham reappearance, but a cracked rib offered an explanation of his decline and he bounced back to something like his brilliant best in the Game Spirit Chase at Newbury in February. Surviving an uncharacteristic blunder at the last, he bounded up the run-in to win easily and a winning RPR of 181 suggests there is little to fear from stablemate Twist Magic (172) and Kalahari King (169).

The latter remains open to further improvement, but Twist Magic has recorded all his best figures on a right-handed track and, although he was travelling okay when falling in the 2007 Arkle, his overall Cheltenham record is uninspiring.

Petit Robin was no match for Twist Magic when the pair met at Ascot in January, but it wouldn't be the greatest surprise if last year's third reversed the placings back at Cheltenham.

WORLD HURDLE	
This year's top rated	RPR
Big Buck's	176
Punchestowns	172
Fair Along	166
Karabak	166
Tidal Bay	166
Diamond Harry	165
Lough Derg	161
Sentry Duty	161
Mr Thriller	160
Time For Rupert	160

How the last ten winners rated

Year	Winner	Win RPR	Pre-race RPR
2009	Big Buck's	176	166
2008	Inglis Drever	174	170
2007	Inglis Drever	169	167
2006	My Way De Solzen	166	159
2005	Inglis Drever	167	165
2004	Iris's Gift	176	173
2003	Baracouda	176	176
2002	Baracouda	171	176
2000	Bacchanal	168	165
1999	Anzum	167	157

10yr winning average RPR: 171

▸World Hurdle

Big Buck's is unbeaten since switching back to hurdles and, with last year's runner-up Punchestowns set to run over fences at the festival, it's not difficult to see why he's odds-on to register back-to-back wins. A RPR of 176 marked him down as a vintage winner of the race and gives him 10lb or more in hand over his likely rivals. He completes a trio of Paul Nicholls hotpots for the major championship races and, as with Kauto Star and Master Minded, it's difficult to see him meeting defeat.

For those looking for an each-way alternative, the obvious starting point is Karabak. Given that his stable wasn't really firing at the time, it was encouraging that he improved his RPR on both starts this season and, if anything were to go wrong with the favourite, he looks the one most likely to take advantage.

It's unlikely that Fair Along can find much improvement on his current RPR of 166 and he's not easy to predict. However, he has place claims if he is on a going day. The 2008 Arkle winner Tidal Bay rolled back the years when making a winning return to hurdling on Cheltenham's Trials day and, while he will need to step up significantly on the RPR of 166 he earned that day if he is going to follow up in the main event, he has each-way claims.

RYANAIR CHASE		
Year Winner	Win RPR	Pre-race RPR
2009 Imperial Commander	169	161
2008 Our Vic	168	171
2007 Taranis	160	158
2006 Fondmort	164	165
2005 Thisthat-andtother	164	164

SUPREME NOVICES'		
Year Winner	Win RPR	Pre-race RPR
2009 Go Native	152	149
2008 Captain Cee Bee	159	144
2007 Ebaziyan	150	116
2006 Noland	150	137
2005 Arcalis	146	143
2004 Brave Inca	152	145
2003 Back In Front	160	149
2002 Like-A-Butterfly	147	156
2000 Sausalito Bay	147	132
1999 Hors La Loi III	159	151
10yr winning average RPR: 152		

NEPTUNE NOVICES'		
Year Winner	Win RPR	Pre-race RPR
2009 Mikael D'Haguenet	158	158
2008 Fiveforthree	149	136
2007 Massini's Maguire	149	147
2006 Nicanor	155	146
2005 No Refuge	148	145
2004 Fundamentalist	157	148
2003 Hardy Eustace	153	149
2002 Galileo	154	142
2000 Monsignor	164	163
1999 Barton	160	158
10yr winning average RPR: 155		

TRIUMPH HURDLE		
Year Winner	Win RPR	Pre-race RPR
2009 Zaynar	157	141
2008 Celestial Halo	149	133
2007 Katchit	154	136
2006 Detroit City	153	135
2005 Penzance	141	127
2004 Made In Japan	140	120
2003 Spectroscope	137	121
2002 Scolardy	144	135
2000 Snow Drop	140	144
1999 Katarino	155	158
10yr winning average RPR: 146		

▸Ryanair

With many understandably reluctant to take on Kauto Star in the Gold Cup and Master Minded in the Champion Chase, this intermediate-distance event could attract a pretty strong field, although it is unlikely that current top-rated Imperial Commander (177) will attempt a repeat of last year's win.

In his likely absence, 2009 runner-up Voy Por Ustedes heads the ratings along with Huntingdon winner Deep Purple. They share a RPR of 171, though both have something to prove after running below par on their most recent starts. Given his decent course record, preference would be for the Alan King-trained former Champion Chase winner.

Planet Of Sound and Albertas Run are both rated 168, a level good enough to win a typical running of this race, while 2008 winner Our Vic (167) rolled back the years to win in good style at Haydock. Recent Red Mills Chase winner J'y Vole (162) gets a valuable 7lb from her male rivals and is bang there on the figures, along with the progressive Poquelin (167) and Tranquil Sea (163). Barbers Shop (160) is a shorter price than his form over further warrants, but he is open to improvement on the drop back in trip and adds further spice to what has the makings of a hot race.

▸Novice hurdles

With a RPR already in excess of all bar three of the last ten winners of the Supreme Novices' Hurdle, Dunguib is understandably a red-hot favourite to land the meeting's curtain-raiser. It's anybody's guess just how much he had in hand when cruising home in his final prep race in the Grade 1 Deloitte Novice Hurdle at Leopardstown and a winning RPR of 156+ may well underestimate him. A few minor jumping errors apart, it was another jaw-dropping performance from last season's hugely impressive Bumper winner, who oozes class. It will be surprising if he fails to give the Irish team their eighth win in the race in the past ten years.

Menorah heads the home team and a figure of 153 suggests he will be hard to keep out of the frame. Thereafter the picture becomes murkier, with plenty of the highly rated contenders also having the option to run in the Neptune Investment Management Novices' Hurdle the following day.

One is Rite Of Passage, last season's Bumper third and subsequent Leopardstown November Handicap winner, who would be a major player in either race but looks set to go for the Neptune.

Impressive Totesport Trophy Hurdle winner Get Me Out Of Here (150+) is another with the option of running in either race and, already proven in an ultra-competitive race, he has sound credentials. Unbeaten former point winner Peddlers Cross (148+) is still a bit short on experience, but he is clearly long on talent. His latest Haydock win proved he has plenty of speed and he should not lack for stamina in the longer race, which is his probable target.

Last season's Triumph Hurdle sixth Reve De Sivola (149) wouldn't

Get Me Out Of Here earned a high RPR after surviving a final-flight error to land the Totesport Trophy at Newbury

quite be in the same class as stablemate Diamond Harry, but he seems certain to line up in the Neptune and looks to have place claims. He will need to jump better than he did when staying on strongly to claim the Grade 1 Challow Hurdle at Newbury over Christmas but, if he does, he should confirm superiority with third-placed Finian's Rainbow (142).

Tell Massini (150) holds a course-and-distance verdict over Reve De Sivola, but he looks more likely to take his chance in the Albert Bartlett.

Recent years have seen a string of vintage Triumph Hurdle winners, but the division has failed to catch fire this time around. Carlito Brigante and Alaivan (both 142) head the ratings and, while Carlito Brigante was impressive when beating that rival at Leopardstown on Boxing Day, the runner-up was clearly not at his best that day. On the home front, Me Voici (137) heads the British ratings but seems unlikely to run unless the ground is testing.

Punchestowns shares the top RPR for the RSA Chase with Long Run but will have to give 1lb to his younger stablemate

»Novice chases

Nicky Henderson's French import Long Run (164) currently heads the RPRs for both the Arkle and RSA on the strength of his Boxing Day success in the Feltham Chase at Kempton and would be tough to beat in either race. If connections opt for the longer race he will have to cross swords with last season's World Hurdle runner-up Punchestowns (164), who currently shares the top RPR with Long Run but will have to give his younger stablemate a pound.

A 170+ hurdler, Punchestowns recovered well from a potentially race-losing error to account for the smart Tchico Polos at Sandown and, along with his stablemate, has the ability to better the 170 winning marks posted in the past ten runnings by Looks Like Trouble and Cooldine.

Diamond Harry (160) was not that impressive when landing a muddling race at Newbury in February, but had previously looked the real deal when making a winning debut over fences at Haydock. He completes a trio of top-class performers who could provide a rare treat if they run to their potential in the RSA.

In a normal year Reynoldstown winner Burton Port (160) would be a leading fancy for the race, but he is only Nicky Henderson's third string. Even so, he should run well if taking his chance.

If Long Run opts for the longer race, the 2008 Supreme Novices' Hurdle winner Captain Cee Bee (163) will share top rating for Tuesday's Arkle with the 2008 Champion Hurdle favourite Sizing Europe (163). The latter seemed to have lost his way but is unbeaten in four starts over fences, although Captain Cee Bee looked to have his measure when falling at the last at Leopardstown over Christmas.

Last season's Supreme Novices' Hurdle third Somersby (157) has taken well to fences and, along with the Henderson-trained Riverside Theatre (156), adds further quality to what has the makings of a highly competitive Arkle. ■

ARKLE TROPHY

Year	Winner	Win RPR	Pre-race RPR
2009	Forpady-deplasterer	162	157
2008	Tidal Bay	168	154
2007	My Way De Solzen	165	158
2006	Voy Por Ustedes	162	160
2005	Contraband	158	154
2004	Well Chief	157	133
2003	Azertyuiop	170	165
2002	Moscow Flyer	167	151
2000	Tiutchev	164	145
1999	Flagship Uberalles	157	144

10yr winning average RPR: 162

RSA CHASE

Year	Winner	Win RPR	Pre-race RPR
2009	Cooldine	170	160
2008	Albertas Run	162	157
2007	Denman	165	169
2006	Star De Mohaison	153	141
2005	Trabolgan	160	155
2004	Rule Supreme	161	154
2003	One Knight	159	151
2002	Hussard Collonges	156	141
2000	Lord Noelie	154	142
1999	Looks Like Trouble	170	142

10yr winning average RPR: 161

Prime time stars

Dave Edwards (Topspeed) on the main performers
and whether they have what it takes for the festival

▸▸Gold Cup

Topspeed ratings provide a measure of excellence of a horse's
performance against the clock and the closer the speed figure to the
Racing Post Rating the better. A close correlation is invariably
indicative of solid form backed up by a good time and the majority of
recent Gold Cup winners lined up with a pre-race speed figure of 165-
plus, confirming that the ability to jump fluently and at speed in a
pressure-cooker environment is a prerequisite.

The best Gold Cup-winning time performance in recent years was
by Denman in 2008, when he earned a Topspeed of 178. In the past
ten runnings, See More Business, with 173 in 1999, and Kauto Star
(172 last year) are the only other winners to have recorded a rating
above 168. If Kauto Star and/or Denman are at their peak, a huge
figure is likely to be needed this time around.

Kauto Star has breached the 170 mark on a remarkable six
occasions, including his three most recent starts. He is more versatile
than Denman, having recorded smart figures over two miles earlier in
his career, and this year's record-equalling success in the King George
had the handicappers drooling. After factoring in the all-important
going allowance, however, Kauto Star's 'actual' time in the King
George was similar to those he had clocked in his three previous wins
in the Kempton showpiece. For all his talent, he has not yet matched
Denman on the clock and it is notable that his arch-rival superseded
his 2008 Gold Cup-winning Topspeed figure when defying top weight
in the Hennessy at Newbury in November, though whether he can do
it again is open to doubt after his Aon Chase catastrophe last time out.

Apart from the big two, only Imperial Commander (173) and Notre
Pere (172) have attained lofty Topspeed marks in their careers but
both have plenty to find on current figures. Imperial Commander was
just denied by Kauto Star in the Betfair Chase in November and then
was well below par in the King George, when he may have been
feeling the effects of his epic duel at Haydock (though he also ran
poorly in the 2008 King George before bouncing back to win the
Ryanair at the festival). Cheltenham plays to Imperial Commander's
strengths, but he is an unknown quantity over the Gold Cup trip.

Notre Pere impressed on the clock when scoring at Punchestown in
April, but the ground is a crucial factor for him, the softer the better,
and he has disappointed so far this term.

In Compliance boasts a lifetime best of 167 but has been beset with
injury problems and the trip probably stretches him.

It is difficult to escape the view that Paul Nicholls will maintain his
stranglehold, with Imperial Commander the each-way alternative.

GOLD CUP
Career-best Topspeed figures

Denman	180
Kauto Star	176
Imperial Commander	173
Notre Pere	172
In Compliance	167
Schindlers Hunt	159
Trabolgan	157
What A Friend	156
Rare Bob	156
Air Force One	155
Mon Mome	155

How the last ten winners rated

Year	Winner	Win TS	Pre-race TS
2009	Kauto Star	172	176
2008	Denman	178	157
2007	Kauto Star	144	168
2006	War Of Attrition	153	133
2005	Kicking King	158	160
2004	Best Mate	165	168
2003	Best Mate	168	166
2002	Best Mate	113	165
2000	Looks Like Trouble	150	170
1999	See More Business	173	166

The hat-trick beckons in the Champion Chase for Master Minded after his return to form in the Game Spirit Chase

Queen Mother Champion Chase 2008
MASTERMINDED

Tingle Creek Chase 2008
MASTER MINDED

Victor Chandler Chase 2009
MASTER MINDED

Queen Mother Champion Chase 2009
MASTERMINDED

Kerrygold Champion Chase 2009
MASTER MINDED

CHAMPION CHASE

Career-best Topspeed figures

Master Minded	185
Voy Por Ustedes	181
Well Chief	174
Twist Magic	169
Kalahari King	168
Newmill	163
Tranquil Sea	160
Big Zeb	159
Golden Silver	159
Fix The Rib	158
Free World	157

How the last ten winners rated

Year	Winner	Win TS	Pre-race TS
2009	Master Minded	161	185
2008	Master Minded	185	143
2007	Voy Por Ustedes	159	160
2006	Newmill	163	155
2005	Moscow Flyer	145	177
2004	Azertyuiop	148	161
2003	Moscow Flyer	162	140
2002	Flagship Uberalles	142	177
2000	Edredon Bleu	173	171
1999	Call Equiname	172	164

▸▸Champion Chase

A pre-race speed figure in excess of 155, and often in the 160s, is invariably needed for a two-miler to have a chance of winning this championship event, although dual winners Moscow Flyer and Master Minded did not fulfil that criterion when gaining their first success. This season all the major players possess a time figure greater than 155 and, while the race has been won three times in the past ten runnings with a figure less than 150, the other seven winners achieved at least 159.

Master Minded took the race to another level when winning with a figure of 185 two years ago and last year's much-reduced 161 was still more than adequate to see off the opposition. The race revolves around him again this year and a hat-trick beckons now that he appears to be over his injury problems.

Most of his rivals have questions to answer. Cheltenham, either the track or the preliminaries, rarely brings out the best in Twist Magic, 2007 winner Voy Por Ustedes now seems more effective over further and Well Chief is probably past his best. Of the Irish challengers, Big Zeb has looked the part on occasion but his jumping has let him down more than once, while Tranquil Sea's best figures are over further.

Kalahari King could be a viable alternative to the favourite. An unlucky second in the Arkle last year, Ferdy Murphy's nine-year-old is at his best on good or better ground and earned a career-best figure on his reappearance at Doncaster in February.

⏵Champion Hurdle

Punjabi won in a blanket finish last year, in a time best described as ordinary, and the form has not worked out too well. The Nicky Henderson-trained winner bucked a recent trend in that his best pre-race time figure was not earned at Cheltenham. Before that all the winners since 2002 had earned their pre-race personal bests at the course (five of which were in excess of 150), indicating that previous Cheltenham experience is an advantage.

Solwhit is the only leading fancy without that experience and is said to need soft ground, but he has recorded an excellent speed figure and has hardly put a foot wrong, winning six of his last seven starts.

Zaynar surprisingly lost his unblemished record at Kelso in his warm-up race. The ground was given as an excuse, but the time was perfectly respectable, so he has questions to answer. He earned his best time figure over 2m4f but that should not be counted against him as he displayed plenty of speed in last year's Triumph, winning in a time 1.3sec faster than the County Hurdle over course and distance later on the card, and he is a big threat on this best form.

Khyber Kim has been a revelation this term, winning the Greatwood (with a Topspeed of 133) and Boylesports International (165) at Cheltenham. His best figures were achieved on the New Course but he is equally effective on the Old, on which the Champion is run, and he goes well fresh.

Go Native (152) won last year's Supreme Novices' Hurdle in a time only a tenth of a second slower than the Champion Hurdle a couple of hours later, but despite his subsequent victories he has not progressed time-wise.

⏵World Hurdle

The stats for this race are striking for their irregularity. Only once in the past ten runnings has a winner earned a Topspeed figure commensurate with his Racing Post Rating, Inglis Drever (175) in 2008, which is unusual for a championship race as the pace is usually true. Only three winners in the past decade had a pre-race best over 160 and a modest pre-race 96 did not prevent Big Buck's doing the business last season.

Hot favourite to retain his crown, Big Buck's still lacks a genuine top-quality speed rating but it has not prevented him gaining six straight wins over hurdles and worthwhile opposition is ebbing away. Karabak has a bit to find with Big Buck's on Newbury running in December and the Cleeve Hurdle, in which 2008 Champion Hurdle winner Katchit could not match strides with Tidal Bay, was slowly run.

The best alternative to the favourite is Sentry Duty, who has smart handicap form over two miles and is best fresh. Although untried over the trip, a moderate pace could play to his strengths.

CHAMPION HURDLE

Career-best Topspeed figures

Punjabi	167
Solwhit	167
Celestial Halo	166
Zaynar	165
Khyber Kim	165
Quevega	165
Sublimity	160
Medermit	159
Katchit	157
Won In The Dark	156
Mourad	155
Go Native	152

How the last ten winners rated

Year	Winner	Win TS	Pre-race TS
2009	Punjabi	155	160
2008	Katchit	157	157
2007	Sublimity	145	139
2006	Brave Inca	173	151
2005	Hardy Eustace	152	155
2004	Hardy Eustace	155	124
2003	Rooster Booster	164	154
2002	Hors La Loi	145	152
2000	Istabraq	152	171
1999	Istabraq	155	161

WORLD HURDLE

Career-best Topspeed figures

Karabak	157
Katchit	157
Diamond Harry	156
Muirhead	155
Pettifour	155
Sentry Duty	154
Cape Tribulation	150
Mourad	150
Big Buck's	147
Cousin Vinny	146
Lie Forrit	146
Mr Thriller	146
Time For Rupert	146

How the last ten winners rated

Year	Winner	Win TS	Pre-race TS
2009	Big Buck's	131	96
2008	Inglis Drever	175	162
2007	Inglis Drever	141	162
2006	My Way De Solzen	145	122
2005	Inglis Drever	148	162
2004	Iris's Gift	161	160
2003	Baracouda	161	147
2002	Baracouda	81	147
2000	Bacchanal	149	147
1999	Anzum	165	151

Tranquil Sea, like four previous winners of the Ryanair, gained his personal best on the clock with victory in one of the big Cheltenham handicaps

RYANAIR CHASE	
Career-best Topspeed figures	
Voy Por Ustedes	181
Imperial Commander	173
Tidal Bay	168
In Compliance	167
Snowy Morning	167
Barbers Shop	160
Our Vic	166
Scotsirish	162
Jack The Giant	161
Tranquil Sea	160
Golden Silver	159
Schindlers Hunt	159
Poquelin	158

ARKLE CHASE	
Career-best Topspeed figures	
Somersby	157
French Opera	156
Tchico Polos	153
Captain Cee Bee	152
Riverside Theatre	140
Tataniano	140
Sizing Europe	137
Citizen Vic	136
Little Josh	134
Take The Breeze	133
Long Run	130

SUPREME NOVICES'	
Career-best Topspeed figures	
Menorah	149
Get Me Out Of Here	146
Dunguib	145
Fionnegas	143
Puyol	140
Bellvano	138
Manyriverstocross	138
Any Given Day	136
Rite Of Passage	132
Some Present	131

▸Other races

In its short history, the **Ryanair Chase** has produced some persuasive facts from the clock. All five winners had a pre-race best in excess of 150 (the minimum winning figure for the race itself is 154), three had ratings above 160 and four had gained their personal bests at the track in either the Boylesports or Paddy Power Gold Cup.

Tranquil Sea and Poquelin, who won the Paddy Power and Boylesports respectively this season, satisfy the above criteria. Another to note is Chapoturgeon, who won the Jewson last year in a quicker time than that recorded by Ryanair winner Imperial Commander. When the respective weights were factored in, Chapoturgeon's figure on the clock was a mere 4lb inferior.

Only twice in the past ten runnings has the **Arkle Chase** been won with a Topspeed mark of less than 150 and this year only four – Somersby, French Opera, Tchico Polos and Captain Cee Bee – have served notice of that capability. Clockwise, the overall pre-race level is lower than par this year and some of the market leaders still have to prove themselves, with top-rated Somersby a notable exception.

Recent winning times in the **Supreme Novices' Hurdle** have stacked up well against those clocked in the Champion Hurdle later in the day, confirming that it takes a top-class hurdler to land the festival opener. A rating of more than 140 has been needed to win the race in each of the past six years and hot favourite Dunguib (145) is one of four to have reached that level. The others are top-rated Menorah (149), who blotted his copybook at Ascot in February but is a more attractive price as a result, Totesport Trophy winner Get Me Out Of Here and Fionnegas, second to Dunguib in the Deloitte. ■

Festival dream teams

James Pyman unearths ten profitable
jockey/trainer combinations worth noting

THE Cheltenham Festival is so competitive that trainers want
to send their horses into battle with everything in their favour
and that means booking jockeys in whom they can have
maximum confidence. Here, listed in no particular order, are
ten of the more interesting jockey/trainer combinations to look
out for.

▶▶**Nina Carberry/Enda Bolger** Festival record reads 31511
If you want cast-iron evidence that jockey bookings can prove
significant you only have to look at Enda Bolger's record in the Cross-
Country Chase. He has won the last three runnings, with each of the
winners partnered by Nina Carberry, and the finishing positions of
Bolger-trained runners not steered by Carberry during this period is
an inferior 449236. Bolger specialises in this type of race and had four
runners in last season's contest, so we can expect a block entry again
from him this year. At this stage it looks as though Carberry will aim
for a hat-trick on board Garde Champetre, who has won the last two
Cross-Country Chases, but it would be interesting if Carberry switched
to a stablemate.

▶▶**Ruby Walsh/Willie Mullins** Record since 2008: F601101143
Ruby Walsh is in the enviable position of being able to ride for the
reigning champion trainers in Britain (Paul Nicholls) and Ireland
(Willie Mullins), and in strike-rate terms his recent record for the Irish
champion really catches the eye. Walsh's record for Mullins at the last
two festivals is four winners (starting prices of 7-1, 5-2, 9-4 and 2-1)
from just ten rides and he had three winners from six rides for Mullins
at last year's festival, which suggests he chooses wisely and carefully
when to link up with the Mullins stable. Following the pair blind at
the last two festivals would have yielded a level-stakes profit of £7.75
and they should be among the winners again this year.

▶▶**Barry Geraghty/Edward O'Grady** Record since 2006: 103
Norman Williamson used to be Edward O'Grady's go-to jockey, but
when Storming Norman retired Barry Geraghty took over as the
trainer's first choice. Geraghty has linked up with O'Grady just three
times at the festival since 2006, partnering the well-backed Sky's The
Limit (returned at 11-1) to win the 2006 Coral Cup before drawing
a blank on O'Muircheartaigh. The following year Geraghty was given
the leg-up on Catch Me, who performed with credit to finish third at
7-1 in the Ballymore Properties Hurdle. The fact that Catch Me won a
Grade 1 in 2008 suggests he was always held in high regard by

Ruby Walsh's
record for
Willie Mullins
at the last two
festivals is four
winners from
just ten rides,
with a level-
stakes profit
of £7.75

Leading jockeys

Festival award winners

Year	Jockey	Winners
2009	Ruby Walsh	7
2008	Ruby Walsh	3
2007	Robert Thornton	4
2006	Ruby Walsh	3
2005	Graham Lee	3
2004	Ruby Walsh	3
2003	Barry Geraghty	5
2002	Richard Johnson	2
2000	Mick Fitzgerald	4
1999	Mick Fitzgerald	4

Total festival winners

Ruby Walsh	24
Tony McCoy	21
Barry Geraghty	16
Robert Thornton	15
Richard Johnson	13
Paul Carberry	11
Timmy Murphy	8
Davy Russell	5
Graham Lee	4
Paddy Brennan	4
Nina Carberry	4

Leading trainers

Festival award winners

Year	Trainers	Winners
2009	Paul Nicholls	5
2008	Paul Nicholls	3
2007	Paul Nicholls	4
2006	Paul Nicholls	3
2005	Howard Johnson	3
2004	Paul Nicholls	4
2003	Jonjo O'Neill	3
2002	Martin Pipe	3
2000	Nicky Henderson	4
1999	Paul Nicholls	3

Total festival winners

Nicky Henderson	34
Paul Nicholls	25
Edward O'Grady	18
Jonjo O'Neill	16
Willie Mullins	15
Philip Hobbs	11
Alan King	11
Nigel Twiston-Davies	10
David Elsworth	9
Ferdy Murphy	8
Howard Johnson	7
Henrietta Knight	7
Arthur Moore	7

connections and any Geraghty/O'Grady link-up at this year's festival will be worth noting.

▶▶Robert Thornton/Francois Doumen Record since 2005: 141
The shrewd French-based trainer has sent at least three runners to the festival in each of the last seven seasons and it would be no surprise to see Thornton partner one of his festival hopefuls. Thornton joined forces with Doumen three times at the 2005 festival and it proved a successful pairing with two winners (Moulin Riche at 9-1 and Kelami at 8-1) and a fourth. Thornton's commitment to Alan King is possibly why we haven't seen him ride for Doumen since, but if Doumen has runners in races where King doesn't have a representative it is likely that he will be getting in touch with Thornton's agent.

▶▶Davy Russell/Ferdy Murphy Record since 2003: 632121
Ferdy Murphy has been a staunch supporter of the talented Irish rider, who was his stable jockey for a couple of seasons until they parted company in 2004, and Russell has not disappointed with two winners (Joes Edge at 50-1 and Naiad Du Misselot at 7-1) and two seconds (Truckers Tavern at 33-1 and New Alco at 10-1) from his last four rides at the festival for the shrewd Yorkshire-based trainer. Part of the reason behind the pair's success is that Murphy's top horses are invariably trained to peak at Cheltenham – he's enjoyed at least one winner at three of the last four festivals – and Russell is a jockey for the big occasion who thrives under pressure.

▶▶Barry Geraghty/Jonjo O'Neill Record since 2003: 1215002612
The majority of Barry Geraghty's mounts at the festival will be for Nicky Henderson, but look out for the jockey if he picks up any spare rides for Jonjo O'Neill. The pair haven't joined forces at the festival since 2005, but five of Geraghty's ten rides for O'Neill between 2003 and 2005 finished in the first two, with the combination enjoying three winners. Geraghty's three winners for O'Neill were achieved in hurdle races, where his record reads 1215001.

▶▶Barry Geraghty/all Irish-based trainers
Record since 2003: 9-54, 17% strike-rate
The third appearance in this list for festival specialist Geraghty, whose tentacles spread far and wide throughout Ireland and, despite his allegiance to Nicky Henderson, we can expect to see Geraghty booked for some of the more fancied Irish raiders. We've already talked about his success when linking up with Edward O'Grady, but overall he boasts a creditable strike-rate of 17 per cent when partnering horses trained in Ireland at the festival since 2003, and his nine winners account for 18 per cent of all the Irish-trained winners at the festival in this period.

▶▶Richard Burton Record for all trainers since 2005: 12015F8F01
A suspension rules the top amateur out of the first three days of this

Barry Geraghty has a fine record at the festival and is worth noting when he links up with Irish trainers

year's festival, but he will be back for the Foxhunter on the final afternoon – a race he won last year on board the well-supported Cappa Bleu. That took his total to three winners at the last five festivals, which means that in terms of total festival winners for the period he is joint-11th behind Ruby Walsh (18 winners), Robert Thornton (12), Barry Geraghty (nine), Tony McCoy (six), Paul Carberry (six), Davy Russell (five) and Graham Lee, Nina Carberry, Paddy Brennan and Timmy Murphy (all four). Following Burton's mounts blind at the festival would have yielded a level-stakes profit of £18.00, so he is the first name to look out for when assessing races restricted to amateur riders at the festival.

▶▶**Robert Thornton/Ian Williams** No runners
This combination have yet to link up at the festival, but Ian Williams is enjoying a great season and should be sending a bunch of runners to the meeting, spearheaded by his RSA Chase hope Weird Al. Thornton's record this season for Williams of five wins from ten rides would make him an eyecatching jockey booking for one of the Worcestershire-based trainer's runners.

▶▶**Tony McCoy/Jonjo O'Neill**
Record since 2006: U3P1P0FF1P2210F26510730
This may be an obvious combination to look out for, but they deserve to be on the list because of their consistency at the festival. Thirty-nine per cent of their runners have finished in the first three and they have enjoyed at least one winner at each of the last four festivals. The partnership have really excelled in non-handicaps, with three winners, two seconds and two thirds from their last 14 runners. ∎

On the right lines

George Kimberley of the Racing Post Bloodstock team finds key contenders from a pedigree angle

THE pedigrees of recent winners from selected Cheltenham Festival races have been analysed to try to provide betting clues that can be applied to this year's festival. Only male-line ancestry – sire to grandsire to great grandsire – has been researched, as the dam side doesn't give enough of a data set to draw worthwhile conclusions.

Sons of Sadler's Wells are a strong stamina influence
There are many good jumps stallions by the late, great Flat sire and their progeny frequently feature among the winners of the festival's staying races. In 2m or 2m1f events over the past seven years, Old Vic and Accordion are both a dismal 0/12, Oscar and King's Theatre are 0/10, Dr Massini is 0/3 and Saddlers' Hall is 0/4, but they have all sired winners of festival races over 2m4f-plus in that period. Champion Chase contenders Twist Magic (Winged Love) and Big Zeb (Oscar) have to overcome the poor record of the Sadler's Wells line in the Champion Chase, which suggests that Kalahari King could be the greatest threat to Master Minded's crown.

The Arkle has been a great race for French-breds The record of French-breds in the Arkle is seven in the last 15 renewals and three in the last ten. If you had limited your bets to the most fancied French-bred in terms of SP in the last ten runnings, as long as they were single-figure odds, you would have had three winners and four losers, with form figures of P511122 and a profit of £11.25.

With Long Run likely to go for the RSA Chase, two of the probable French-bred runners in the Arkle are Tataniano and Osana. Tataniano would be a live contender if his Newbury defeat could be forgiven and Osana was second in the Champion Hurdle two years ago, which suggests he could be suited by the festival conditions. Riverside Theatre is well fancied but enthusiasm for him is tempered by the fact that he is by King's Theatre, a son of Sadler's Wells, and may need further.

2m5f hurdles are a stern stamina test Wednesday's two 2m5f hurdles should be viewed as staying events in terms of stallions. Eight of the last ten Neptune Investment Management Novices' Hurdle winners have come from sire lines that are strong stamina influences (Busted, Sir Ivor, Sadler's Wells, Nijinsky, Alleged and three from Mill Reef). The other two winning sires were the German-bred Lavirco, who sired last year's winner Mikael D'Haguenet, and Hardy Eustace's sire Archway, who is by Thatching. Neptune favourite Rite Of Passage has stamina doubts, being by Giant's Causeway, and Anshan, the sire

There have been seven French-bred winners in the last 15 runnings of the Arkle and a good profit could have been made by backing them

of Quantitativeeasing, is 0/20 in the past seven years. Willie Mullins' Fionnegas (by Accordion) should have the required stamina for this race and would be interesting if he lines up, as would Reve De Sivola (Assessor), Get Me Out Of Here (Accordion) and Quel Esprit (Saint Des Saints).

Of the past ten Coral Cup winners, four were French-bred. The remainder were again from the sire lines of Sadler's Wells, Alleged (twice), Busted and Nijinsky, with the sixth by Toulon, a son of Top Ville from the line of Derring-Do, another that carries stamina.

The Albert Bartlett has one of the strongest sire trends The five renewals of the Albert Bartlett have been won by sons of Presenting (Busted line), Video Rock (twice), Oscar and King's Theatre (both by Sadler's Wells). All of these sire lines are firmly in the staying power category and this race's winners have a strong trend in this regard, albeit from only five runnings. At the head of the Albert Bartlett betting, Tell Massini (Dr Massini), Quel Esprit (Saint Des Saints), Restless Harry (Sir Harry Lewis) and Shinrock Paddy (Deploy) all derive from suitably stamina-packed sire lines.

Few surprises in sires of Pertemps winners The last ten Pertemps Final winners were by stallions descending from Sadler's Wells (three), Mill Reef (three), Nijinsky (two), Diesis and Ahonoora. The anomaly is Ahonoora, who is normally a strong speed influence. With the possible exception of Diesis, the others are familiar staying sire lines.

Sadler's Wells strong in the National Hunt Chase The last three winners of the National Hunt Chase – at four miles, the longest race of the festival – were by sons of Sadler's Wells: Oscar (Tricky Trickster 2009), Saddlers' Hall (Old Benny 2008) and Poliglote (Butler's Cabin 2007). This year the Donald McCain-trained Fabalu (by Oscar) has a good chance to enhance the record of the Sadler's Wells line. Saddlers' Hall is the sire of Giles Cross and Saddlers Storm, while Synchronised is by Sadler's Wells himself.

RSA Chase: stamina, stores, and don't forget the French-breds The RSA Chase is one for traditional jump-bred horses and several winners have been drawn from familiar stamina influences Video Rock, Roselier, Presenting, Supreme Leader and Zaffaran, along with one son of Sadler's Wells, Accordion. French-breds have won two of the seven RSA Chases in which they have been represented in the past decade, both at big prices: 14-1 (Star De Mohaison) and 33-1 (Hussard Collonges).

The ante-post favourite Punchestowns looks to have a great chance on form, but he would not be a typical winner as a former Flat runner, and his main challengers Long Run (Cadoudal), Diamond Harry (Sir Harry Lewis) and Weird Al (Accordion) have strong claims. Dual Grade 1-winning chaser Pandorama is by Flemensfirth, who has yet to sire a festival winner over 3m+, so stamina is a worry with him. ■

Inside the stables

Three of the festival's leading trainers talk about their main contenders, plus an in-depth look at the Irish challenge and reports from the Racing Post's regional correspondents

Leading lights

Three trainers – with 25 winners between them at
the past three festivals – talk about their big hopes

Paul Nicholls

Pepe Simo Supreme Novices' Hurdle Has an outside chance if the ground dries. It was a bit too soft when we threw him in at the deep end in the Christmas Hurdle. Dunguib will be extremely hard to beat – I was impressed with him at Leopardstown and his hurdling seems fine to me.

Ghizao Supreme Novices' or Neptune Novices' He'd have an outside chance wherever he goes. The ground will determine his target. If it's soft I'd say it will be the Supreme Novices', but if it dries out he'd go for the longer race.

Tataniano Arkle No more than an outside chance, though he could improve on better ground. He was quite impressive on his first two runs over fences, although the form of his Grade 2 win hasn't worked out. There's always Aintree and Punchestown later in the spring.

Woolcombe Folly Arkle I'm becoming increasingly sweet on his chance, provided the ground dries out. The weather has meant we're taking him to the festival with just one run under his belt, which isn't ideal, but then not many novice chasers win a Grade 2 on their debut as he did at Doncaster.

The Tother One William Hill Chase He's high enough in the handicap, but there's a good handicap to be won with him. Put a line through his effort in the Welsh National as it came much too soon after his good run behind The Package, which would give him every chance in this.

Kicks For Free William Hill Chase Goes well fresh and we've had this in mind for a while. Beaten a nose in the Coral Cup a couple of years ago and ran okay at Sandown last time on ground that was too soft. Needs to go left-handed.

Celestial Halo Champion Hurdle I'm not saying he'll win, but he'll go well again if he gets better ground. He's run a bit below his best on his last two starts, but he doesn't like winter soft ground. He loves Cheltenham and has started coming to himself now.

Massasoit NH Chase I've yet to win this, but he seems the ideal type and I give him a leading chance. Ran well in a handicap at Sandown last time when blinkered for the first time. If he'd jumped the last better he'd have gone close to winning.

Nicholls factfile

▸▸Manor Farm Stables, Ditcheat, Somerset

▸▸Champion trainer four times (2005-06, 2006-07, 2007-08, 2008-09)

▸▸Festival winners: 25 (19 in chases, six over hurdles)

▸▸Top festival trainer six times (1999, 2004, 2006, 2007, 2008, 2009)

▸▸Last five festivals (earliest first): 2/3/4/3/5

▸▸The only man to have won the leading trainer award four years in a row

▸▸Almost half of Nicholls' festival winners (12 out of 25) have been in races currently on the final-day programme – only three have been in races on the opening day

▸▸Only seven of Nicholls' 25 festival winners have been in handicaps – his best handicap races are the County Hurdle (three winners) and the Grand Annual Chase (two winners)

The Nightingale RSA Chase Still needs to book his place, as I don't know whether he'll stay the trip. Now he's over his breathing problems he could go far, as he's very talented.

Master Minded Champion Chase He looked right back to his old self at Newbury, despite ignoring the last. In that sort of form he'll be very hard to beat. I never had him quite right last season – he's not the easiest to train and suffers from muscle problems.

Twist Magic Champion Chase He's been a complete revelation and his form in winning the Tingle Creek and Victor Chandler entitles him to go there with an outstanding chance. He's run way below his best in the last two renewals of the Champion Chase, but now he's mentally more mature I hope he won't be fazed by the occasion. He'll need to cope better with the parade.

Sanctuaire Fred Winter Juvenile Looks our main hope for this after he won at Taunton on his first run for us. It was the same contest that Nictory Vote won last year before injury ruled him out of this race.

Al Ferof Champion Bumper He's the best chance I've ever had of winning this. John [Hales] bought him privately after he'd won his Fairyhouse bumper in December and after he followed up at Newbury on Aon day, John said he'd like to go to Cheltenham. His form looks strong, so I'd be really hopeful.

Rivaliste Jewson Novices' Hasn't run since early December, but that was always the plan as I thought his handicap rating of 135 was worth preserving for this. He got there too soon, then idled in front, when just caught at Sandown last time, so we aim to hold on to him for longer at Cheltenham.

Al Ferof is the best chance I've had of winning the Bumper. His form looks strong, so I'd be really hopeful

Poquelin Ryanair On nice ground he'd have an outstanding chance. We knew he'd improved massively in the autumn and after finishing strongly to be second in the Paddy Power he went one better in the Boylesports, despite being unsuited by the soft ground. We've deliberately kept him off since to have him nice and fresh for the spring, as last season he didn't hold his form through to the festival.

Big Buck's World Hurdle Will be the festival banker for many and I wouldn't argue with that. He goes there nice and fresh, he looks fantastic and I couldn't be happier with his preparation. Tidal Bay looks our most dangerous rival.

Chapoturgeon Plate or Grand Annual The handicapper has him too high, but he would probably have finished second in the Boylesports Gold Cup but for making a hash of the last, which wouldn't have put him far behind Poquelin.

Advisor Triumph Hurdle Has strong claims in an open race. His Flat form wasn't as good as Celestial Halo's, our Triumph winner two years ago, but he has done nothing but improve since he was gelded. Has worked brilliantly.

Kauto Star "goes there on the back of a career-best, fit and fresh – and when he's like that he's lethal"

Tito Bustillo County Hurdle One of our secret weapons. We've won the County recently with similar types to this one. Wants decent ground, as his speed is blunted on anything too soft.

Najaf Albert Bartlett or Neptune Novices' Ran over a distance too short when winning at Exeter on his first outing since coming from France, where he had smart form. Has fair prospects of staying three miles.

Kauto Star Gold Cup The ratings say he's got 11lb or more in hand on the opposition, so if I get him to the festival in the same form as he was in at Kempton on Boxing Day, he'll be very hard to beat. He goes there on the back of a career-best, he's fit and fresh – and when he's like that he's lethal.

Denman Gold Cup The doubters write him off at their peril, as he'll be there with every chance. The ratings say he has to improve to beat Kauto, so he has a mountain to climb. I said that two years ago, and he went and climbed it.

Tricky Trickster Gold Cup Could easily run a big race. It was always the plan to use the Gold Cup to help get him spot on for the Grand National. He showed a great turn of foot when getting up to win the Aon and he looks in fantastic shape.

Taranis Gold Cup Has fair prospects of running into a place. He's not easy to train and it took some time to get him back after his win in the Argento Chase, but he's fine now. Loves Cheltenham.

Alan King

Salden Licht Supreme Novices' Hurdle He won three times for Andre Fabre before joining James Eustace. He was impressive first time out for us at Newbury, but then made rather heavy weather of it before following up at Plumpton. The runner-up there won next time, so perhaps we shouldn't be disappointed. He's also in the County Hurdle and he has the class to be competitive whichever race he contests.

Bensalem William Hill Chase We're getting rather fed up finishing second to Diamond Harry and, while we've not entirely dismissed the option of taking him on again in the RSA Chase, that looks red-hot with Punchestowns and Long Run in there and it may be more sensible to take the handicap route. I think he's a whole lot better than his mark of 143. Having won a chase at Plumpton, he'll pick up a £60,000 bonus if he does the same at Cheltenham. I'd rather win the William Hill than finish third in the RSA. He'd be one of my leading hopes for the week.

Nenuphar Collonges William Hill Chase He was third in this race last year and, although he hasn't run since the Hennessy, he is best when fresh. Blinkers bring him to life and he'll be thereabouts again.

Medermit Champion Hurdle He has done well since beating Punjabi at Haydock, where I left a bit to work on, and I'm very pleased with his progress, he has never looked better. I appreciate there is a strong challenge from Ireland, but he has a serious each-way chance. Looking back, he was unlucky not to beat Go Native in last season's Supreme, where he was hampered at the final flight, and that form looks pretty strong now. I must admit I've been surprised by his progress because at the start of the season I was all set to send him over fences, as he'd schooled so well.

Pennek National Hunt Chase He came from way back to take third in the Pertemps Final last year and was beaten just over two lengths. His three runs over fences have been on easy courses and he'll be suited by this test of stamina.

Manyriverstocross Neptune Novices' Hurdle I'm working on the owner because I believe this will suit rather better than the Supreme. He ran a smashing race when a staying-on third in the Totesport Trophy and the extra distance will be to his advantage. He needs a strongly run race to show his best and if he gets that, which seems likely, he'll go really well. He goes on any ground.

Saticon Coral Cup He was third in last season's Fred Winter, beaten less than four lengths. I was pleased with his run at Doncaster behind another of ours, Sir Harry Ormesher, especially as the testing ground was against him. He also has an entry in the Martin Pipe Conditional Jockeys' Hurdle.

King factfile

▶▶ Barbury Castle Stables, Wroughton, Wiltshire

▶▶ Festival winners 11 (seven in chases, four over hurdles)

▶▶ Last five festivals: 1/2/3/3/1

▶▶ Had his first winner at the festival in 2004 with Fork Lightning (William Hill Chase) and has had at least one winner every year since then

▶▶ Has sent out three dual festival winners – Voy Por Ustedes (2006 Arkle, 2007 Champion Chase), My Way De Solzen (2006 World Hurdle, 2007 Arkle) and Katchit (2007 Triumph, 2008 Champion Hurdle)

▶▶ Eight of his 11 festival winners have been in Grade 1 races

Sir Harry Ormesher Coral Cup He came from off the pace to win at Doncaster. He's gone up 7lb, but if the ground is no easier than good to soft he'll run.

Lake Legend Coral Cup This has been his main target all season and I believe he'll be very competitive. We put him away after he won at Kempton on Boxing Day because we didn't want a higher rating. He has thrived since returning from his break and worked nicely the other morning.

Silk Hall Coral Cup His participation is ground dependent – we took him out at Ascot the other day because it was too soft. He was a decent novice but we have struggled to find decent ground for him this winter.

Causeway King Fred Winter Juvenile Handicap Hurdle He needs a true-run race and, with that more than likely, I think he has a realistic chance of winning. He won first time up, since when he has finished runner-up to three smart types.

Gilded Age Fred Winter Juvenile Handicap Hurdle I thought he'd win first time over hurdles, but he returned home that night a sick horse and we gave him three months off. He qualified for a BHA mark, and therefore this race, when winning gamely at Doncaster last time.

Chamirey Pertemps Final He beat Tricky Trickster at Fontwell and then finished third in the Haydock qualifier. He's genuine enough, but we may fit blinkers to sharpen him up.

Voy Por Ustedes Ryanair He travelled and jumped well for a mile and a half in the Game Spirit, but we know he's no longer a two-miler and they quickened away at the end. This race looks perfect for him, especially if the ground comes up good. His engine might not be what it once was, but he retains his enthusiasm and I've certainly not lost faith in him.

Having endured a difficult time before Christmas, Alan King is optimistic his string will shine at the festival

Katchit World Hurdle I appreciate he hasn't managed to win since the 2008 Champion Hurdle and also that he has lost a gear or two, but he retains his enthusiasm and ran a super race in the Cleeve. If the ground is decent I'd be surprised if he's not right there with them at the final flight.

Karabak World Hurdle As with Katchit, I'd expect him to be there at the final flight and, who knows, one of these days Big Buck's might not pick up. Karabak does not stand too much racing, so the fact he had to miss the Cleeve because of a poor scope may be to his advantage because he goes well fresh.

Mille Chief Triumph Hurdle He wasn't right after his work the day before the Adonis, which meant we had to miss that race. It is a major concern, but we will continue to monitor the situation. On his work at home he'd be right up with the best of my juveniles over the years. He has no end of gears and, on his work, he'd murder three of ours who were placed in a Triumph – Franchoek, Blazing Bailey and Walkon. Katchit won a Triumph, but this one has more gears; he'd be more on a par with our 2005 winner Penzance. He was one of the worst affected by the muscle enzyme problem that affected the string before Christmas and it took a long time for him to come right.

The Betchworth Kid Albert Bartlett Novices' Hurdle One of my best chances of the week. He was staying on strongly at the end of a muddling race at Kempton last time, after being one of the first of the fancied runners to come off the bridle, and I'm sure he'll be suited by three miles, as he was a thorough stayer on the Flat for Michael Bell.

Oh Crick Grand Annual He had a low weight when winning this last year, but will be close to the top of the handicap this time. He's also in the Champion Chase and we'll monitor that to see if it cuts up.

Katchit "ran a super race in the Cleeve and if the ground is decent I'd be surprised if he's not right there at the last"

Willie Mullins

Blackstairmountain Supreme Novices' He won two bumpers, as well as a Flat race at Galway, and I always hoped he would make a good novice hurdler. He jumped well when he won at Punchestown at the end of January, but there hasn't been quite enough time to give him another run. It's not ideal that he is travelling with so little racecourse experience of jumping, but I'm happy with him.

Flat Out Supreme Novices' His bumper form was very good and at one stage I thought of keeping him for the Champion Bumper. In the end I decided to go jumping with him. I was delighted with the way he won a maiden hurdle at Punchestown. I think he'll stay a good bit further than two miles in the future, but he'll probably run in the Supreme Novices' rather than the Neptune.

Morning Supreme Supreme Novices' She was fifth to Dunguib in the Bumper last year. The weather upset our plans with her to an extent, but she has won both her starts over hurdles and could run in the Supreme.

Mikael D'Haguenet Arkle or RSA Chase It's a pity we haven't been able to get a run into him, but I'm satisfied with the way things have been going with him in the last few weeks.

Shakervilz Arkle He has taken to fences really well and is a natural jumper with great courage. He won over three miles as a hurdler, but the way he won over two miles at Navan helped to confirm for me that the Arkle is the right race for him. The pace they'll go should bring his stamina into play, though I would be a little worried about him if the ground was too lively.

Sports Line Arkle The plan is to run him in the Arkle. He was beaten by An Cathaoir Mor in the Leopardstown version, but that was only his second run over fences. I think he'll be better on good ground.

Jayo William Hill or Byrne Group Plate He was a good novice last year and stays well. I was thrilled with the way he ran when fifth to Poquelin in the Boylesports, as that was his first handicap and first run after a break. He ran well again at Leopardstown last time and I plan to run him in one of the handicaps.

Quevega Mares' Hurdle I haven't been able to get a run into her and, while that may not be ideal, it's not something that concerns me too much. She had been going well before a disappointing piece of work that forced us to scrap the plan to run her in the Red Mills at Gowran. It would be great if she could do what she did last year.

Fionnegas Neptune or Albert Bartlett He was no match for Dunguib in the Deloitte, but his two wins over hurdles have been over two and a half miles and he's entitled to go for one of the two staying races. I'm not sure which one it will be.

Mullins factfile

▶▶Stables: Closutton, Bagenalstown, Co Carlow

▶▶Irish champion trainer 2007-08, 2008-09

▶▶Festival winners: 15 (three in chases, six over hurdles, six in the bumper)

▶▶Last five festivals: 1/0/1/2/3

▶▶Won four of the first nine runnings of the Champion Bumper but only two of the last eight

▶▶Does best with young, up-and-coming horses – 14 of his 15 festival winners have been in the bumper, novice hurdles and novice chases (the exception was Quevega in last year's mares' hurdle)

▶▶Has returned a level-stakes profit on all runners at six of the last nine festivals

Quel Esprit Neptune or Albert Bartlett He's probably best with cut in the ground but he ran well when fourth to Dunguib in the Bumper last year. After winning his first two races over hurdles as I expected, I was a bit disappointed he was beaten by Coole River at Leopardstown. I'm prepared to give him the benefit of the doubt. At the moment I'm leaning towards the Neptune.

Uimhiraceathair RSA Chase Following his dead-heat at Navan he has to improve to have a serious chance in the RSA Chase, but he jumps well for a horse who hasn't had much experience over fences. He stays really well and good ground seemed to suit him well last season.

Golden Silver Champion Chase After beating Tranquil Sea in the Grade 1 at Leopardstown it was a bit disappointing that he didn't jump as well as he can when he was beaten by Big Zeb at Punchestown. Still, he's done enough to take his chance in the Champion Chase.

Bishopsfurze Champion Bumper He hated the heavy ground when he won at Fairyhouse but it got him qualified for the race in time. He had been working very well.

Day Of A Lifetime Champion Bumper Like Bishopsfurze we left it late in the day to get him qualified but he booked his ticket by winning in good style at Fairyhouse.

Up Ou That Champion Bumper He won his only point-to-point start and looked an obvious Cheltenham horse when he won a bumper at Fairyhouse.

Barker Ryanair or Champion Chase He unseated in the Durkan at Punchestown on his first run since winning the Swordlestown Cup there last season. He injured his back in the Durkan and missed some time, but he'll go for either the Ryanair or the Champion Chase.

Deutschland Ryanair or Coral Cup Although I feel he jumps better over fences than hurdles, I think he's well enough handicapped over hurdles and could pick up a good prize. I'm thinking about the Coral Cup as an alternative to the Ryanair. He's versatile and stays well.

J'y Vole Ryanair or Coral Cup She had lost her way a bit, so it was great to get her back to form to win at Gowran recently. She's a Grade 1-winning mare over fences but she's well enough handicapped over hurdles, so that's why I've decided to give the Mares' Hurdle a miss and she could run in the Coral Cup if she doesn't run in the Ryanair.

Cousin Vinny World Hurdle We've decided to put his chasing career on hold for the time being because he hasn't been jumping well and was disappointing in the Moriarty at Leopardstown. He is a course winner, so we're going to let him take his chance in the World Hurdle.

Mourad World Hurdle He ran what was probably his best race of last season when third to Zaynar in the Triumph, so we're going to head back and try to pick up some place money. I know he's up against it,

We've decided to put Cousin Vinny's chase career on hold for the time being. He's a course winner, so we're going to let him take his chance in the World Hurdle

Secant Star is "a lovely prospect who has lived up to expectations. I was happy with the way he won at Gowran"

and he's only a five-year-old, but he's been in good form and it was no disgrace to be beaten by War Of Attrition at Navan.

Secant Star Triumph Hurdle I thought he was a lovely prospect when I got him for France and he has lived up to expectations. He took off too soon at Leopardstown and jumped a shadow, but I was happy with the way he won at Gowran.

Tarkari County Hurdle He's only a five-year-old and is still a novice, but he ran so well when fourth in the MCR Hurdle at Leopardstown that we're thinking of letting him take his chance in the County.

Enterprise Park Albert Bartlett He's unbeaten in three starts, a bumper and two races over hurdles, and I've been pleased with him since he won a Grade 3 over two miles and six furlongs at Limerick in December. The second and third have both won well since then, so it looks as though that was a decent race.

Cooldine Gold Cup It was encouraging that he showed so much improvement between his poor run in the Lexus and his second in the Hennessy and I'm confident there is more to come from him. If he jumps around cleanly it will give him a good chance of picking up some place money. I suppose you can never tell what is going to happen on the day, but Kauto Star is going to be very hard to beat, and Denman too, despite what happened to him last time.

William HILL
Telephone betting

OPEN 24 HOURS

Back your winner with us first

William Hill prices available from 6pm the night before on all top races.

Call us using the phone number on your account card.

If you don't have an account call

0800 289 892

All systems go

Alan Sweetman assesses the Irish team and rates
Go Native a good chance for championship glory

▸▸Feature races

This time last year it looked as if the Smurfit Kappa Champion Hurdle offered the best hope of an Irish victory in one of the showpiece events, only for the race to be comprehensively dominated by the home team as Irish-trained horses drew a blank in the four major championship races for the second year in a row. Optimism has been renewed this season, however, as there has been a resurgence in the Irish hurdling division, spearheaded by Go Native, last season's Supreme Novices' winner, and Solwhit, winner of five of his six races at Grade 1 level.

When the Noel Meade-trained Go Native was soundly beaten by the mare Voler La Vedette at Down Royal in early November, his future in the senior ranks was open to question. And yet, only seven weeks later, not only had he become a prime Champion Hurdle contender, he had also put himself into the unique position of being eligible for a £1 million bonus should he triumph on March 16. First, he relegated Solwhit to third in landing the Fighting Fifth at Newcastle and four weeks later he beat Starluck and last season's Champion Hurdle third Binocular in the Christmas Hurdle at Kempton.

Solwhit's defeat at Newcastle was the only blot on his record in 2009. He signalled his arrival on the scene by winning the John Smith's Aintree Hurdle and went on to beat last year's Champion Hurdle winner, Punjabi, by a short head in the Rabobank Champion Hurdle at Punchestown. A modest pace at Newcastle was not ideal for him and trainer Charles Byrnes got his campaign back on track with victory in the December Festival Hurdle at Leopardstown's Christmas meeting. Then, getting the strong gallop he needs, he captured the Toshiba Irish Champion Hurdle in decisive fashion from Go Native's stablemate Donnas Palm.

Quick going at Cheltenham would be a worry for Solwhit, and with that reservation in mind Go Native is the horse most likely to reclaim the hurdling crown for Ireland. He is 3-3 in Britain, all in Grade 1 races, and looks a rock-solid contender.

Sublimity, the 2007 Champion Hurdle winner and best of the Irish when fourth in 2008, has shown lively signs this season, kicking off with a good second to Go Native in the Fighting Fifth. Solwhit reversed form with him at Leopardstown a month later and again had much the better of the exchange in the Irish Champion. That was by no means a discouraging display by Sublimity, as much less use is likely to be made of him at Cheltenham, where better ground will be more suitable into the bargain.

It is virtually impossible to see the Cheltenham Gold Cup as

3

Go Native has won on his three visits to Britain, all in Grade 1 races, and looks a rock-solid contender as he chases a £1m bonus

Quick going at Cheltenham would be a concern for five-time Grade 1 winner Solwhit (left)

anything other than a match between Kauto Star and Denman, with Irish interest largely confined to last year's dashing RSA Chase winner Cooldine. Following a dismal effort on his return to action in the Lexus Chase, he gave a reassuring display when second to Joncol in the Hennessy Cognac Gold Cup to put himself into the reckoning in the Gold Cup's 'without two' market. He relished the track as a novice last year and is set to peak at the right time.

This time last year Master Minded looked impregnable in the Queen Mother Champion Chase but that was before Big Zeb gave him a serious fright at Punchestown. As is well documented, Big Zeb, who fell four from home in last year's race, is prone to error, and if he had not blundered badly at the final fence at Punchestown he probably would have beaten the dual champion. Colm Murphy's nine-year-old started the season with a smart display in the Fortria at Navan, blotted his copybook with a bad run in the Tingle Creek and then bounced back to form at Punchestown, where a seven-length defeat of Leopardstown Grade 1 winner Golden Silver confirmed his status as Ireland's leading two-mile chaser. If he can get around without error he should not be far away.

Not since Dorans Pride in 1995 has there been an Irish-trained winner of the World Hurdle and there is little chance of things being any different this year. Although the Willie Mullins-trained Mourad attracted some attention in the ante-post market after winning over 2m4f at Punchestown in January, he has never gone beyond 2m5f and it is hard to be sure whether he will stay effectively enough to be a force at the highest level. Powerstation did well to take third place a year ago, though soundly beaten behind Big Buck's and Punchestowns. He has shown decent form this season and holds an each-way chance again on the basis that the track always seems to bring out the best in him (four seconds and a third from six runs, without winning).

Going green

▶▶Ireland is dominant in the Champion Bumper (14 winners in 17 runnings) and the Cross Country Chase (five out of five), as well as having a strong record in the Supreme Novices' Hurdle (seven winners in the last ten runnings)

▶▶The Neptune has been another strong novice hurdle for Irish raiders, with four winners (including three of the last four) and seven placed horses in the last ten runnings. In that period they have had seven places in the Triumph too, but have won only once

▶▶At the past ten festivals the only long-standing races in which Ireland has drawn a blank are the World Hurdle (eight placed horses), the Kim Muir and the Byrne Group Plate. There has been no Irish-trained winner in the five-year history of the Ryanair Chase

▶▶The best handicap races for Ireland have been the Coral Cup (four wins, 11 places in the last ten runnings) and the Grand Annual (four wins, four places)

⇢Novice hurdles

The roar of anticipation that traditionally greets the start of the festival is set to be even louder this time around. Not since the Champion Hurdle-winning days of Istabraq has a horse travelled from Ireland under a weight of expectation similar to that attending Dunguib, who returns to the scene of his commanding victory in last season's Weatherbys Champion Bumper to contest the Supreme Novices' Hurdle.

Ability shown in bumpers does not automatically transfer to the novice hurdling sphere, but Dunguib has the makings of an exceptional hurdler. The Presenting gelding, who gives the impression that he could hold his own in top-level staying races on the Flat, has looked a class apart from his contemporaries and was able to get away with a suspect hurdling technique when landing the Deloitte Novice Hurdle at Leopardstown without coming off the bridle. If he arrives at Cheltenham in the same shape, the only hope for his opponents is that his jumping will let him down.

Trainer Philip Fenton, whose main concern in the Deloitte was that Dunguib should settle effectively and not have a hard race, is confident that a true-run race will help to eliminate the errors, and he is almost certainly right. At Leopardstown, Dunguib was simply never travelling fast enough to get into a proper rhythm, but the pace is likely to be significantly quicker on better ground at Cheltenham. For the Irish contingent it will be nothing short of a disaster if he is beaten.

No criticism could be levelled against the jumping technique displayed by Rite Of Passage in his two wins over hurdles at Leopardstown and Punchestown. The Giant's Causeway gelding, who was soundly beaten in third behind Dunguib when favourite for last year's Bumper, had shown strong evidence of physical improvement when blitzing the opposition in the Leopardstown November Handicap and is much closer to being the finished article than he was 12 months ago.

Still his trainer Dermot Weld is keen to avoid a clash with Dunguib and aiming him instead at the Neptune Investment Management Novices' Hurdle. As a proven stayer over two miles on the Flat, there is no doubt about Rite Of Passage's ability to see out the trip, and such was his assurance at Leopardstown that he does not look likely to be disadvantaged by his relative inexperience. One negative attached to his chance is that his trainer, who has conquered at tracks all over the world, has a conspicuously poor record at Cheltenham, with a 20-year gap since Triumph Hurdle winner Rare Holiday provided his sole festival success. Rite Of Passage looks good enough to end the drought.

Willie Mullins has carved a reputation as a formidable festival operator and has won the past two runnings of the race now known as the Neptune with Fiveforthree and Mikael D'Haguenet. Though the stable's hopes of a hat-trick were dented when Quel Esprit, fourth in last year's Bumper and winner of his first two starts over hurdles, was beaten in a Grade 2 event at Leopardstown, Mullins has another smart

Irish runners often go well in the Pertemps and a £38 profit to a £1 level stake makes this the most lucrative punting race on the raiding party at the past ten festivals

*Dunguib has the
makings of an
exceptional hurdler
and travels from
Ireland under
a weight of
expectation not
seen since the
golden days of
Istabraq*

staying type in the unbeaten Enterprise Park, a live candidate for the
Albert Bartlett Novices' Hurdle, for which the Paul Nolan-trained
Shinrock Paddy, who has won both his starts over hurdles, including
a Grade 1 event at Navan in December, is another with a major
chance.

Ireland has not managed a win in the JCB Triumph Hurdle since
Mullins was successful with Scolardy in 2002, but this season's crop
contains several above-average types. Secant Star, a Mullins import
from France, where he won on his only start last season, looks
potentially very smart. He had the race in the bag when falling at the
last at Leopardstown, apparently distracted by the shadow of the
hurdle in low sun, and impressed when making all to beat weak
opposition at Gowran.

Pittoni, a maiden winner for John Oxx over ten furlongs, has won
three of his four starts over hurdles for Charles Byrnes. He merits
respect, but possibly needs more cut in the ground than he is likely to
get at Cheltenham. In contrast, the Gordon Elliott-trained Carlito
Brigante, who burst a bubble when beating Edward O'Grady's well-
regarded Alaivan at Leopardstown and completed a hat-trick with a
win at Musselburgh, will appreciate a quickish surface.

⏩Novice chases

Last season the raiders provided the winner of both Grade 1 novice chases at the meeting. Forpadydeplasterer became the first Irish-trained winner of the Arkle since Moscow Flyer in 2002 and Cooldine captured the RSA Chase, a third winner of the race for Willie Mullins, previously successful with Florida Pearl in 1998 and Rule Supreme in 2004. This time around the visitors have a particularly strong hand in the Arkle.

The two principal Arkle challengers have had contrasting experiences of the Cheltenham Festival. The Edward Harty-trained Captain Cee Bee enjoyed a memorable triumph when beating Binocular in the 2008 Supreme Novices' Hurdle, while later the same afternoon Henry de Bromhead's hope Sizing Europe was an abject failure when favourite for the Champion Hurdle.

Sizing Europe's troubles continued through last season, before he turned a corner with a fair run in a Grade 1 hurdle at Punchestown in May. He then beat modest opposition on his chasing debut at the same venue before being left off for the summer. The experience stood to him on his return and he arrives an unbeaten winner of four races over fences, including a Grade 1 event at Leopardstown in December.

RECORD OF IRISH-TRAINED RUNNERS AT THE LAST TEN FESTIVALS

Race	Wins	2nd & 3rd	Runners	Profit/loss	Winner's SP
Supreme Nov Hurdle	7	5	63	+26.75	14-1, 7-4, 3-1, 7-2, 40-1, 17-2, 12-1
Arkle Chase	2	1	40	-24.5	11-2, 8-1
William Hill Chase	2	0	11	+5	7-1, 7-1
Champion Hurdle	6	6	54	+7.31	4-9, 8-13, 33-1, 7-2, 7-4, 16-1
Cross Country	5	6	34	-9.5	4-1, 7-2, 5-2, 4-1, 7-2
Mares' Hurdle	1	1	6	-3	2-1
NH Chase	2	8	46	+2.5	13-2, 40-1
Neptune Nov Hurdle	4	7	47	-19	6-1, 17-2, 7-1, 5-2
RSA Chase	2	4	29	+0.25	25-1, 9-4
Champion Chase	3	3	23	-0.75	7-4, 6-4, 16-1
Coral Cup	4	11	58	-9	16-1, 4-1, 11-1, 14-1
Fred Winter Hurdle	1	1	29	-8	20-1
Champion Bumper	8	9	95	+7.5	14-1, 14-1, 7-1, 7-2, 33-1, 11-2, 12-1, 9-2
Jewson Novice Chase	1	2	15	-5	9-1
Pertemps Hurdle	3	7	37	+38	12-1, 10-1, 50-1
Ryanair Chase	0	3	11	-11	
World Hurdle	0	8	25	-25	
Byrne Group Plate	0	4	24	-24	
Kim Muir Chase	0	4	32	-32	
Triumph Hurdle	1	7	58	-41	16-1
County Hurdle	3	6	54	+21	10-1, 12-1, 50-1
Albert Bartlett Hurdle	1	4	24	-15	8-1
Gold Cup	2	7	29	-15.5	4-1, 15-2
Foxhunter	1	7	44	-23	20-1
Martin Pipe Hurdle	0	0	2	-2	
Grand Annual Chase	4	4	36	-8	7-2, 6-1, 7-1, 15-2
TOTAL	**63**	**125**	**926**	**-193.69**	

Irish winners

2009	9	1998	4
2008	7	1997	3
2007	5	1996	7
2006	10	1995	4
2005	9	1994	3
2004	4	1993	6
2003	6	1992	2
2002	5	1991	2
2001*		1990	2
2000	3	1989	0
1999	5		

*Meeting abandoned

However, the bare detail does not tell the whole story, as Captain Cee Bee seemed set to take control when falling at the last at Leopardstown.

As a nine-year-old, Captain Cee Bee does not have the profile of a typical Arkle winner, but he really does seem to have come back as good as ever, having been absent for 20 months prior to winning first time over fences at Naas in early December. For the most part he has jumped with conviction in his races, though it is a touch worrying that he made a mistake at the last when winning his prep race at Naas in February. With an error-free round he will take all the beating.

Ireland's other main contender for the Arkle is the Willie Mullins-trained Sports Line, who impressed when winning first time over fences at Navan in November. He was probably in front too soon when collared late by Sizing Europe's stable companion An Cathaoir Mor in the Arkle at Leopardstown and may have learnt enough from the experience to make his presence felt. An Cathaoir Mor's established preference for heavy ground makes it unlikely that he will travel.

Mullins was expected to have a big say in the RSA Chase with last season's novice hurdling star Mikael D'Haguenet. However, he had not made it to the track by late February and, with the home team looking strong, Irish hopes will hinge principally on last year's Albert Bartlett winner Weapon's Amnesty, who will appreciate the return to a longer trip after being beaten by the Mullins-trained Citizen Vic at Leopardstown. Citizen Vic won again at the track three weeks later but looks unlikely to run.

▸▸Champion Bumper

Dunguib's rout of the opposition was accompanied by an Irish clean sweep of the first eight places in last season's Weatherbys Champion Bumper, but this year's assault may not have the same strength in depth.

Race specialist Willie Mullins has exerted nothing like the same influence in Irish bumpers as he did last season, but he could have a big say with Day Of A Lifetime, a smooth winner at Fairyhouse in February, and Up Ou That, a son of 1995 Champion Hurdle winner Alderbrook who won his only point-to-point start and took a Punchestown bumper in January, though he had only three rivals.

With several promising horses in the yard, Mullins could pull a rabbit out of the hat late in the day, but Dermot Weld is in pole position with two smart candidates in Elegant Concorde and Hidden Universe, both impressive winners at Leopardstown. Elegant Concorde, who had one run last season, is a year older and appears to be the stable's main hope.

Other strong contenders include the John Kiely-trained mare Araucaria, winner of two of her four starts, and Tavern Times, a Tom Mullins-trained gelding who looked very useful when making a winning debut at Fairyhouse in October.

Garde Champetre goes for a Cross Country Chase hat-trick but faces a strong challenge from stablemate L'Ami and Sizing Australia

▸▸Other races

The David Nicholson Mares' Hurdle was won last year by the Willie Mullins-trained Quevega and she has held her position at the head of the ante-post market despite having been absent since last May. She was hugely impressive 12 months ago and will take all the beating if Mullins can get her back to peak condition in time. Colm Murphy will also be hoping that he can get the talented Voler La Vedette to the race after a setback. She is unbeaten in four races this season, including a defeat of a below-par Go Native at Down Royal. Zarinava, winner of a Grade 2 contest at Doncaster for Jessica Harrington, is another who could make her presence felt.

Schindlers Hunt, a fine third in last year's Ryanair Chase, should again be in with a shout after a good effort in third behind Joncol and Cooldine in the Hennessy at Leopardstown. Joncol will miss the race to wait for Punchestown, leaving Tranquil Sea, Edward O'Grady's Paddy Power Gold Cup winner, as the other principal Irish hope.

Enda Bolger tightened his grip on the cross-country scene when saddling a one-two-three in last year's festival event, and the winner Garde Champetre, also successful in 2008, has consolidated his reputation as a tremendous course specialist by winning on his two visits this term. L'Ami, second in the race last year, and the Henry de Bromhead-trained Sizing Australia, runner-up to Garde Champetre at the venue in December, are the ones most likely to thwart the hat-trick bid. ∎

Reaching for the stars

Jessica Lamb takes a tour of the Irish yards in
search of some lesser-known names to note

Henry de Bromhead has a winning chance with Sizing Europe in
the Arkle Chase, but just as exciting is the youngster waiting in the
wings for the trainer and owners Ann and Alan Potts.

Loosen My Load has model looks and an engine to match. He's a
fantastic athlete and already has a Cheltenham victory under his belt
after pipping speedster Some Present over 2m in November, which
came as something of a surprise as he looked to be in need of another
year to reach the level of power and strength required at this most
demanding of tracks.

Propelled into the spotlight when taking the 2008 Coral Welsh
National on Notre Pere, jockey Andrew Lynch has slowly but surely
come of age and the perfectly judged ride he gave Loosen My Load at
Cheltenham should turn out to have been an invaluable education.

De Bromhead – still undecided whether to send Loosen My Load for
the Supreme Novices' Hurdle or the Neptune Investment Management
Novices' Hurdle – was annoyed that the six-year-old was not quite
ready to clash with Dunguib in the Deloitte Novice Hurdle in February.

The County Waterford trainer expected him to get quite close to
Dunguib that day, but now appears to be favouring the 2m5f Neptune.
"He's really well and I'm very pleased with him," he said. "He's just
tipping away at the moment and I'd say he'll be going straight to
Cheltenham, though I'm really not keen to take Dunguib on anymore."

Look out too for De Bromhead's Sizing Australia, as the trainer is
looking forward to giving Enda Bolger's team a run for their money in
the Cross Country Chase.

▶▶**Gordon Elliott** is best known for Silver Birch's shock win in the
2007 Grand National, but nobody would be surprised if this was the
year he broke his Cheltenham Festival duck.

Elliott has become a specialist at mounting successful raids on the
more minor British meetings, but there is no doubt he has the talent
in his County Meath yard to make an impact at the festival.

Carlito Brigante, already a hardened traveller, goes to the Triumph
Hurdle on the back of a hat-trick, with two of the wins coming at
Musselburgh and the middle leg in the Grade 2 juvenile hurdle at
Leopardstown's Christmas meeting.

His first Musselburgh win in November – only five days after
finishing 14th on his hurdling debut at Navan, where the ground was
too heavy for his liking – allowed him to fly under the radar when he
lined up on yielding going at Leopardstown. A 20-1 chance, he scored
by 11 lengths from odds-on favourite Alaivan.

Elliott has no doubt the Gigginstown House Stud four-year-old will

Loosen My Load
is a fantastic
athlete, with
model looks
and an engine
to match, and
the Neptune
appears to be
the favoured
target

handle the hustle and bustle of the Triumph Hurdle and he has other live festival hopes too. You would not rule out Silver Birch landing the Cross Country Chase, in which he finished second before going on to Grand National glory, and Chicago Grey is just the type of classy young hurdler who could steal a place in the Coral Cup if given a stealthy ride.

The real dark horse in Elliott's festival string is Meath All Star, who has been trained for the Martin Pipe Conditional Jockeys' Handicap Hurdle since winning his maiden hurdle at Ffos Las in January.

He has Cheltenham experience, having finished 11th behind Dunguib in the Champion Bumper last year, and Elliott thinks 121 is a "fair enough mark for a horse who has only run five times". He will be partnered by Keith Donoghue, who has stacks of experience under his belt and looks set for a great ride.

▶▶In the Champion Bumper's 17-year history, no trainer has been more successful than six-time winner Willie Mullins, but it often pays to follow a smaller operation.

Philip Fenton's 45-strong string produced Dunguib to win the prize last year, Joe Crowley's select team landed it with Hairy Molly in 2006 and this year 20-horse **Danny Miley** could hold the ace with Forty Foot Tom, a general 20-1 shot.

Alain Cawley, the leading jockey for the County Wicklow trainer, rode Forty Foot Tom in several pieces of work before his 24-length Navan bumper victory in December and said: "I like him a lot. He's green and wouldn't be the best of work horses yet, but I like the way he goes on and quickens."

Miley, who sells most of his inmates as young horses, wanted to find a buyer for the five-year-old before the Champion Bumper, but he was unable to get the price he felt his potential star warranted and is now looking forward to his first festival runner. "He's a lovely, big horse and is a bit immature, but he has a fair engine," he said.

▶▶Dun Doire will be a familiar name in the Foxhunter line-up when he returns to the festival for the first time since winning the William Hill Chase four years ago. That took him to a peak RPR of 142 and, given his liking for Cheltenham, the 11-year-old will attract plenty of interest.

Sam Curling, son of legendary painter Peter, has taken over Dun Doire's training from Tony Martin and believes that, once he got his head in front again on his fifth point-to-point start in January, the veteran has come back to his old self.

"That was the turning point," said County Tipperary-based Curling, for whom Dun Doire will be a first festival runner. "He improved again to win his next start and he'll go straight to Cheltenham now, with a racecourse gallop in between."

Both wins were over 3m and Curling says the extra two and a half furlongs of the Foxhunter will bring further improvement, though he warns that Dun Doire is better with a bit of cut in the ground.

The real dark horse in Elliott's festival string is Meath All Star, who has been trained for the Martin Pipe Hurdle since winning his maiden hurdle at Ffos Las in January

Dun Doire: back on good form and will try to add the Foxhunter to his 2006 William Hill Chase success

His Cheltenham win, on his only previous visit to the track, was on good to soft over 3m½f and in those conditions he will be a live contender, especially with the considerable assistance of Nina Carberry in the saddle.

▶▶The four miles of the National Hunt Chase is a step into the unknown for most of the runners in Wednesday's opening race, but **Mouse Morris** is hopeful the trip is within reach for improving young chaser Tinakellylad.

"He's had a little break because he didn't seem 100 per cent behind when he won at Clonmel in December," the County Tipperary trainer said after his comeback run at Gowran Park in January, when he earned a career-best RPR of 137 after finishing fourth to useful novice Uimhiraceathair. "We thought about a handicap briefly, but this race looks made for him – he's built to stay all day."

Tinakellylad has never gone further than three miles, but he won two point-to-points over that trip as a four-year-old and he will be one of the safer conveyances in a race where the ability to jump well can help to conserve energy over the marathon trip.

He has never fallen in seven chase starts and has experience in big fields, with five of those outings coming against 14 or more rivals. He isn't extravagant with his leaps, but he's safe and races up with the pace, which will keep him out of trouble at the festival.

Strong competition comes in the shape of 11-2 favourite Any Currency and recent Fairyhouse scorer Saddlers Storm, but siding with a Gold Cup-winning trainer seems a good way to ensure you have a staying chaser up to the job at Cheltenham. ■

Henderson's got talent

Rodney Masters thinks Lambourn's festival virtuoso
will do well – and not just with the obvious fancies

WITH 34 winners at the Cheltenham Festival, Nicky Henderson is a
furlong clear of his colleagues and he arrives this year with such a
dynamic team it is likely that his lead will be stretched rather than
eroded. Henderson, who is nine winners ahead of Paul Nicholls, is
fielding his strongest-ever squad in more than 30 years as a trainer,
spearheaded by talents such as Punchestowns, Long Run, Zaynar,
Punjabi and Barbers Shop.

But let us embark on this Lambourn preview with a couple of the
less obvious candidates from Seven Barrows, who may prove lucrative
each-way bets. Of the handicappers within that category, the JP
McManus-owned **Ainama** is of particular interest in the Pertemps
Hurdle Final. His sole start since returning to training last autumn
came in a Newbury Pertemps qualifier. Tackling three miles for the
first time, he was noted staying on strongly at the finish to take fifth
behind smart stayer Lie Forrit. It was an eye-catching performance,
conceding 4lb to the winner, and connections will be content that the
BHA handicapper left Ainama's rating untouched at 139.

It will be remembered that the strong-pulling Ainama was in front
four flights from home in Go Native's Supreme Novices' Hurdle at last
year's festival, for which he was sent off a 14-1 shot. He was disputing
the lead with two to jump, but a mistake at the final flight ruined his
dwindling chance and he faded to finish a creditable eighth. That was

*Ainama is held in
high regard by
Nicky Henderson
and is expected
to thrive over
three miles in the
Pertemps Final*

only his third start over hurdles and he was to gain further valuable experience at Aintree, when a good third to Bouggler over 2m4f, and again when sixth over that same distance at Punchestown. The fact that he was travelled to such illustrious venues underlines the regard in which he is held within the Henderson camp.

Everything about Ainama hints that the three miles of the Pertemps is tailor-made. Although his owner is hardly in need of the funds, we all know how he thrives on the adrenaline rush of the Cheltenham ring and therefore we can anticipate a hefty each-way punt. It is worth noting Henderson's words at his open day for owners last autumn when discussing Ainama; he used phrases such as "undoubtedly a very talented performer" and "I think stamina will be his forte".

With Long Run almost certainly bound for the RSA Chase, Henderson's **Riverside Theatre** looks decent value at odds of around 10-1 for the Irish Independent Arkle Trophy. With the yard so commanding in the novice chase division, Riverside Theatre has been unfairly overshadowed by his more high-profile stable companions. Make no mistake, he is a class act.

Riverside Theatre races for the Jimmy Nesbitt Partnership, which includes Large Action's owner Brian Stewart-Brown, and, coincidentally, the horse carries red and white colours because the actor is a friend of Sir Alex Ferguson.

A decent hurdler, Riverside Theatre was third to Hurricane Fly in the Grade 1 Champion Novice at Punchestown and has transferred that ability to chasing. When winning at Newbury and Kempton he was impossible to fault, and the way he quickened the tempo in a matter of a few strides in the Wayward Lad Novices' Chase in December was mighty impressive.

The one niggling worry is that the six-year-old has no experience of Cheltenham, most of his races having come on courses with few undulations. However, he appears a most versatile type and the lack of Cheltenham experience is most likely a needless concern. I have no doubt double-figure odds represent a shrewd investment and at the time of writing he is my sole festival bet.

Detractors may point to the fact that he is without a race between Christmas and the Arkle, but he operates particularly well fresh and the evidence is there to support that theory because he has won first time out in his three seasons of competition so far.

Remaining with our less obvious contenders, the 20-1 available about **Candy Creek** looks too good to be true – each-way at least, and mindful of Quevega at the top of the betting – in the David Nicholson Mares' Hurdle, a race Henderson invariably targets. An alternative engagement, however, may be the Martin Pipe Conditional Jockeys' Handicap Hurdle.

Candy Creek has won four of her six starts and one of those defeats was behind Dunguib in the days when she was trained by John Kiely in Ireland. She changed hands for £200,000 last spring after winning the Listed mares' bumper at Aintree's Grand National meeting.

She was stuck in the mud when beaten at 8-13 at Newbury but

With the yard so commanding in the novice chase division, Riverside Theatre has been unfairly overshadowed by his more high-profile stablemates. Make no mistake, he is a class act

Pick of the bunch

▶▶**JP special** The 3m of
the Pertemps Final is
tailor-made for Ainama
and he looks a good
each-way punt

▶▶**Star turn** Riverside
Theatre is good value for
the Arkle from a stable
packed with top novices

▶▶**Class act** Punchestowns
can complete a Grade 1
novice-chase double for
Nicky Henderson

▶▶**Running up that hill**
The 2m5f with a stiff
finish will be perfect for
Micheal Flips *(pictured)*
in the Coral Cup

erased all memory of that next time when, on a better surface at
Musselburgh, she accelerated like a Ferrari against a 4x4 to outclass
the opposition in a novice hurdle. The only surprise that day was her
SP of 11-10.

Away from team Henderson, Andrew Turnell's **Micheal Flips**
ranks as our region's most likely winner of the Coral Cup. Bought for
£200,000 after winning a point-to-point in Ireland in the spring of
2008, he ran well for a long way in last season's Supreme Novices'
Hurdle until getting tapped for toe from the penultimate flight.

He took his first significant step up in distance in the 2m5f
Lanzarote Handicap Hurdle at Kempton in January and duly produced
an improved performance, quickening clear to overwhelm course
specialist Duc De Regniere by eight lengths.

While he was disappointing when reappearing the following
weekend at Ascot, it is safe to assume that was for no other reason
than the race coming too soon after Kempton; that was certainly the
view of his connections. Under the circumstances, that reverse must
not be viewed as detrimental to his chance in the Coral Cup, where
the 2m5f with a stiff finish looks right up his street.

For some reason that's difficult to fathom, Turnell's fine record of
achievement in major races is generally overlooked. His strikes at the
festival include Katabatic (1991 Queen Mother Champion Chase) and
Old Bridge (1996 Mildmay of Flete).

His stable was becalmed with an infection shortly before Christmas,
and likewise his Marlborough Downs neighbour Alan King was
experiencing a similar lull. Both teams are now operating at near full
capacity and King has an ace to play at the festival with the
thoroughly likeable **Mille Chief**, as long as he makes the line-up for
the JCB Triumph Hurdle.

From the same source in south-east France as last year's Triumph
runner-up Walkon, Mille Chief would appear to be blessed with all the
requirements for this demanding test and I have been particularly
impressed by his slick jumping and ability to quicken in a few strides.
King has always spoken of him with similar enthusiasm and has
regarded him as his leading juvenile since before Christmas.

Of our district's more obvious representatives, **Zaynar**, whose two
best performances have come at Cheltenham, remains the choice for
the Smurfit Kappa Champion Hurdle despite his reverse at Kelso and
in the RSA Chase, which is shaping up as a thriller, **Punchestowns**
is taken to prove too strong for Long Run and Diamond Harry.
Punchestowns, who put up a bold show against Big Buck's in last
season's Ladbrokes World Hurdle, will be all the wiser after his
blunder at the first of Sandown's downhill fences in the Scilly Isles
Novices' Chase.

Of the negatives, Petit Robin does not look value at 16-1 against the
likes of Master Minded and Kalahari King in the Seasons Holidays
Queen Mother Champion Chase and I can't see anything from our
patch getting close to Dunguib in the Spinal Research Supreme
Novices' Hurdle. ■

Western sharpshooters

Andrew King says Paul Nicholls holds the aces but
other West Country yards can make a mark too

ONCE again it is impossible to get away from the all-conquering Paul
Nicholls team when assessing the major prizes at the festival. The
champion trainer went close to a clean sweep of the four big races 12
months ago and we can expect more of the same, with Kauto Star,
Master Minded and Big Buck's solid chances to hold on to their
respective crowns. Only in the Champion Hurdle does Nicholls not
hold a favourite's chance.

Barring accidents it is difficult to envisage Nicholls not taking Gold
Cup honours again, as he holds such a strong hand with Kauto Star
and Denman, with Taranis and Tricky Trickster a more than useful
back-up pair. **Kauto Star** is deservedly a short-priced favourite,
having looked as good as ever in his two outings this season. His
demolition job in the King George at Kempton on Boxing Day could
not have been more impressive and, as long as it is not a slog in the
mud at Cheltenham, only a major error or getting brought down can
stop him registering his third Gold Cup success.

Denman has a substantial question mark hanging over him after
unceremoniously unseating Tony McCoy at Newbury in the Aon
Chase. The mistakes he made at consecutive fences in the straight
were worrying enough, but even before those errors he had not fully
shaken off the attentions of Niche Market and Tricky Trickster.
Connections are willing to gloss over that disappointing show, but to
my eye Denman appeared to be making heavy weather of it and,
given his worrying problems in the past, he makes little appeal as
second favourite.

The Nicholls supporting cast of Taranis, Tricky Trickster and
possibly What A Friend are not good enough on bare form, but Tricky
Trickster's battling success after Denman's departure at Newbury
proves he stays all day and gives him place claims.

Master Minded showed he is over the rib problem that saw him
run so poorly at Cheltenham in November when coming right away
to win Newbury's Game Spirit Chase, which is a good guide to the
Queen Mother Champion Chase, and he looks sure of a bold bid to
join the list of hat-trick scorers in the two-mile championship.

Despite a heart-stopping mistake at the final fence at Newbury, he
could have done no more than hack round and audaciously brush
aside some solid enough yardsticks. He is going to take some beating
again now he is back in that sort of form.

Twist Magic is well and truly in the reckoning on his form this
winter, but his Cheltenham record over the seasons is anything but
inspiring and he is most certainly a better horse on a flat course,
where his cruising speed is a valuable asset.

> Denman has
> a substantial
> question mark
> hanging over
> him after
> unceremoniously
> unseating
> Tony McCoy
> at Newbury in
> the Aon Chase

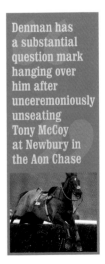

What can stop **Big Buck's** from pocketing another World Hurdle? Nothing, apart from an act of God, it seems. The star staying hurdler is the festival banker, standing head and shoulders above the rest of the field on all known form. The eight-year-old sometimes gives the impression he is struggling, as he does nothing very quickly, but then his resolute galloping style kicks in and it is all over bar the cheering.

The one that got away from Nicholls among the championship races last year was the Champion Hurdle when Celestial Halo narrowly went under to Punjabi after attempting to draw the sting out of his rivals with a bold front-running performance. This year's renewal looks stronger and on good ground he is going to be a sitting duck when the speedsters pounce, so he makes only small place appeal. It might be a different story if conditions are testing on the opening day, because then Celestial Halo's grinding style might have some of them in trouble once the action unfolds up the hill.

As usual, there is tremendous strength in depth to the Nicholls team and he has a shot at his first success in the Champion Bumper with **Al Ferof**, who confirmed himself a contender with a game success at Newbury on his first start for the champion trainer. His Irish form is solid enough and he is an each-way call in a race that has been dominated by Ireland over the years.

On the same day at Newbury, **Tito Bustillo** shaped encouragingly in a decent novice hurdle and he is capable of a bold showing in something like the County Handicap Hurdle if that is the route he takes at the festival. Nicholls has won the County three times in the past six years and Tito Bustillo looks his best handicap prospect this time.

Philip Hobbs has a high regard for his star novice hurdler **Menorah**, who looks the most serious challenger to the much-vaunted Dunguib in the Supreme Novices' Hurdle. The progressive five-year-old could hardly have been more impressive when he overwhelmed Bellvano at Kempton at Christmas and that looks good form, despite his defeat at Ascot last time.

The Hobbs yard could have another ace up their sleeve with **Planet Of Sound**, who goes for the Ryanair Chase. He has been trained with

that race firmly in mind and good ground on the second day of the meeting will see stable confidence high.

Although David Pipe is lacking a real star for this year's festival, he is always a trainer to keep on the right side in the handicaps and **I'm So Lucky** will be of plenty of interest if he goes for the Byrne Group Plate or even the Grand Annual Chase.

On his last trip to Cheltenham on New Year's Day, I'm So Lucky could not have been less so as he was knocked sideways and brought down when just about to creep into contention. He will be a serious prospect wherever his shrewd trainer decides to run him.

The Sliotar is another Pipe-trained horse who catches the eye and he could well be tailor-made for the four-mile National Hunt Chase. He has always given the impression that stamina is his strong suit and his second to Burton Port at Southwell in February reads well, as that course would not have played to his strengths. He will be much more at home around the galloping Cheltenham circuit.

The small Devon yard of Nick Williams has made giant strides over the past few seasons and the increasing quality of his string could see the trainer score his first festival success this year. One of his main hopes is **Reve De Sivola**, who looks set to play a hand in the finish of the Neptune Investment Management Novices' Hurdle. Sixth in last year's Triumph, he has stepped up this season and landed the Grade 1 Challow Hurdle in December over the Neptune trip. Sometimes he has looked a difficult ride but, with a fast pace almost guaranteed at the festival, he should be able to travel better and then unleash his turn of foot at the business end.

Williams's other big hope is Diamond Harry, who is expected to take in the RSA Chase unless connections have a change of heart and revert to hurdles for the World Hurdle. On the plus side his Cheltenham record reads 113, all over hurdles, but conversely the seven-year-old is pretty light-framed and has always looked the type who needs time between his races. Perhaps winning at Newbury only 21 days after his Haydock success and just five weeks away from his big target will leave its mark, but hopefully that will not be the case and he can turn up in good order. ∎

All eyes will be on the big guns from Ditcheat to see whether the champion trainer can plunder the biggest prizes again

Northern lights

Colin Russell on the main contenders for the Ferdy
Murphy, Howard Johnson and Donald McCain yards

NO trainer in the north has a better record at the festival in recent years than Ferdy Murphy and once again the master of Wynbury Stables in West Witton has an ace or two up his sleeve ready to be played in March. His main hope is **Kalahari King**, who came so close to winning last year's Arkle and bids to go one better against Master Minded and company in the Seasons Holidays Queen Mother Champion Chase.

The nine-year-old was a decent hurdler, but he has excelled since being sent over fences and proved his class with that short-head Arkle defeat by Forpadydeplasterer. He didn't face quite such a strong field in the John Smith's Maghull Novices' Chase at Aintree and netted the big prize he deserved with an eight-length win over Tatenen.

A slight setback delayed his comeback this season, but when it came in February he provided convincing proof that he has improved again. Despite his trainer considering him to need the race, and racing off a stiff enough mark of 157, he took a Doncaster handicap in good style by three and a half lengths after travelling well throughout. Murphy is convinced Kalahari King has come on for that outing and, providing the ground is good or better, an excellent run is expected in the Queen Mother.

Master Minded is going to take all the beating, but Kalahari King jumps well and gets the trip well round Cheltenham. It would certainly not be a surprise to his connections if he were to topple the dual champion.

Another Murphy runner, the mare **I'm Delilah**, who has run two good races at Doncaster this season and is still improving, is considered to have an each-way chance in the Arkle, while stablemate **Poker De Sivola** could surprise a few with a good run in either the Kim Muir or the National Hunt Chase.

Poker De Sivola was beaten favourite in the Kim Muir last year, when Murphy felt he was unlucky not to finish nearer than seventh. He's not totally straightforward and, though he finally managed to win a chase when handed the race at Catterick in February, he's not one to have great confidence in. However, he could run into a place.

A Murphy handicapper well worth noting is **Watch My Back**, who hasn't run since winning in great style at Doncaster in December. He's a progressive sort who is suited by decent ground and has been trained for the Byrne Group Plate.

A good-ground festival would play to the strengths of **Tidal Bay**, whose course win in the Cleeve Hurdle in January put him in the reckoning for the Ladbrokes World Hurdle. After schooling him over hurdles prior to the Cleeve, trainer Howard Johnson was really

Ferdy Murphy has high hopes with Kalahari King and several well-treated handicappers

buzzing about his jumping, so it came as no surprise when he won that race despite the going being softer than ideal for him.

The 2008 Arkle winner races with an ungainly head carriage and has been the subject of some rude comments over the last couple of seasons, but the Cleeve win suggested the return to hurdles was just what he needed after losing his confidence over fences. He now heads for the race that his former stable companion Inglis Drever dominated for so long and, though he will need to step up on the Cleeve form to beat Big Buck's, he is an interesting contender, particularly if the ground is genuinely good. Johnson is convinced he is much better on decent ground.

Door Boy, who lost his unbeaten record over fences at Musselburgh in February, and the juvenile hurdler **Ascendant** are two other possible Johnson winners, but the harsh winter means the County Durham-based trainer is likely to field a somewhat weaker team than usual this year.

Across to the west, the bad weather has made little impact on the form of the Donald McCain stable, which has maintained a healthy strike-rate all season. The one to make most appeal is the novice hurdler **Peddlers Cross**, who bolted up on his second start over hurdles at Haydock in January. He wouldn't be quite in the class of Dunguib, but he jumps better and is not short of pace. Whether he takes on the Irish hotpot in the Supreme Novices' Hurdle or goes for the Neptune over 2m5f has yet to be decided, but he looks a pretty smart prospect.

McCain's **Whiteoak** looks to have a solid each-way chance in the David Nicholson Mares' Hurdle, which she won two years ago, and **Kudu Country** is expected to go well by his trainer Tom Tate in the Fred Winter Juvenile Handicap Hurdle.

The key trials

Raceform's unique
analysis team assess
the form of the
major prep races
on the road to
the festival

▶Paddy Power Gold Cup

Four of the five winners of the Ryanair Chase contested the Paddy Power in the same season (only Imperial Commander won this race), while 2008 winner Our Vic had landed the Paddy Power three years previously, and the form lines look strong around Tranquil Sea.

Coming into this contest off a Naas victory over Joncol (later a dual Grade 1 winner in the John Durkan and Irish Hennessy), Edward O'Grady's second-season chaser saw off Poquelin, who won the Boylesports.com Gold Cup on his next outing. Admittedly the 2m trip at Naas was in his favour, and in both races he had his preferred soft ground, but Tranquil Sea took full advantage in the Paddy Power. Runner-up Poquelin might have given him more of a race but for having too much ground to make up when the tempo lifted.

Tranquil Sea has run only once more, finishing second over 2m behind Champion Chase contender Golden Silver at Leopardstown's Christmas meeting. On Racing Post Ratings that ranked on a par with his Paddy Power win and a long way above the level of his novice season, when he was largely disappointing.

Paul Nicholls' Chapoturgeon (fell eighth) has plenty to prove after disappointing at Cheltenham on New Year's Day but cannot be left out of calculations for March, especially as he is a previous festival winner.

Verdict Tranquil Sea and Poquelin must come into the reckoning for the Ryanair, with the ground likely to decide which goes best [David Toft]

▶Fighting Fifth Hurdle

With no obvious front-runner in the line-up, this season's Fighting Fifth was run at a crawl and things only began to get serious nearing the home bend. That resulted in a slower winning time than the following maiden won by Quantitativeeasing, making the form look suspect, but Go Native was visually impressive. He was suited by the way the race unfolded, jumped really well throughout and had plenty left at the finish. He showed it to be no fluke when following up in the Christmas Hurdle and, with his liking for Cheltenham, has strong claims for the big one in March. He should get his ground again there (his three below-par runs since the start of last year were all on soft ground), but whether he will able to repeat this with a more searching gallop is open to doubt.

Solwhit was one of the worst affected by the lack of early pace and should not be judged solely on this display. He turned form around with Sublimity when winning the two key races in Ireland. Sublimity, the 2007 Champion Hurdle winner, proved keen off the sedate early gallop here, but found a neat turn of foot when the dash developed nearing three out. He was another suited by the way the race was run and remains a player for the Champion at the age of ten.

Verdict Solwhit can turn this form around after showing his true colours at Leopardstown on his next two runs. He looks the most solid of the Champion contenders [Dave Orton]

Result

Paddy Power Gold Cup
Cheltenham
November 14, 2009
2m4½f, soft

1 **Tranquil Sea** 7 10-13
Andrew McNamara
11-2f

2 **Poquelin** 6 11-1
Ruby Walsh 12-1

3 **Hold Em** 7 10-1
Jamie Moore 14-1

4 **Ballyfitz** 9 10-11
Paddy Brennan 6-1

Trainer: Edward O'Grady
Owner: Nelius Hayes
Distances: 4½l, 2l, 3½l
16 ran

Result

WBX.com Fighting Fifth Hurdle
Newcastle
November 28, 2009
2m, good to soft

1 **Go Native** 6 11-7
Davy Condon 25-1

2 **Sublimity** 9 11-7
Philip Carberry 20-1

3 **Solwhit** 5 11-7
Davy Russell 15-8

Trainer: Noel Meade
Owner: Docado Syndicate
Distances: 2½l, 3½l
7 ran

▸Hennessy Gold Cup

Result

Hennessy Gold Cup
Newbury
November 28, 2009
3m2¹/₂f, good to soft

1 **Denman** 9 11-12
Ruby Walsh 11-4f

2 **What A Friend** 6 10-4
Sam Thomas 7-1

3 **Niche Market** 8 9-11
Andrew Glassonbury 33-1

4 **Barbers Shop** 7 10-8
Barry Geraghty 13-2

Trainer: Paul Nicholls
Owners: Paul Barber and
Mrs Margaret Findlay
Distances: 3¹/₂l, 3³/₄l, shd
19 ran

Since the Hennessy was first run in 1957, only Arkle (twice) and Denman in 2007-08 have won this race and the Cheltenham Gold Cup in the same season. Denman, who won his second Hennessy here despite conceding 13lb or more to his 18 rivals, now bids to match Arkle's feat of doubling up twice and only Kauto Star can be considered in the same league on this form. This was one of the greatest weight-carrying performances of the past 40 years, but then came the Aon disaster that raised fresh doubts over Denman.

What A Friend, who received 22lb from the winner, finished three and a half lengths away in second and franked the form next time by winning the Lexus Chase, suggesting that the Leopardstown race was a long way off Gold Cup form. Barbers Shop (fourth), who appeared to run out of steam here and was then a well-beaten third behind Kauto Star in the King George, is likely to step down to the Ryanair Chase, in which he has strong claims. Joe Lively (tenth) was in the midst of a disappointing run of form here, but he ran his best race for some time in the Argento Chase in January and has an excellent Cheltenham record (four wins from nine starts). He is worth considering if he goes for the William Hill Chase.

Verdict Denman was brilliant here, but you have to forgive his Aon run to see him beating Kauto Star, who looks the more solid of the big two now [Rodney Pettinga]

▸Tingle Creek Chase

This is the premier mid-season target for the top two-milers and, although Master Minded was missing, this looked a pretty good renewal. Winner of the race in 2007 and the only danger to Master Minded when falling two out in 2008, Twist Magic has always gone well at Sandown and enjoyed himself out in front, jumping well throughout, while his rivals struggled to keep up. The time wasn't great (1.8sec slower than the novices in the Henry VIII) but he won easily and this run, together with his subsequent success in the Victor Chandler Chase, suggests he's better than ever. Questions remain about his ability to handle Cheltenham, but being ridden positively seems to suit him and on ratings he's the main danger to Master Minded in the Champion Chase.

Result

**Keith Prowse
Hospitality Tingle
Creek Chase**
Sandown
December 5, 2009
2m, soft

1 **Twist Magic** 7 11-7
Ruby Walsh 9-4

2 **Forpadydeplasterer**
7 11-7
Tony McCoy 9-2

3 **Well Chief** 10 11-7
Timmy Murphy 4-1

Trainer: Paul Nicholls
Owners: Barry Fulton,
Tony Hayward,
Michael Lynch
Distances: 15l, 9l
5 ran

Forpadydeplasterer, best in a strongly run race over 2m on decent ground, didn't have conditions to suit and can do better at the festival, if he makes the line-up. Well Chief won well on his comeback in November but now looks a shadow of his former self, being well beaten here and again by Twist Magic in the Victor Chandler. Big Zeb (fourth) was again let down by his jumping and, though he bounced back to form when taking the Tied Cottage Chase at Punchestown in January, he has to prove he can reproduce his home form in Britain.

Verdict Master Minded looks unbeatable in the Champion Chase, so the principals will be running for the minor places [Steffan Edwards]

▸Boylesports International Hurdle

In the past ten years only Rooster Booster and Katchit have won the Champion Hurdle after running in this race, but this season's renewal looked a strong race on paper, with Punjabi and Celestial Halo (first and second respectively in the 2009 Champion) locking horns once again.

Both were firmly put in their place by Khyber Kim, whose improvement this season is reminiscent of the great strides Rooster Booster made on his way to Champion Hurdle success in 2003. He appeared to beat Celestial Halo on merit and Medermit, who beat Punjabi again on his next start at Haydock, rates a solid benchmark.

Punjabi (fourth) clearly needed this first outing in seven months and faded badly from the second-last, having looked to be travelling best of all to that point. He was still not at his best when beaten by Medermit at Haydock in January and may be able to turn this form around if he arrives at Cheltenham in peak condition.

This form took a knock when Celestial Halo was trounced by Solwhit in the Irish Champion Hurdle on his next start, although he cannot be written off given his good record at Cheltenham (122 from three starts). Ebadiyan (fifth), who ran out in last season's Triumph Hurdle while holding place claims, ran disappointingly here but showed better form at Naas in January when getting the better of Muirhead over 2m3f. He is reportedly being aimed at the Coral Cup.

Verdict Khyber Kim's winning RPR of 167 puts him right in the mix [Rodney Pettinga]

Result

Boylesports.com International Hurdle
Cheltenham
December 12, 2009
2m1f, soft

1 **Khyber Kim** 7 11-4
Paddy Brennan 12-1

2 **Celestial Halo** 5 11-8
Ruby Walsh 4-7f

3 **Medermit** 5 11-4
Robert Thornton 8-1

Trainer: Nigel Twiston-Davies
Owner: Caroline Mould
Distances: 2¼l, 3l
7 ran

Master Minded (left) is set to face a strong challenge from Twist Magic (right), who won the Tingle Creek in his stablemate's absence

⏵Boylesports.com Gold Cup

This long-established handicap chase, like the Paddy Power Gold Cup, is a good guide to the Ryanair Chase – Fondmort (the 2006 Ryanair winner) and Taranis (2007) were beaten in this race earlier in the season. Second in the Paddy Power on his previous run, Poquelin showed here that he is on the upgrade and can handle soft going. Better ground will suit him best at the festival, however.

Razor Royale ran a fine race, building on his success in an amateur riders' race over 3m here the previous month, and boosted the form with victory in the Racing Post Chase in February. He would have a live chance if he goes for the William Hill Chase.

Skippers Brig is effective at around this trip and on soft ground and travelled well for a long way, before staying on at one pace. Chapoturgeon goes well on this track, having won the Jewson last spring, but is prone to jumping errors. He was beginning to struggle when making a bad mistake at the final fence and was disappointing when fading over the same track and trip on New Year's Day.

Jayo (fifth) finished on the heels of the first four but could not build on that on heavy ground at Leopardstown in January. Our Vic took the wrong course early here but, after being well beaten in the King George, bounced back to win the Peter Marsh Chase in January.

Verdict Poquelin will be a big threat in the Ryanair on good ground and Razor Royale's liking for the course makes him a festival prospect too [Ashley Rumney]

⏵Christmas Hurdle

Go Native will go to Cheltenham with a shot at the £1m bonus for winning the Fighting Fifth, Christmas and Champion, and victory in this middle leg was achieved with more authority than the short-head margin would suggest. Having cruised through to lead at the last, he idled badly on the run-in and was almost caught by the fast-finishing Starluck, but the impression was that he was doing just enough.

Noel Meade's stable star is proven at Cheltenham and has won all three Grade 1 races he has contested in Britain, but a slight negative is that he has not impressed against the clock this season, as the winning time here was fractionally slower than the novice event on the card. The impression was that he was dossing in front, which is something he would not want to do at Cheltenham if hitting the front early, though it is possible to argue that a stronger pace might suit him as much as his rivals.

Starluck enhanced his reputation here but, while he has place prospects, it is hard to envisage him winning the Champion Hurdle. Pepe Simo (fifth), an unbeaten novice coming into this race, found this company too hot but looks a decent outside bet for the Supreme Novices' Hurdle and would be of interest in one of the handicaps.

Verdict Go Native should confirm this form with the beaten horses but he has those time questions to answer [Rodney Pettinga]

Result
Boylesports.com Gold Cup
Cheltenham
December 12, 2009
2m5f, soft

1 **Poquelin** 6 11-8
Ruby Walsh 7-2f

2 **Razor Royale** 7 10-11
Paddy Brennan 8-1

3 **Skippers Brig** 8 10-11
Brian Harding 15-2

4 **Chapoturgeon** 5 11-10
Daryl Jacob 13-2

Trainer: Paul Nicholls
Owner: The Stewart family
Distances: 7l, 3l, 1½l
17 ran

Result
William Hill.com Christmas Hurdle
Kempton,
December 26, 2009
2m, good to soft

1 **Go Native** 6 11-7
Davy Condon 5-2

2 **Starluck** 4 11-7
Timmy Murphy 100-30

3 **Binocular** 5 11-7
Tony McCoy 11-8f

Trainer: Noel Meade
Owner: Docado Syndicate
Distances: shd, 1½l
7 ran

Kauto Star, having won his fourth King George, now tries to join the select band of three-time Gold Cup winners

▸King George VI Chase

This mid-season championship is by far the most significant pointer to the Cheltenham Gold Cup. On the last ten occasions that both races were run, the following seven horses won the Gold Cup after running in the King George (finishing positions at Kempton in brackets): See More Business (1st), Looks Like Trouble (pulled up), Best Mate (2nd), Best Mate (1st), Kicking King (1st), Kauto Star (1st) and Kauto Star (1st). Only Best Mate in the season when he won his third Gold Cup, War Of Attrition and Denman have won the big one at Cheltenham since 1999 having not run at Kempton.

It was all the more significant, then, that this victory was the most emphatic of Kauto Star's four King George wins, having jumped superbly throughout. Paul Nicholls is following the same plan that paid handsome dividends last year, keeping Kauto Star fresh by sending him straight from the King George to the Gold Cup, and another slice of history beckons for the remarkable ten-year-old.

Madison Du Berlais and Nacarat (fourth) may wait for Aintree, but Barbers Shop, who ran to a similar level behind Denman in the Hennessy, is being aimed at the Ryanair Chase. Imperial Commander (fifth) was disappointing on the face of it, but he clearly doesn't like the going right-handed and made mistakes at crucial stages. He has each-way claims at Cheltenham, given that his course record over fences reads 11411.

Verdict Kauto Star was imperious here and the balance tilted firmly in his favour after Denman's Aon disaster [Rodney Pettinga]

Result

William Hill King George VI Chase
Kempton,
December 26, 2009
3m, good to soft

1 **Kauto Star** 9 11-10
Ruby Walsh 8-13f

2 **Madison Du Berlais**
8 11-10
Tom Scudamore 10-1

3 **Barbers Shop** 7 11-10
Barry Geraghty 14-1

Trainer: Paul Nicholls
Owner: Clive Smith
Distances: 36l, 1l
13 ran

⟩⟩Feltham Novices' Chase

Result

William Hill.com Feltham Novices' Chase
Kempton, December 26, 2009, 3m, good to soft

1 **Long Run** 4 11-0
Sam Waley-Cohen 11-8f

2 **Tazbar** 7 11-7
James Reveley 9-2

3 **Ogee** 6 11-7
Jimmy McCarthy 15-2

Trainer: Nicky Henderson
Owner: Robert Waley-Cohen
Distances: 13l, 24l
7 ran

This race has a fine roll of honour and Long Run is potentially as good as any previous winner, though it is notable that no Feltham winner has gone on to add the RSA Chase, from 16 to try. He was making his British debut, having won three of his four starts over fences in France, the latest of them in a valuable Grade 1 against his fellow four-year-olds.

Keen to post and in the race too, his jumping was somewhat sketchy, although he never looked likely to come down. He eased past Tchico Polos three out and survived a mistake at the next before careering away from the useful Tazbar, who had closed on him between the last two fences.

His jumping was generally better in the Kingmaker over 2m at Warwick in February, although he made a notable mistake at the first of the line of five fences down the back. He took over on the home turn and quickly came away, putting in fine jumps over the last two fences and winning with plenty in hand. This was the shortest trip he had tackled since his racecourse debut and he gave the impression he would be more suited by the 3m of the RSA Chase than the Arkle over 2m, although connections were delaying that decision. The experience will have done him good.

Verdict Long Run is sure to take a great deal of beating in the RSA Chase, but his jumping will have to stand up to the test over the Cheltenham fences [Ashley Rumney/Richard Lowther]

⟩⟩Lexus Chase

Result

Lexus Chase
Leopardstown
December 29, 2009
3m, soft

1 **What A Friend** 6 11-10
Sam Thomas 11-2

2 **Money Trix** 9 11-10
Davy Russell 14-1

3 **Joncol** 6 11-10
Alain Cawley 7-2

Trainer: Paul Nicholls
Owner: Ged Mason & Sir Alex Ferguson
Distances: ½l, 1¼l
11 ran

What A Friend *(pictured)* got on top late in the day to become the fourth successive British-trained winner of this race. His victory paid a handsome compliment to Denman, having received 22lb from his stable companion when beaten into second in the Hennessy at Newbury on his previous run, and underlined the gulf in class between the top Irish chasers and their British counterparts. It is hard to see him troubling the big two in the Gold Cup, but the 40-1 on offer wouldn't be the worst each-way value to give Paul Nicholls another 1-2-3 in the race.

Joncol won't be going to the festival, but is one of the benchmarks of the Irish chasing form. He had landed the John Durkan on his previous outing and was fancied to step up again. He looked in pole position approaching three out, but began to run out of puff and gave way on the run-in. Despite proving himself at 3m with a gutsy win in the Irish Hennessy in February, he was soon ruled out of the festival.

The lightly raced Money Trix also needs it soft and, with those conditions here, he put up a career-best display. He was only sixth of seven behind Joncol in the Irish Hennessy next time but could go to the Gold Cup if the ground comes up soft.

Verdict A key race tying up the British and Irish form, and the logical conclusion is that the Irish are struggling to keep up [Dave Orton]

»Long Walk Hurdle

As the only Grade 1 staying hurdle race before the festival, the Long Walk Hurdle has had the greatest influence on the World Hurdle in recent years, with Anzum, Baracouda (twice) and My Way De Solzen all running in this race before taking the stayers' crown.

This year's race, which was switched from Ascot to Newbury, promised to be a cracker, with reigning champion Big Buck's taken on by Diamond Harry and Karabak. Big Buck's hit his customary flat spot during the race but eventually won with authority. Having defeated two of the pretenders to his crown, he was cut to a best price of 4-6 after this performance and was put away for Cheltenham.

Karabak is admirably consistent but will need to find significant improvement to challenge at the festival. Diamond Harry was switched to fences after this race, with the RSA Chase the target. Kayf Aramis (fourth) is qualified for the Pertemps Final, which he won last season, and on this form he looks one of the likelier prospects for that race. Fair Along (fifth) has finished behind Big Buck's four times now and there is no reason to suggest he can bridge the gap in the World Hurdle, especially as he was also well beaten by Tidal Bay in the Cleeve Hurdle in January.

Verdict This confirmed Big Buck's as the dominant staying hurdler and opposition dwindled after this, as Diamond Harry and Punchestowns were sent chasing [Rodney Pettinga]

»Irish Champion Hurdle

Solwhit won his fifth Grade 1 race in nine months to put himself forward as the most likely winner of the Champion Hurdle. The race was run at more of a Cheltenham pace than any other he has contested this season and, having travelled well and jumped as fluently as he ever has, he is likely to take some beating in the big one. Perhaps he hit a flat spot for a few strides after the second-last, but he picked up well after a good jump at the last.

Donnas Palm passed the test on his first run against horses of this calibre this season and, with his trainer also responsible for Go Native, connections must have been encouraged by this run.

Sublimity, the 2007 Champion Hurdle winner, ran a fine race. Ridden more positively than usual, he was just in front and travelling well at the second-last. The effort took its toll in the end, but if he gets better going at Cheltenham he can be expected to go a lot closer.

The form of last year's Champion Hurdle has taken a bit of a battering and this was another setback for Celestial Hero, who was beaten nine lengths into fourth. There appeared to be no excuse for the 2009 Champion runner-up, even allowing for the fact that this inside track may not have suited him.

Verdict Five of Ireland's seven recent Champion Hurdle winners ran in both the December Festival Hurdle and this race, so Solwhit's pair of wins put him in with a big shout [Dave Orton]

Result

Racing UK Long Walk Hurdle
Newbury, December 29, 2009, 3m¹/₂f, heavy

1 **Big Buck's** 6 11-7
Ruby Walsh 1-2f

2 **Karabak** 6 11-7
Tony McCoy 14-1

3 **Diamond Harry** 6 11-7
Timmy Murphy 11-4

Trainer: Paul Nicholls
Owner: The Stewart family
Distances: 3¹/₂l, 2³/₄l
8 ran

Result

Toshiba Irish Champion Hurdle
Leopardstown, January 24, 2010, 2m, soft to heavy

1 **Solwhit** 6 11-10
Davy Russell 5-6f

2 **Donnas Palm** 6 11-10
Barry Geraghty 8-1

3 **Sublimity** 10 11-10
Philip Carberry 10-1

Trainer: Charles Byrnes
Owner: Top of the Hill Syndicate
Distances: 4¹/₂l, 1¹/₂l
7 ran

▸Cleeve Hurdle

Inglis Drever and Big Buck's had taken the previous two runnings of this race before going on to win the World Hurdle and, while lacking an established staying hurdler of their class, this year's renewal featured a Champion Hurdle winner, some progressive types and a few decent chasers trying their luck back over the smaller obstacles.

Tidal Bay, the 2008 Arkle winner, was in the latter category, having his first start over hurdles since April 2007. His stamina wasn't guaranteed, especially in this testing ground, but the distance proved no problem. He was still going well when taking over coming to the final flight and found plenty to pull clear up the hill. He was a high-class novice hurdler (beaten a neck in the 2007 Ballymore before winning a Grade 2 at Aintree) and this victory established him as a threat to Big Buck's.

Time For Rupert, successful in a handicap over course and distance in December, never stopped trying, but the winner proved too strong for him from the final flight. His trainer believes there is still improvement in him.

Katchit, without a win since the 2008 Champion Hurdle, was tackling this trip for the first time and put in a decent effort, only just losing out in the battle for second. He could also return for the World Hurdle and, with faster ground likely, he may see out the trip even better than he did here.

Verdict Tidal Bay showed his class but there was not too much depth here and Big Buck's is much tougher [Ashley Rumney]

▸Irish Hennessy Gold Cup

This race may turn out to be more informative for the Ryanair Chase than for the Gold Cup, which is widely seen as a two-horse race. Joncol, the gusty winner, is not going to the festival but Ireland will have a chance of a first Ryanair winner in the race's six-year history with Schindlers Hunt, third here just as he was in last year's Ryanair.

This was his best performance of the season, over a trip further than his best and on ground more tiring than he cares for. Connections are entitled to look with some confidence at the Ryanair, as he might just get the spring ground he likes with the race falling a little later this year, on March 18.

The only horse of Gold Cup interest was last year's runaway RSA Chase winner Cooldine, who put up by far his best display since then. He travelled and jumped well, with the exception of one fence, and put the gun to the heads of his rivals with an excellent jump at the second-last. He was mugged late on, but if he was slightly lacking fitness here (having been pulled up in the Lexus on his reappearance) then it was a fine performance, which he should improve on again.

Verdict Cooldine (*pictured*) has place claims in the Gold Cup, while Schindlers Hunt won't have to find as much improvement to have a winning chance in the Ryanair [Dave Orton]

▸▸Deloitte Novice Hurdle

A wonderful performance in every aspect bar one from Dunguib, who wasn't clever at several of his hurdles, probably as a result of jockey Brian O'Connell's successful attempt to switch him off at the back of the field. Those sketchy jumps did not stop him winning impressively and the quest of finding a rival that can get him off the bridle continues. There is a strong chance it will take until next season to find one, as he has an incredible engine and cruising speed. The effortless way he made up ground after the second-last against good novices was breathtaking and, even though this was his smallest winning margin, he was in complete command.

This rated as his best performance over hurdles, in a race run at a proper gallop. His jumping leaves only the slightest doubt about him, but it is probably no coincidence that his best jump was at the final flight when he was doing slightly more than half-speed.

Fionnegas, while outclassed by the winner, stayed on to finish clear of the others. His only previous defeat was third behind Hollo Ladies in a 2m Grade 1 at Leopardstown over Christmas and he should be a player in one of the longer novice hurdles at Cheltenham. Odds of 20-1 for the 2m5f Neptune Novices' Hurdle underestimate him.

Verdict How Dunguib jumps in the hurly-burly of the Supreme Novices' Hurdle will be a big talking point, but it is hard to see him being beaten [Dave Orton]

Result

Deloitte Novice Hurdle
Leopardstown, February 7, 2010, 2m2f, soft

1 **Dunguib** 7 11-10
Brian O'Connell 30-100f

2 **Fionnegas** 6 11-10
Ruby Walsh 8-1

3 **Some Present** 7 11-10
Tony McCoy 16-1

Trainer: Philip Fenton
Owner: Daniel Harnett
Distances: 2½l, 11l
7 ran

▸▸Dr PJ Moriarty Novice Chase

This race invariably attracts novices who go on to bigger things, though the 2009 running was more significant than usual in terms of the festival, with Cooldine, the winner, going on to take the RSA Chase and runner-up Forpadydeplasterer winning the Arkle (this season's Paddy Power Gold Cup winner Tranquil Sea was fifth).

There was an upset this time as Citizen Vic, the lesser fancied of Willie Mullins's two runners, made all and kept on well when asked to raise his effort after two out. He is a massive improver at just the right time for the spring festivals but, according to his trainer, the Powers Gold Cup over this trip at Fairyhouse is a more likely option than the RSA Chase.

The one to take out of this for the RSA Chase was the fast-finishing Weapon's Amnesty. The modest gallop meant he wasn't able to show his true colours on this drop in trip, but the way he finished his race was most encouraging. He has to turn around a short-head defeat by Ireland's other proven staying novice chaser, Pandorama, in a 3m Grade 1 at Leopardstown over Christmas, but the likely better ground at Cheltenham could see him do that (Pandorama prefers it soft). Having shown his class when taking the Albert Bartlett at last year's festival, he will relish going back over 3m.

Verdict Weapon's Amnesty (pictured) looks the strongest of the Irish challengers for the RSA and 12-1 is more than fair [Dave Orton]

Result

Dr PJ Moriarty Novice Chase
Leopardstown, February 7, 2010, 2m5f, soft

1 **Citizen Vic** 7 11-10
Paul Townend 12-1

2 **Weapon's Amnesty** 7 11-10
Davy Russell 4-1

3 **Roberto Goldback** 8 11-10
Robbie Power 5-2f

Trainer: Willie Mullins
Owner: Donal O'Connor
Distances: 1¾l, 3l
8 ran

Result

Aon Chase
Newbury, February 13,
2010, 3m, good to soft

1 **Tricky Trickster** 7 11-3
Ruby Walsh 8-1

2 **Niche Market** 9 11-6
Andrew Glassonbury
25-1

3 **Air Force One** 8 11-0
Paul Moloney 14-1

Trainer: Paul Nicholls
Owner: Chris Giles
Distances: sh hd, 18l
6 ran

▸▸Aon Chase

Denman looked nigh on impossible to oppose at 1-6, being miles clear on official ratings and with bullish reports coming from connections, and what happened early in the home straight came as a major shock. Denman drifted to a best-priced 7-2 for the Gold Cup after his exit following two catastrophic mistakes, with Kauto Star shortening to odds-on, and a quick return to his Hennessy-winning best is unlikely.

Champion jockey Tony McCoy was on board for the first time, in a 'getting to know you' exercise before the Gold Cup, and it appeared to be business as usual when the pairing opened up a clear lead approaching the fifth-last. That impression didn't last long, as McCoy began to look over his shoulder to see how far clear he was, and it was apparent Denman wasn't stretching on as expected when Niche Market began to close up again. Denman then got the fourth-last all wrong when standing right off it, doing well to stay on his feet, and that rival steamed past him. The favourite was beaten even before he walked through the next fence and unseated McCoy.

The eventual first two have the Grand National as their principal target, so the only real significance of this result in terms of the festival was the damage it did to Denman's chance.

Verdict Denman ran a big race in last year's Gold Cup on the back of a defeat, but it is asking a lot for him to do it again [Dave Orton]

Result

**Totepool Game
Spirit Chase**
Newbury, February 13,
2010, 2m1f, good to soft

1 **Master Minded** 7 11-10
Ruby Walsh 8-13f

2 **Mahogany Blaze** 8 11-0
Paddy Brennan 14-1

3 **Fix The Rib** 7 11-4
Tony McCoy 6-1

Trainer: Paul Nicholls
Owner: Clive Smith
Distances: 13l, 1¼l
5 ran

▸▸Game Spirit Chase

Master Minded had a lot to prove after flopping at Cheltenham on his seasonal return in November, when he hung right throughout and finished a laboured third. It transpired afterwards that he was suffering from a cracked rib, but still there were question marks over his form, as he has never matched his awesome performance when winning his first Queen Mother Champion Chase in 2008.

He was 10lb clear of his nearest rival at the weights here and everything looked in place for him to resume winning ways if fully recovered. He delivered in some style, leaving his rivals for dead when quickening to the front with a stunning leap four out. He was just as impressive over the next two fences but made a hash of the last. Ruby Walsh, who was quick to blame himself for the mistake, did well to recover and they won easily.

Master Minded was cut to a best-priced 4-5 to complete a Champion Chase hat-trick and his RPR of 181 (joint second-best of his career) puts him a long way clear of his rivals.

Of the others, Voy Por Ustedes (fourth) dropped out tamely on this first run over the minimum distance since finishing second to Master Minded in the 2008 Champion Chase. There is a chance he could bounce back over a longer trip on livelier ground at Cheltenham, but on this evidence he is regressing.

Verdict Master Minded *(pictured)* was most impressive and, with further improvement likely, he is all set for the hat-trick [Dave Orton]

RACING POST
PRESENTS

CHELTENHAM
HEAVY
HITTERS

KO the bookies at Cheltenham with the Racing Post every day

EXCLUSIVE
CHAMPION COLUMNISTS

In the build-up to the Cheltenham Festival get the **exclusive** insight from the champion trainers Paul Nicholls and Willie Mullins

 ## BRILLIANT TIPPING

Unbeatable world-class tipping team assessing every runner for every Cheltenham race

 ## PRICEWISE

Feared by the bookies, don't bet without his advice

PLUS Simply the **best writers**, exclusive **interviews** and features – bringing your sport to life. PLUS all **previews**, reports, latest **news**, best pictures and **much more**

RACING POST
CHELTENHAM FESTIVAL 2010 OFFICIAL MEDIA PARTNER

Trainer analysis

Kevin Morley delves into
the festival records of the top
trainers in search of pointers

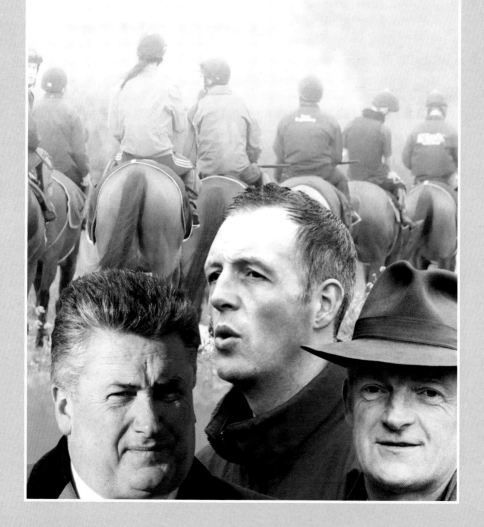

Paul Nicholls

To see how difficult it is to train a winner at Cheltenham, compare Paul Nicholls' strike-rate at the festival with the rest of the jumps season. Generally around a quarter of the champion trainer's runners win (24% this season at the time of writing), but over the last ten festivals his strike-rate has been 10%, which is pretty much as good as it gets at jump racing's championship meeting.

Nicholls has been the most successful trainer at this meeting in recent seasons, finishing top of the pile last year (with five winners) for the fourth time in a row. He sent out 33 runners across the 26 races last year and his 15% strike-rate made him profitable to follow to a level stake.

Fair play to any punter who adopted that policy for the 2009 meeting, but that level of success was a deviation from the norm. Although it is hard to envisage a festival without at least a couple of successes for Nicholls' powerful Ditcheat yard, his winners tend to be at short prices these days and the usual result of following his stable blind is a loss.

Chasers are Nicholls' speciality and he is particularly good in the championship races. The best betting strategy is to be selective with his fancied horses in these races. He appears to have the Gold Cup sewn up, so take your pick out of Kauto Star and Denman (I favour the reigning champ) and he also has the favourites for the Champion Chase (Master Minded) and the Ryanair (Poquelin).

But he is not the champion trainer for his skill with chasers alone. Hurdling victories have been on the increase in recent years and this has been reflected at the festival. His hurdling team did him proud last year, when the highlight was Big Buck's winning the World Hurdle – the quirky seven-year-old looks unopposable this year in his bid for back-to-back victories. Nicholls was also on the mark with American Trilogy in the County Hurdle and just failed to land the Champion Hurdle with Celestial Halo.

Despite Nicholls' strength in depth in most areas, he does have a festival Achilles heel. Considering his brilliance at training chasers, his record in festival handicaps over fences is disappointing and Chapoturgeon was a rare winner in that category when taking the

Festival winners 25
Last five years 2/3/4/3/5

1999 Flagship Uberalles (Arkle), Call Equiname (Champion Chase), See More Business (Gold Cup)

2003 Azertyuiop (Arkle)

2004 Azertyuiop (Champion Chase), Earthmover (Foxhunter), St Pirran (Grand Annual), Sporazene (County Hurdle)

2005 Sleeping Night (Foxhunter), Thisthatandtother (Ryanair)

2006 Noland (Supreme), Star De Mohaison (RSA Chase), Desert Quest (County Hurdle)

2007 Denman (RSA Chase), Kauto Star (Gold Cup), Andreas (Grand Annual), Taranis (Ryanair)

2008 Master Minded (Champion Chase), Denman (Gold Cup), Celestial Halo (Triumph)

2009 Master Minded (Champion Chase), Chapoturgeon (Jewson), Big Buck's (World Hurdle), American Trilogy (County Hurdle), Kauto Star (Gold Cup)

	Hurdles						Chases						Bumper			Overall		
	H'cap			Non-H'Cap			H'cap			Non-H'Cap								
1999	0/2	0%	-2.00	0/1	0%	-1.00	0/6	0%	-6.00	3/8	38%	+25.50	0/0	0%	0.00	3/17	18%	+16.50
2000	0/0	0%	0.00	0/1	0%	-1.00	0/3	0%	-3.00	0/5	0%	-5.00	0/0	0%	0.00	0/9	0%	-9.00
2002	0/0	0%	0.00	0/3	0%	-3.00	0/6	0%	-6.00	0/11	0%	-11.00	0/0	0%	0.00	0/21	0%	-21.00
2003	0/1	0%	-1.00	0/3	0%	-3.00	0/6	0%	-6.00	1/9	11%	-6.75	0/1	0%	-1.00	1/20	5%	-17.75
2004	1/4	25%	+4.00	0/3	0%	-3.00	1/4	25%	+1.00	2/11	18%	+6.88	0/0	0%	0.00	4/22	18%	+8.88
2005	0/7	0%	-7.00	0/1	0%	-1.00	0/13	0%	-13.00	2/13	15%	-3.00	0/0	0%	0.00	2/34	6%	-24.00
2006	1/4	25%	+1.00	1/7	14%	0.00	0/10	0%	-10.00	1/7	14%	+8.00	0/1	0%	-1.00	3/29	10%	-2.00
2007	0/2	0%	-2.00	0/6	0%	-6.00	1/16	6%	-3.00	3/10	30%	-0.05	0/0	0%	0.00	4/34	12%	-11.05
2008	0/5	0%	-5.00	1/7	14%	-1.00	0/10	0%	-10.00	2/11	18%	-3.75	0/1	0%	-1.00	3/34	8%	-19.75
2009	1/5	20%	+16.00	1/6	17%	+1.00	1/9	11%	0.00	2/13	15%	-8.89	0/2	0%	-2.00	5/33	15%	+6.11
Total	3/30	10%	+4.00	3/38	8%	-18.00	3/83	4%	-62.00	16/98	16%	+1.94	0/5	0%	-5.00	25/252	10%	-73.06

Jewson last year. That probably relates to how he campaigns his chasers: given the quality at his disposal, Nicholls isn't usually interested in protecting handicap marks. It was notable that Chaptoturgeon, who carried 10st 11lb to victory, had the joint-lowest weight among the Nicholls handicap team last year, but often his horses are near the top of the weights and are vulnerable to rivals that have been plotted up. In all handicaps at the past ten festivals, Nicholls has had one winner from 60 runners weighted at 11st or above (the winner was American Trilogy, who carried exactly 11st) and five winners from 55 carrying less than 11st.

Chapoturgeon's success came over 2m5f but Nicholls' other five festival handicap victories (chases and hurdles) have been over 2m in the Grand Annual and County Hurdle, so if you want to back a Nicholls handicapper it is probably best to concentrate on those racing over the minimum trip.

Alan King

Over the past few seasons, Alan King has been just about the most progressive jumps trainer around. In 2003-04 – the season of his first Cheltenham Festival winner, Fork Lightning in the William Hill Chase – King sent out 47 winners but that has increased year on year and last season he had 136 winners, only 19 behind champion trainer Paul Nicholls.

King's rise has been mirrored at the festival, where he has had at least one winner every year since Fork Lightning's 2004 breakthrough success, but last year he had to wait until the final race of the festival to strike with Oh Crick in the Grand Annual. For a stable accustomed to winning championship races with Katchit (2008 Champion Hurdle), Voy Por Ustedes (2007 Champion Chase) and My Way De Solzen (2006 World Hurdle), that was a disappointing return.

If King is to get his festival strike-rate back on an upward curve, it is likely that a handicap success will have to contribute and Bensalem is interesting in the William Hill Chase

That's not to say King's horses ran badly last year; they just came up a bit short. Medermit (Supreme Novices'), Karabak (Ballymore Properties), Voy Por Ustedes (Ryanair) and Walkon (Triumph) all finished runner-up in championship races, so King was bang in contention even if success was frustratingly elusive.

Another way of reading last year's festival results is that King's rate of improvement has levelled off or even dipped – a view supported by King's overall figures this season. His total of winners is likely to fall well short of last season and challengers for the big races look thin on the ground.

Even with the improvement in his stable's form since the turn of the year, King has still had problems during the festival build-up, with Mille Chief going lame before his intended prep for the Triumph – a race in which King has had two winners, two runners-up and a third from seven runners in the past five years.

Oh Crick's Grand Annual win last year was a rare festival handicap

Festival winners 11
Last five years 1/2/3/3/1

2004 Fork Lightning
(William Hill Chase)

2005 Penzance (Triumph)

2006 Voy Por Ustedes
(Arkle), My Way De Solzen
(World Hurdle)

2007 My Way De Solzen
(Arkle), Katchit (Triumph),
Voy Por Ustedes (Champion
Chase)

2008 Katchit (Champion
Hurdle), Old Benny (NH
Chase), Nenuphar Collonges
(Albert Bartlett)

2009 Oh Crick
(Grand Annual)

Alan King has had a winner at every festival since 2004, but had a
frustrating run of seconds before striking with Oh Crick last year

winner for King. While he has an enviable record in the level-weights
races, his figures in handicaps are nowhere near as impressive. Oh
Crick was only his second such winner – the first was Fork Lightning's
breakthrough William Hill Chase victory in 2004 – and, like Paul
Nicholls' runners, King's horses rarely hold secrets from the
handicapper, which makes them vulnerable at a meeting as
competitive as the festival.

If King is to get his festival strike-rate back on an upward curve,
however, it is likely that a handicap success will have to contribute.
King could have some interesting novices in handicaps – Oh Crick and
Fork Lightning were both novices when they won at the festival, even
though they stepped into open handicap company, and Old Benny
won the National Hunt Chase in 2008. This year **Bensalem**, for
example, is an interesting betting proposition in the William Hill
Chase on the opening day.

	Hurdles						Chases						Bumper			Overall		
	H'cap			Non-H'Cap			H'cap			Non-H'Cap								
2000	0/4	0%	-4.00	0/1	0%	-1.00	0/1	0%	-1.00	0/4	0%	-4.00	0/0	0%	0.00	0/10	0%	-10.00
2002	0/1	0%	-1.00	0/1	0%	-1.00	0/2	0%	-2.00	0/0	0%	0.00	0/0	0%	0.00	0/4	0%	-4.00
2003	0/2	0%	-2.00	0/2	0%	-2.00	0/0	0%	0.00	0/0	0%	0.00	0/1	0%	-1.00	0/5	0%	-5.00
2004	0/2	0%	-2.00	0/4	0%	-4.00	1/1	100%	+7.00	0/1	0%	-1.00	0/1	0%	-1.00	1/9	11%	-1.00
2005	0/0	0%	0.00	1/5	20%	+5.00	0/0	0%	0.00	0/1	0%	-1.00	0/0	0%	0.00	1/6	17%	+4.00
2006	0/6	0%	-6.00	1/5	20%	+4.00	0/3	0%	-3.00	1/1	100%	+7.50	0/1	0%	-1.00	2/16	13%	+1.50
2007	0/7	0%	-7.00	1/4	25%	+2.50	0/3	0%	-3.00	2/3	67%	+7.50	0/0	0%	0.00	3/17	18%	0.00
2008	0/3	0%	-3.00	2/7	29%	+14.00	0/5	0%	-5.00	1/3	33%	+7.00	0/0	0%	0.00	3/18	17%	+13.00
2009	0/10	0%	-10.00	0/6	0%	-6.00	1/5	20%	+3.00	0/4	0%	-4.00	0/0	0%	0.00	1/25	4%	-17.00
Total	0/35	0%	-35.00	5/35	14%	+11.50	2/20	10%	-4.00	4/17	24%	+12.00	0/3	0%	-3.00	11/110	10%	-18.50

Willie Mullins

For many years Willie Mullins was regarded at the festival as little more than a Bumper specialist and, while that was always an unfair judgment, it is certainly a misguided view nowadays. Mullins has been Ireland's champion trainer for the past two seasons and is on course for a hat-trick, which reflects the overall improvement in the depth and quality of his string. That has been evident at Cheltenham too and last year's three winners from 21 runners was Mullins' best return at the festival, following on from two winners in 2008.

Last year's total came without one of his eight Bumper runners emerging victorious, but that race is still where Mullins' runners attract most attention. He looks sure to field a strong line-up again, though it has not always been his most fancied runner who has landed the spoils – Missed That in 2005 is the only one to have won when going off as Mullins' shortest-priced runner in the years since he started having multiple entries in the race (Missed That is also the only one of Mullins' six Bumper winners to have won as favourite).

Mullins has faced stiffer competition from his compatriots in recent seasons and, on top of that, working out his best Bumper horse isn't easy. Even Ruby Walsh's choice of mount has been no help in recent years – since teaming up with winning favourite Missed That in 2005, Walsh has been beaten on Mullins-trained Bumper runners at odds of 5-2, 4-1 (twice) and 10-1. The picture may become clearer nearer the day, but at the moment Mullins' best hopes in the Bumper appear to be Day Of A Lifetime and Up Ou That.

Another area where Mullins is to be feared is in the novice races. Last year he took his strongest team of novices to the festival and won the RSA Chase with Cooldine and the Ballymore Novices' Hurdle with Mikael D'Haguenet. Both were well-backed favourites and Quel Esprit looks another likely type this year (probably for the Albert Bartlett), though it's not uncommon for Mullins to win one of the novice races at a big price (hence his level-stakes profit of +12.25pt).

Rule Supreme was a 25-1 shot when winning the 2004 RSA Chase and Ebaziyan was a 40-1 victor of the Supreme Novices' Hurdle in 2007. Mullins' first festival winner was in the Supreme Novices' in 1995, when Tourist Attraction came in at 25-1, and this year

	Hurdles						Chases						Bumper			Overall		
	H'cap			Non-H'Cap			H'cap			Non-H'Cap								
1999	0/0	0%	0.00	0/3	0%	-3.00	0/0	0%	0.00	0/2	0%	-2.00	0/1	0%	-1.00	0/6	0%	-6.00
2000	0/0	0%	0.00	0/2	0%	-2.00	0/0	0%	0.00	0/2	0%	-2.00	1/4	25%	+11.00	1/8	13%	+7.00
2002	0/1	0%	-1.00	1/4	25%	+13.00	0/2	0%	-2.00	0/3	0%	-3.00	0/1	0%	-1.00	1/11	9%	+6.00
2003	0/0	0%	0.00	0/5	0%	-5.00	0/0	0%	0.00	0/4	0%	-4.00	0/4	0%	-4.00	0/13	0%	-13.00
2004	0/1	0%	-1.00	0/6	0%	-6.00	0/1	0%	-1.00	1/4	25%	+22.00	0/5	0%	-5.00	1/17	9%	+9.00
2005	0/0	0%	0.00	0/2	0%	-2.00	0/0	0%	0.00	0/0	0%	0.00	1/1	100%	+3.50	1/3	33%	+1.50
2006	0/2	0%	-2.00	0/4	0%	-4.00	0/2	0%	-2.00	0/5	0%	-5.00	0/4	0%	-4.00	0/17	0%	-17.00
2007	0/3	0%	-3.00	1/6	17%	+35.00	0/1	0%	-1.00	0/2	0%	-2.00	0/3	0%	-3.00	1/15	7%	+27.00
2008	0/0	0%	0.00	1/5	20%	+3.00	0/0	0%	0.00	0/2	0%	-2.00	1/4	25%	+9.00	2/11	18%	+10.00
2009	0/1	0%	-1.00	2/9	22%	-2.50	0/0	0%	0.00	1/3	33%	+0.25	0/8	0%	-8.00	3/21	14%	-11.25
Total	0/8	0%	-8.00	5/46	11%	+26.50	0/6	0%	-6.00	2/27	7%	+2.25	3/35	9%	-2.50	10/122	8%	+12.25

Morning Supreme is an interesting each-way alternative to the obvious in the festival opener.

On the subject of big prices, a best price of 25-1 for **Mikael D'Haguenet** in the Arkle is tempting. He has an interrupted preparation to overcome, but his ability and trainer's record in novice races make him worthy of respect.

Handicaps do not appear high on Mullins' agenda, with no wins in 13 attempts at the past ten festivals. More of a concern, though, is his record in the major championship races. Considering he has an endless flow of novice talent, it is surprising that none has gone on to win one of the real top contests. Even the great Florida Pearl, winner of the 1997 Bumper and the 1998 RSA Chase, came up short in three attempts at the Gold Cup, and it is disappointing that Cooldine, Hurricane Fly and Cousin Vinny haven't kicked on this season.

Nicky Henderson

The Seven Barrows stable of Nicky Henderson has always been strong on quality and recently he has added quantity without diminishing the general high class of horse in his yard. Last season there was a sizeable increase in Henderson's number of winners (115, well up on the usual level in the 70s or 80s) and there was a knock-on effect at the festival, where he bounced back from blanks in 2007 and 2008 with three winners last year. That took his Cheltenham tally to 34 since his first winners in 1985, confirming his status as the leading active trainer at the meeting.

Until last year, Henderson had shown a growing reliance on his chasers at the festival, with ten of his 11 winners from 2000 to 2006 coming over fences, and his chase successes have been a good ally to punters over the past ten festivals with 11 winners from 94 runners (12%/+41.83pt). There was something of a turnaround last season, as Henderson had some great hurdling talent at his disposal for the 2008-09 campaign and the hurdlers supplied him with all three of his festival victories (Punjabi in the Champion Hurdle, Zaynar in the Triumph and Andytown in the Conditional Jockeys' Handicap Hurdle).

No chase wins last year far from dents confidence in Henderson's festival runners over fences, as that side of his game seems as good as ever, and the strength in depth he now has with his hurdlers as well as his chasers makes him arguably the best all-round trainer at the festival.

Although Paul Nicholls holds the upper hand in the championship chases, Henderson does far better than the champion trainer in handicaps, particularly over fences, where he has had some big-priced winners. One contest in which he has achieved notable success is the Kim Muir, which he has won in two of the past six runnings when he has had a runner with The Bushkeeper (2002) and Juveigneur (2005). Both horses went into the race with little exposure to the

Paul Nicholls holds the upper hand in the championship chases, but Henderson does far better than the champion trainer in handicaps, particularly over fences, where he has had some big-priced winners

1985 First Bout (Triumph), See You Then (Champion), The Tsarevich (Festival Plate)

1986 See You Then (Champion), River Ceiriog (Supreme), The Tsarevich (Festival Plate)

1987 Alone Success (Triumph), See You Then (Champion)

1989 Rustle (World Hurdle)

1990 Brown Windsor (Cathcart), Master Bob (Kim Muir)

1991 Remittance Man (Arkle)

1992 Remittance Man (Champion Chase), Flown (Supreme)

1993 Travado (Arkle), Thumbs Up (County Hurdle)

1994 Raymylette (Cathcart)

1997 Barna Boy (County Hurdle)

1999 Katarino (Triumph), Stormyfairweather (Cathcart)

2000 Tiutchev (Arkle), Stormyfairweather (Cathcart), Bacchanal (World Hurdle), Marlborough (William Hill Chase)

2002 The Bushkeeper (Kim Muir)

2005 Liberthine (Festival Plate), Juveigneur (Kim Muir), Trabolgan (RSA Chase)

2006 Non So (Festival Plate), Fondmort (Ryanair), Greenhope (Grand Annual)

2009 Punjabi (Champion Hurdle), Zaynar (Triumph), Andytown (Martin Pipe Conditional Jockeys)

Nicky Henderson has strength in depth over hurdles and fences, making him arguably the best all-round trainer at the festival

handicapper and it is always worth looking among his string to see if there is a horse with a similar profile. Novices Polyfast and Wogan, first and second in a handicap at Kempton on Boxing Day, best fit that description and have races in them off their respective marks.

Henderson holds a strong hand in the RSA Chase, with Punchestowns and Long Run, and has decent claims in the Champion Hurdle. Punjabi won at Kempton on Racing Post Chase day to boost his hopes of retaining his crown, but Henderson probably has a better chance with Zaynar, despite his shock defeat at Kelso last time out.

With Henderson's stable in pretty much the same form as last season and matching strides with Nicholls in terms of winners, he should get at least a couple of winners on the board. And with the many dark horses he has with untapped potential who could be aimed at novice races or handicaps, it's not inconceivable that he could end up with more than last year's total of three.

	Hurdles						Chases						Bumper			Overall		
	H'cap			Non-H'Cap			H'cap			Non-H'Cap								
1999	0/6	0%	-6.00	1/3	33%	+0.75	0/2	0%	-2.00	1/3	33%	+7.00	0/0	0%	0.00	2/14	14%	-0.25
2000	0/2	0%	-2.00	1/8	13%	-1.50	1/4	25%	+2.50	2/2	100%	+13.50	0/1	0%	-1.00	4/17	24%	+11.50
2002	0/4	0%	-4.00	0/9	0%	-3.00	1/3	33%	+2.50	0/5	0%	-5.00	0/1	0%	-1.00	1/22	5%	-16.50
2003	0/1	0%	-1.00	0/6	0%	-6.00	0/6	0%	-6.00	0/6	0%	-6.00	0/2	0%	-2.00	0/21	0%	-21.00
2004	0/4	0%	0.00	0/3	0%	-3.00	0/4	0%	-4.00	0/4	0%	-4.00	0/2	0%	-2.00	0/17	0%	-17.00
2005	0/5	0%	-5.00	0/2	%	-2.00	2/12	17%	+27.00	1/2	50%	+5.00	0/0	0%	0.00	3/21	14%	+25.00
2006	0/6	0%	-6.00	0/2	0%	-2.00	2/13	15%	+35.00	1/2	50%	+2.33	0/0	0%	0.00	3/23	13%	+29.23
2007	0/8	0%	-2.00	0/6	0%	-6.00	0/6	0%	-6.00	0/2	0%	-2.00	0/1	0%	-1.00	0/23	0%	-23.00
2008	0/2	0%	-8.00	0/9	0%	-6.00	0/7	0%	-6.00	0/1	0%	-2.00	0/1	0%	-1.00	0/20	0%	-20.00
2009	1/12	8%	+14.00	2/10	20%	+19.50	0/7	0%	-7.00	0/3	0%	-3.00	0/0	0%	0.00	3/32	9%	+23.50
Total	1/50	2%	-24.00	4/58	7%	-18.25	6/64	9%	+35.00	5/30	17%	+6.83	0/8	0%	-8.00	16/210	8%	-8.42

Nigel Twiston-Davies

Festival success comes in bursts for Nigel Twiston-Davies and he appears to be in the midst of another purple patch after sending out three winners at the past two festivals. He has never tasted success in one of the feature championship races but has decent chances this year with Khyber Kim in the Champion Hurdle and, at least on an each-way basis, Imperial Commander in the Gold Cup.

Imperial Commander is his best horse and is probably the biggest threat to the Paul Nicholls stranglehold on the Gold Cup, though victory is unlikely. Khyber Kim, who looked below top class in his first season with Twiston-Davies and before that with Nicky Henderson, has made significant progress this term for the waiting tactics applied by stable jockey Paddy Brennan, who has been an excellent acquisition for the yard. Khyber Kim deserves respect, as Twiston-Davies's festival record shows that he can have success with all types given the right ammunition.

One oddity in that record was his long drought with staying chasers until Tricky Trickster (now with Nicholls) won the four-mile National Hunt Chase last year. It is reasonable to expect more success in that sphere, though there is no standout candidate this year.

Many will be looking closely at stable form going into the festival, but Twiston-Davies is one trainer who can turn around a poor run at this time of year. He always has a significant dip after Christmas, yet usually turns out his festival runners in peak condition.

Festival winners 10
Last five years 0/0/0/1/2

1992 Tipping Tim (William Hill Chase)

1993 Gaelstrom (Neptune Novices' Hurdle), Young Hustler (RSA Chase)

1994 Arctic Kinsman (Supreme)

1998 Upgrade (Triumph)

2000 Rubhahunish (Pertemps Final)

2004 Fundamentalist (Neptune Novices' Hurdle)

2008 Ballyfitz (Pertemps Final)

2009 Tricky Trickster (NH Chase), Imperial Commander (Ryanair)

	Hurdles						Chases						Bumper			Overall		
	H'cap			Non-H'Cap			H'cap			Non-H'Cap								
1999	0/2	0%	-2.00	0/7	0%	-7.00	0/1	0%	-1.00	0/1	0%	-1.00	0/1	0%	-1.00	0/12	0%	-12.00
2000	1/4	25%	+5.00	0/4	0%	-4.00	0/2	0%	-2.00	0/2	0%	-2.00	0/0	0%	0.00	1/12	8%	-3.00
2002	0/0	0%	0.00	0/2	0%	-2.00	0/3	0%	-3.00	0/2	0%	-2.00	0/1	0%	-1.00	0/8	0%	-8.00
2003	0/0	0%	0.00	0/1	0%	-1.00	0/0	0%	0.00	0/1	0%	-1.00	0/0	0%	0.00	0/2	0%	-2.00
2004	0/3	0%	-3.00	1/3	33%	+10.00	0/3	0%	-3.00	0/2	0%	-2.00	0/1	0%	-1.00	1/12	8%	+1.00
2005	0/3	0%	-3.00	0/3	0%	-3.00	0/3	0%	-3.00	0/1	0%	-1.00	0/0	0%	0.00	0/10	0%	-10.00
2006	0/1	0%	-1.00	0/5	0%	-5.00	0/6	0%	-6.00	0/4	0%	-4.00	0/1	0%	-1.00	0/17	0%	-17.00
2007	0/3	0%	-3.00	0/2	0%	-2.00	0/3	0%	-3.00	0/1	0%	-1.00	0/0	0%	0.00	0/9	0%	-9.00
2008	1/2	50%	+17.00	0/3	0%	-3.00	0/9	0%	-9.00	0/4	0%	-4.00	0/0	0%	0.00	1/18	6%	+1.00
2009	0/2	0%	-2.00	0/4	0%	-4.00	0/7	0%	-7.00	2/6	33%	+13.00	0/0	0%	0.00	2/19	11%	0.00
Total	2/20	10%	+8.00	1/34	3%	-21.00	0/37	0%	-37.00	2/24	8%	-5.00	0/4	0%	-4.00	5/115	4%	-59.00

Jonjo O'Neill

Festival winners 16
Last five years 0/1/3/1/1

1991 Danny Connors (Pertemps Final)

1995 Front Line (NH Chase)

2000 Master Tern (County Hurdle)

2002 Rith Dubh (NH Chase)

2003 Inching Closer (Pertemps Final), Sudden Shock (NH Chase), Spectroscope (Triumph)

2004 Creon (Pertemps Final), Native Emperor (NH Chase), Iris's Gift (World Hurdle)

2006 Black Jack Ketchum (Albert Bartlett)

2007 Butler's Cabin (NH Chase), Wichita Lineman (Albert Bartlett), Drombeag (Foxhunter)

2008 Albertas Run (RSA Chase)

2009 Wichita Lineman (William Hill Chase)

Jonjo O'Neill has never been the easiest of trainers to read but he is a reliable performer at the festival, with only one blank in the past eight years. Thirteen winners in that period is a tally many trainers would be envious of and, in terms of punting, few can compete with his level-stakes profit column.

As is the case with most trainers, there are strengths and weaknesses in O'Neill's record. Wichita Lineman's success in the 2009 William Hill Chase – O'Neill's sole winner last March – was a rare one in a handicap chase, as it was his first in 34 attempts at the past ten festivals. His yard is light on championship quality at present, however, and that has heightened the need to improve in handicap chases if O'Neill is to maintain his proud record at the festival.

The chase in which the Jackdaws Castle trainer has really excelled is the four-mile National Hunt Chase, which he usually lays one out for and has won four times in the past eight runnings. Can't Buy Time was his fancied representative last year, going off 4-1 favourite, and he looked a big threat until his stamina gave out and he faded into fourth. We can expect O'Neill to have at least one well-fancied runner again this year and to attract the better amateur riders to aid his cause.

The improving **Theatrical Moment** could be the one for the race this year and it is possible he could be a handsome price despite his trainer's record in the race. That shouldn't deter punters, as Sudden Shock (2003) and Butler's Cabin (2007) were big-priced winners for the stable in this race.

O'Neill has generally done well over hurdles. He has won the three-mile Albert Bartlett Novices' Hurdle twice with short-priced favourites (Black Jack Ketchum in 2006 and Wichita Lineman in 2007), but he seems to lack the ammunition to make an impact at Grade 1 level this term and, as over fences, his best chance of success may lie in handicap hurdles. This is an area where he can supply winners (he has won the Pertemps Final on three occasions) and sometimes at a big price – his latest Pertemps winner was Creon, who scored at 50-1 in 2004.

	Hurdles						Chases						Bumper			Overall		
	H'cap			Non-H'Cap			H'cap			Non-H'Cap								
1999	0/0	0%	0.00	0/0	0%	0.00	0/2	0%	-2.00	0/0	0%	0.00	0/0	0%	0.00	0/2	0%	-2.00
2000	1/1	100%	+4.50	0/0	0%	0.00	0/1	0%	-1.00	0/0	0%	0.00	0/0	0%	0.00	1/2	50%	+3.50
2002	0/4	0%	-4.00	0/3	0%	-3.00	0/2	0%	-2.00	1/2	50%	+9.00	0/2	0%	-2.00	1/13	8%	-2.00
2003	1/5	20%	+2.00	1/8	13%	+13.00	0/3	0%	-3.00	1/4	25%	+22.00	0/2	0%	-2.00	3/22	14%	+42.00
2004	1/6	17%	+45.00	1/7	14%	-1.50	0/3	0%	-3.00	1/5	20%	+1.00	0/2	0%	-2.00	3/23	13%	+37.50
2005	0/2	0%	-2.00	0/7	0%	-7.00	0/5	0%	-5.00	0/1	0%	0.00	0/1	0%	-1.00	0/16	0%	-16.00
2006	0/6	0%	-6.00	1/4	25%	-2.00	0/4	0%	-4.00	0/5	0%	-5.00	0/1	0%	-1.00	1/21	5%	-19.00
2007	0/3	0%	-3.00	1/4	25%	-1.63	0/4	0%	-4.00	2/6	33%	+49.00	0/2	0%	-2.00	3/19	16%	+38.37
2008	0/1	0%	-1.00	0/2	0%	-2.00	0/4	0%	-4.00	1/5	20%	0.00	0/0	0%	0.00	1/12	8%	-7.00
2009	0/6	0%	-6.00	0/0	0%	0.00	1/7	0%	-1.00	0/4	0%	-4.00	0/0	0%	0.00	1/17	6%	-11.00
Total	**3/34**	**9%**	**+29.50**	**4/35**	**11%**	**-4.13**	**1/34**	**3%**	**-28.00**	**6/32**	**19%**	**+71.00**	**0/11**	**0%**	**-11.00**	**14/146**	**10%**	**+57.37**

Ferdy Murphy

Festival winners 8
Last five years 0/2/2/1/0

1996 Stop The Waller (Kim Muir), Paddy's Return (Triumph)

1998 French Holly (Neptune Novices' Hurdle)

2006 You're Special (Kim Muir), Hot Weld (NH Chase)

2007 Joes Edge (William Hill Chase), L'Antartique (Jewson)

2008 Naiad Du Misselot (Coral Cup)

There is no doubt that when Ferdy Murphy has horses good enough for the festival, he lays them out for the meeting. And he's pretty good at it as well. He enjoyed success at Cheltenham in the late 1990s with the likes of Paddy's Return and French Holly but then endured a lean spell, with Truckers Tavern's second place in the 2003 Gold Cup as good as it got for a while.

That quiet period probably explains how a trainer as adept as Murphy was able to fire in two unfancied 33-1 shots at the 2006 meeting, both in amateur rider races with Oliver Harding in the saddle (Hot Weld in the National Hunt Chase and You're Special in the Kim Muir). He proved that was no fluke the following year when landing two more big handicap chases with Joes Edge (50-1 in the William Hill Chase) and L'Antartique (20-1 in the Jewson).

Although Murphy drew a blank last year, a couple of his runners in handicap chases rewarded each-way support – Nine De Sivola (16-1) was third in the National Hunt Chase and Three Mirrors (9-1) fourth in the Festival Plate. In some cases, however, the market was alive to his runners, with Poker De Sivola only seventh as 7-2 favourite for the Kim Muir.

The recent evidence suggests Murphy targets the amateur rider races and, given the prices of most of his winners, whatever he has in mind for the meeting will not be easy to spot at this stage. His most obvious candidate for one of the staying handicap chases is **Galant Nuit**, who was successful at the course in November and is entered in the William Hill Chase and the Kim Muir. That course win over a marathon trip points more towards the amateur riders' race.

Murphy can do it in hurdles as well, winning with the high-class pair Paddy's Return and French Holly and with the well-supported Naiad Du Misselot (7-1) in the 2008 Coral Cup. He has not won one of the big championship races but he has had placed runners and has another squeak in this year's Queen Mother Champion Chase with **Kalahari King**, who lost out narrowly in the 2009 Arkle and came back from a long absence to score a smart victory at Doncaster in February.

	Hurdles				Chases				Bumper			Overall		
	H'cap			Non-H'Cap			H'cap			Non-H'Cap					
1999	0/0	0%	0.00	0/2	0%	-2.00	0/2	0%	-2.00	0/2	0%	-2.00	0/0	0%	0.00	0/6	0%	-6.00
2000	0/1	0%	-1.00	0/1	0%	-1.00	0/1	0%	-1.00	0/1	0%	-1.00	0/0	0%	0.00	0/4	0%	-4.00
2002	0/0	0%	0.00	0/1	0%	-1.00	0/4	0%	-4.00	0/3	0%	-3.00	0/0	0%	0.00	0/8	0%	-8.00
2003	0/1	0%	-1.00	0/0	0%	0.00	0/1	0%	-1.00	0/1	0%	-1.00	0/0	0%	0.00	0/3	0%	-3.00
2004	0/0	0%	0.00	0/0	0%	0.00	0/2	0%	-2.00	0/1	0%	-1.00	0/0	0%	0.00	0/3	0%	-3.00
2005	0/2	0%	-2.00	0/0	0%	0.00	0/4	0%	-4.00	0/4	0%	-4.00	0/0	0%	0.00	0/10	0%	-10.00
2006	0/3	0%	-3.00	0/0	0%	0.00	1/4	25%	+30.00	1/3	33%	+31.00	0/0	0%	0.00	2/10	20%	+58.00
2007	0/0	0%	0.00	0/1	0%	-1.00	2/4	50%	+68.00	0/3	0%	-3.00	0/0	0%	0.00	2/8	25%	+64.00
2008	1/1	100%	+7.00	0/1	0%	-1.00	0/4	0%	-4.00	0/1	0%	-1.00	0/0	0%	0.00	1/7	14%	+1.00
2009	0/1	0%	-1.00	0/0	0%	0.00	0/6	0%	-6.00	0/3	0%	-3.00	0/0	0%	0.00	0/10	0%	-10.00
Total	1/9	11%	-1.00	0/6	0%	-6.00	3/32	9%	+74.00	1/22	5%	+12.00	0/0	0%	0.00	5/69	7%	+79.00

David Pipe

Looking at how well a stable's runners have performed throughout the season is often a fair indicator of their prospects for the festival. For that reason David Pipe was a trainer to avoid at Cheltenham last year, as the yard had underachieved in the 2008-09 campaign, and so it proved when he failed to strike with any of his 32 festival runners.

His string has been in much better form this term, however, and his stronger festival contenders will be worthy of more respect this year. Comparisons with his father are inevitable, but Pipe jnr – now in his fourth season at the helm of Nicholashayne – has a different approach. Whereas Martin was always a better trainer of hurdlers than chasers, the reverse appears to be true of David, which perhaps shouldn't come as a surprise as he trained hunter chasers before taking over the full licence at Nicholashayne.

Pipe's chasers have outperformed the hurdlers this season and it is probably best to look at his runners over fences for his best chances at the festival. Although he broke his festival duck in his first year with Gaspara in the Fred Winter Juvenile Handicap Hurdle, Pipe's two subsequent winners have been over fences courtesy of Our Vic (Ryanair) and An Accordion (William Hill Chase) in 2008.

Although main owner David Johnson has downsized his interest in racing, he provides Pipe with sufficient ammunition to hit the target at the meeting. The likes of Our Vic and Well Chief are probably a bit long in the tooth to be winning at the top level and, with Paul Nicholls, Nicky Henderson and Willie Mullins boasting incredible strength in depth, an impact in the major championship races seems unlikely. But there are some more progressive types in the Johnson silks who could be worth siding with.

The Package and **Seven Is My Number** are interesting on two counts. Both are proven at the course and they have the stamina for three miles and the speed for half a mile shorter, giving Pipe options for their festival targets (possibly the William Hill Chase or the Byrne Group Plate).

As for his hurdlers, the Fred Winter could be a race where Pipe strikes again. As well as winning with Gaspara, he sent out Ashkazar to finish runner-up in 2008. Look, too, for a strong challenge in the race named after his father, the Martin Pipe Conditional Jockeys' Handicap Hurdle, in which he ran seven last year, though his best placing was third with favourite Big Eared Fran.

	Hurdles						Chases						Bumper			Overall		
	H'cap			Non-H'Cap			H'cap			Non-H'Cap								
2007	1/4	25%	+1.50	0/5	0%	-5.00	0/9	0%	-9.00	0/5	0%	-5.00	0/3	0%	-3.00	1/26	4%	-20.50
2008	0/10	0%	-10.00	0/4	0%	-4.00	1/6	17%	+2.00	1/4	25%	+1.00	0/2	0%	-2.00	2/26	7%	-13.00
2009	0/16	0%	-16.00	0/7	0%	-7.00	0/6	0%	-6.00	0/3	0%	-4.00	0/0	0%	0.00	0/32	0%	-32.00
Total	1/30	3%	-24.50	0/16	0%	-16.00	1/21	5%	-13.00	1/12	8%	-8.00	0/5	0%	-5.00	3/84	4%	-65.50

(Also 0/5 in hunter chases between 2002 and 2004)

Howard Johnson

1993 Ushers Island (NH Chase)

2005 Arcalis (Supreme), No Refuge (Neptune Novices' Hurdle), Inglis Drever (World Hurdle)

2007 Inglis Drever (World Hurdle)

2008 Inglis Drever (World Hurdle), Tidal Bay (Arkle)

Before Graham Wylie came along, Howard Johnson was more likely to have Aintree in April in mind than the Cheltenham Festival and he had tasted festival glory only once before linking up with the millionaire owner, though he had gone close in the 2000 Champion Chase when Direct Route ran Edredon Bleu to a short head, having finished third the previous year.

The sea change at Johnson's yard was evident in his second season training for Wylie in the 2004-05 campaign, when he had three winners at the festival with Arcalis (Supreme Novices' Hurdle), No Refuge (Royal and SunAlliance Novices' Hurdle) and Inglis Drever (World Hurdle).

From there up to the 2008 festival, Johnson was profitable to follow at the meeting with six winners from 43 runners (14%/+7.88pt) and the Johnson/Wylie combination appeared likely to be one that would be feared at the festival for years to come.

The wheels came off last year, however. Although not short on quantity (Johnson sent out his biggest-ever festival team of 15), the quality was lacking and he failed to strike even once. His team looks weaker still this time round, though Tidal Bay is an intriguing prospect for the World Hurdle following his impressive return to hurdling in the Grade 2 Cleeve Hurdle on Cheltenham's Trials day in January.

Tidal Bay's Cleeve win was a return to the sort of form he showed when storming up the hill in the 2008 Arkle, though he was largely disappointing over fences once he moved out of novice class. Big Buck's has shown it is possible for an under-performing chaser to switch back to staying hurdles with great success, and Johnson and Wylie know what it takes to win the World Hurdle, thanks to record three-time scorer Inglis Drever.

Going the handicap route with one of his promising novices might represent Johnson's best chance of success, but he doesn't seem to go all out for that type of race (0 from 24 since 1999) and Washington Irving, probably the best prospect among his young horses, is not going to the festival this year.

	Hurdles						Chases						Bumper			Overall		
	H'cap			Non-H'Cap			H'cap			Non-H'Cap								
1999	0/0	0%	0.00	0/0	0%	0.00	0/1	0%	-1.00	0/2	0%	-2.00	0/0	0%	0.00	0/3	0%	-3.00
2000	0/0	0%	0.00	0/0	0%	0.00	0/0	0%	0.00	0/2	0%	-2.00	0/0	0%	0.00	0/2	0%	-2.00
2003	0/0	0%	0.00	0/0	0%	0.00	0/0	0%	0.00	0/1	0%	-1.00	0/0	0%	0.00	0/1	0%	-1.00
2004	0/1	0%	-1.00	0/1	0%	-1.00	0/0	0%	0.00	0/1	0%	-1.00	0/0	0%	0.00	0/3	0%	-3.00
2005	0/4	0%	-4.00	3/5	60%	+30.50	0/1	0%	-1.00	0/3	0%	-3.00	0/1	0%	-1.00	3/14	21%	+21.50
2006	0/5	0%	-5.00	0/4	0%	-1.00	0/0	0%	0.00	0/4	0%	-4.00	0/0	0%	0.00	0/13	0%	-13.00
2007	0/2	0%	-2.00	1/4	25%	+2.00	0/2	0%	-2.00	0/3	0%	-3.00	0/0	0%	0.00	1/11	9%	-5.00
2008	0/2	0%	-2.00	1/2	50%	+0.38	0/0	0%	0.00	1/1	100%	+6.00	0/0	0%	0.00	2/5	40%	+4.38
2009	0/4	0%	-4.00	0/5	0%	-5.00	0/2	0%	-2.00	0/4	0%	-4.00	0/0	0%	0.00	0/15	0%	-15.00
Total	0/18	0%	-18.00	5/21	24%	+22.88	0/6	0%	-6.00	1/21	5%	-10.00	0/1	0%	-1.00	6/67	9%	-16.12

(No runners in 2002)

Jessica Harrington

Moscow Flyer contributed considerably to Jessica Harrington's impressive Cheltenham figures – six winners from 33 runners (18%/+0.75pt) at the past ten festivals – but her success hasn't totally revolved around the two-mile champion chaser. On her festival roll of honour, Harrington also has a handicap chase (Space Trucker, 1999 Grand Annual), a handicap hurdle (Spirit Leader, 2003 County Hurdle) and even the Bumper (Cork All Star, 2007).

Harrington was 0 from 3 last year, though 66-1 shot Horner Woods finished second to Cooldine in the RSA Chase, showing that even her weakest chances can make the frame.

The pick of her team this year are **Zarinava**, who is a solid each-way option in the David Nicholson Mares' Hurdle, and **Summit Meeting**, who is a lively outsider for the Neptune Investment Management Novices' Hurdle.

Edward O'Grady

Although not the force he was, Edward O'Grady knows how to have horses primed for the festival (18 winners between 1974 and 2006) and has been enjoying something of a resurgence, with this season likely to turn out his best of the past decade in terms of number of winners. For that reason, he may well strike somewhere at this year's festival, and punters should take note if the money comes in for one of O'Grady's runners.

Tranquil Sea has a serious chance in the Ryanair and would be a terrific betting proposition if the ground came up heavy, as he was impressive in testing conditions when winning the Paddy Power Gold Cup at Cheltenham in November. **Shot From The Hip**, a late qualifier for the Bumper, is another to watch.

Take note if the money comes in for one of O'Grady's runners, as it did for Tranquil Sea before the Paddy Power

Tony Martin

Both of Tony Martin's festival wins have been in handicaps with heavily backed horses who had a progressive profile – Xenophon was a 4-1 winning favourite of the 2003 Coral Cup and Dun Doire obliged as 7-1 second favourite in the 2006 William Hill Chase.

This year it is difficult to find something that fits the bill among his string and it is also a concern that Martin failed to strike with any of his 44 British raiders in the 2008-09 campaign – a poor run that continued into this season. He looks a trainer to avoid unless the market signals that he has a big improver on his hands.

Noel Meade

Many will be wondering whether Go Native's win in the Supreme Novices' Hurdle last year was the first sign of a turnaround for Noel Meade or merely a temporary break in his poor festival record. That question will be one for punters to weigh up on the opening day this year when Go Native returns for a crack at the Champion Hurdle and a £1m bonus.

Already a proven winner up the Cheltenham hill, Go Native looks a serious contender for the Champion Hurdle, but still it's difficult to ignore his trainer's festival record. Opposing Meade runners has been a profitable policy over the years and Go Native is another to take on, particularly if he shortens closer to the race.

Last year's Supreme victory was only Meade's third at the festival – his record over the past ten festivals is three winners from 101 runners and he has shown a big level-stakes loss (3%/-63.50pt). Citing the cause for this is difficult, though one factor might be that Meade sets great store in winning championships and keeps his horses going through the season, whereas others concentrate more on bringing their top horses to a peak in March.

Meade has certainly had enough quality to have made more of an impact at the festival over the years and, as usual, his team looks strong on paper this season, particularly in the novice ranks. His most interesting contender is Pandorama, a dual Grade 1 winner over fences who has the RSA Chase on his agenda. That looks a hot race this year, with the British runners dominating the ante-post market, but Pandorama has been beaten only once for Meade over hurdles and fences – that defeat was over hurdles by last year's Ballymore winner Mikael D'Haguenet.

Williams should be feared when mapping out a campaign with a progressive novice and one who catches the eye is Green Belt Elite

Venetia Williams

Having made her name in the 1990s with Grade 1 winners Teeton Mill and Lady Rebecca, Venetia Williams has had her only festival successes in handicaps and her runners in that sphere merit the utmost respect. She had her best festival last year when landing the Pertemps Final with Kayf Aramis and sending home the first two in the Festival Plate as Something Wells beat better-fancied stablemate Ping Pong Sivola.

That brought Williams' festival total to five and it is no wonder she is so adept in big handicaps, as she was assistant trainer to Martin Pipe at a time when he was the dominant force in jump racing. Like her mentor, she has a knack for improving horses significantly, often running up sequences in handicaps, and can do it over hurdles and fences – Idole First achieved festival success in both spheres, winning the 2005 Coral Cup and the 2007 Festival Plate.

Samakaan's 2000 Grand Annual success proved Williams should be feared when mapping out a campaign with a progressive novice and a similar type who catches the eye among her current string is **Green Belt Elite.**

The six-year-old, who has won three times this season, should get a decent weight for one of the handicap chases and has winning form at 2m and 2m4f. All of his wins have been on soft or heavy ground and in those conditions he is one to note.

Donald McCain

Since the handover from father to son four years ago, the McCain yard has gone up a gear. The stable is still to be respected when the Grand National comes around, but nowadays victories come in all types of races. That is evident from Donald McCain's two festival winners: smart staying handicap chaser Cloudy Lane justified favouritism when well backed for the Kim Muir in 2007, while the speedier Whiteoak won the 2008 running of the David Nicholson Mares' Hurdle.

Last year was the first in which McCain failed to score at Cheltenham, but he hasn't had that many runners at the meeting and doesn't seem to run something unless he feels he has a chance. Any winning is most likely to be done in a handicap and he has several progressive types who could strike, with staying novice chaser **Youngstown** perhaps his best chance of doing so.

The McCain horse with serious potential is the undefeated **Peddlers Cross**, who hacked up in a Grade 2 novice hurdle at Haydock in January. He looks set to go for the Neptune Novices' Hurdle and appears to have a potent mix of speed and stamina. However he fares this year, he could be one to watch at future festivals.

Philip Hobbs

A reliable trainer trend in recent jumps seasons has been to follow Philip Hobbs in April as he has always saved a bit for an end-of-season push to reach a century of winners, regardless of how he has performed at the festival. But his total so far this season suggests he is going to fall short of that milestone for the first time since the 2000-01 campaign and overall the Minehead handler appears to be losing touch with the leading trainers.

That has been evident at recent festivals, with Hobbs's wins with Rooster Booster in the 2003 Champion Hurdle and Flagship Uberalles in the 2002 Queen Mother Champion Chase a fading memory. Although he has had other smart performers like Detroit City and Monkerhostin come good at the festival, Hobbs has had nothing in the class of Rooster Booster and Flagship Uberalles, and he looks short of quality again this season.

If the Ryanair is to be counted as a championship contest, he has an each-way squeak with Planet Of Sound, but it looks a hot race with some smart horses likely to go this route rather than taking on Kauto Star and Denman in the Gold Cup and a place is probably the best he could hope for. In any case, Hobbs's record suggests his chasers are best avoided. His last winner over fences came when One Knight took the 2003 RSA Chase despite an indifferent round of jumping and he has not won a handicap chase in 39 tries over the past ten festivals.

Any success for Hobbs is far more likely to come over hurdles, and in that sphere he has been profitable to follow in handicaps and non-handicaps alike thanks to some big-priced winners. What's Up Boys, Massini's Maguire and Made In Japan all provided turn-ups at double-figure odds.

Hobbs is unlikely to shy away from taking on Supreme Novices' Hurdle hotpot Dunguib with Menorah, the most promising young jumper in his yard after two wins in four starts over hurdles since moving from Thomas Mullins. The five-year-old suffered a surprise defeat at Ascot last time out but was unsuited by the conditions that day and is better judged on his resounding 12-length success over Bellvano at Kempton in December – form that has been franked since.

Festival winners 11
Last five years 0/1/1/0/0

1990 Moody Man (County Hurdle)

1996 Kibreet (Grand Annual)

2000 What's Up Boys (Coral Cup)

2002 Rooster Booster (County Hurdle), Flagship Uberalles (Champion Chase)

2003 Rooster Booster (Champion Hurdle), One Knight (RSA Chase)

2004 Monkerhostin (Coral Cup), Made In Japan (Triumph)

2006 Detroit City (Triumph)

2007 Massini's Maguire (Neptune Novices' Hurdle)

	Hurdles						Chases						Bumper			Overall		
	H'cap			Non-H'Cap			H'cap			Non-H'Cap								
1999	0/4	0%	-4.00	0/2	0%	-2.00	0/2	0%	-2.00	0/1	0%	-1.00	0/0	0%	0.00	0/9	0%	-9.00
2000	1/2	50%	+32.00	0/3	0%	-3.00	0/4	0%	-4.00	0/1	0%	-1.00	0/1	0%	-1.00	1/11	9%	+23.00
2002	1/5	20%	+4.00	0/2	0%	-2.00	0/4	0%	-4.00	1/2	50%	+0.75	0/0	0%	0.00	2/13	15%	-1.25
2003	0/5	0%	-5.00	1/6	17%	-0.50	0/1	0%	-1.00	1/2	50%	+6.50	0/1	0%	-1.00	2/15	13%	-1.00
2004	1/3	33%	+4.50	1/5	20%	+16.00	0/2	0%	-2.00	0/2	0%	-2.00	0/0	0%	0.00	2/12	17%	+16.50
2005	0/8	0%	-8.00	0/3	0%	-3.00	0/7	0%	-7.00	0/3	0%	-3.00	0/1	0%	-1.00	0/22	0%	-22.00
2006	0/2	0%	-2.00	1/3	33%	+1.50	0/6	0%	-6.00	0/5	0%	-5.00	0/1	0%	-1.00	1/17	6%	-12.50
2007	0/7	0%	-7.00	1/3	33%	+18.00	0/3	0%	-3.00	0/2	0%	-2.00	0/0	0%	0.00	1/15	7%	+6.00
2008	0/5	0%	-5.00	0/1	0%	-1.00	0/5	0%	-5.00	0/3	0%	-3.00	0/2	0%	-2.00	0/16	0%	-16.00
2009	0/7	0%	-7.00	0/3	0%	-3.00	0/5	0%	-5.00	0/3	0%	-3.00	0/0	0%	0.00	0/18	0%	-18.00
Total	3/48	6%	+2.50	4/31	13%	+21.00	0/39	0%	-39.00	2/24	8%	12.75	0/6	0%	-6.00	9/148	6%	-34.25

Other trainer trends

Flat trainers regularly do well Aidan O'Brien, with Istabraq, and James Fanshawe (Royal Gait and Hors La Loi) have won the Champion Hurdle, and Fanshawe also had a recent chase success when Reveillez took the Jewson in 2006. Last year, two races were won by trainers more renowned for their Flat achievements: Mick Quinlan landed the Fred Winter with Silk Affair and John Quinn took the Kim Muir with the quirky Character Building. Another Flat trainer who got on the board recently was David Arbuthnot, who won the 2007 Pertemps Final with Oscar Park.

This year Dermot Weld is likely to have a big say in the Neptune Novices' Hurdle with Rite Of Passage, who has a favourite's chance after adapting impressively to hurdling, and with Elegant Concorde or Hidden Universe in the Bumper.

Murphy's select band merit respect Colm Murphy made an immediate impact by winning the 2004 Supreme Novices' Hurdle with Brave Inca, his first festival runner. Two years later Brave Inca landed the Champion Hurdle and, while those wins remain the only ones for Murphy at the meeting, the County Wexford trainer has had several placed horses from just a handful of runners, so backers usually get a good run for their money with his stable.

Murphy will send over a select band of runners again this year and his best chance of a winner lies with the prolific mare Voler La Vedette. The Champion Hurdle has been mentioned as a possibility but the David Nicholson Mares' Hurdle is her probable target. Big Zeb holds form claims in the Champion Chase and will be there at the finish provided his jumping holds up.

Taaffe has a good strike-rate Victory in the 2005 Gold Cup with Kicking King wasn't a bad way for Tom Taaffe to break his festival duck and he has had a winner at two of the four festivals since then, with Finger Onthe Pulse (2008 Jewson) and Ninetieth Minute (2009 Coral Cup).

Taaffe's festival tally is three winners from 19 runners (16%/ +11.00pt), which puts him in the same bracket as fellow Irish trainers Jessica Harrington and Colm Murphy, whose horses always seem to go well at the meeting. Taaffe has had a quiet season, however, and his best chance lies with Smoking Aces in the Coral Cup or the Pertemps Final.

Doumen is a fading force in the big races Kasbah Bliss was beaten at odds-on in the World Hurdle last year and Francois Doumen has nothing of his class this year, while it has been quite some time since he had a top-notch chaser. The French trainer's last festival winners were in 2005, with Moulin Riche in the Albert Bartlett and Kelami in the William Hill Chase, and handicaps are likely to be his

Dermot Weld is likely to have a big say in the Neptune Novices' and the Champion Bumper

best route to more success. His two best candidates would appear to be 2m4f-3m chaser Doctor Pat and Spunk, who could go for the Fred Winter.

Running on empty Charlie Mann has had some high-class jumpers over the years and is never afraid to aim high with them, but his policy hasn't paid dividends at Cheltenham as he is winless with 36 runners at the past ten festivals. His best horse, Air Force One, is on the mend following injury and could have a crack at the Gold Cup, but aiming a little lower would give him a more realistic chance of victory. Mann is a decent trainer and will probably train a festival winner one day, most likely in a handicap, but his record suggests we can afford to miss it if he does.

Peter Bowen has the unusual distinction of having trained a Gold Cup runner-up (Take The Stand in 2005) without having a festival winner to his name. He has had runners at the past five meetings and not won once in 21 attempts. Perhaps the reason is that many of his horses prefer fast going and do not thrive on the winter jumping ground at the festival.

In contrast, Malcolm Jefferson's best horses tend to need really soft ground to show their best. Dato Star was his last festival winner when he won the Bumper on soft ground back in 1995 and it is doubtful whether current stable stars According To Pete and Cape Tribulation will get close to winning unless there is a monsoon.

Perhaps Gary Moore's record should read better than it does (just one win, with Tikram in the 2004 Festival Plate) and it is disappointing that he has failed to land a festival handicap hurdle, as he is strong in that division at other meetings. His runners should be treated warily. ■

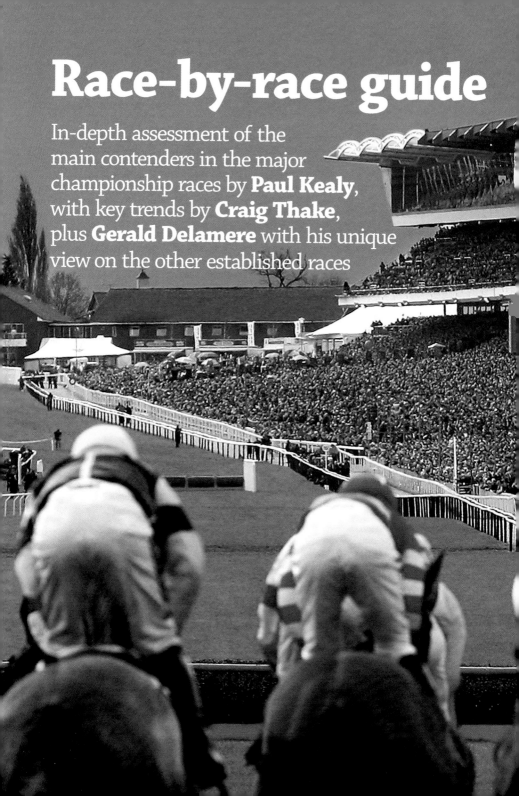

Race-by-race guide

In-depth assessment of the main contenders in the major championship races by **Paul Kealy**, with key trends by **Craig Thake**, plus **Gerald Delamere** with his unique view on the other established races

Tuesday, March 16, 2010 (Old Course)

1.30 Race 1

Spinal Research Supreme Novices' Hurdle
(Grade 1)

C4/RUK

2m¹/₂f

Key stats Twelve of the last 13 winners had won on their previous start (the exception was third). There has been an Irish-trained winner in seven of the last nine runnings

Dunguib has towered over this contest ever since he powered to a ten-length win in the Bumper at last year's festival and his reputation has grown with each run this season. With connections resisting the temptation to switch him to the Champion Hurdle, he is Ireland's big banker in the festival opener and the only slight doubt is that his jumping was sloppy when winning the Grade 1 Deloitte Novice Hurdle on his final outing before the festival. After that win, Dunguib was odds-on and it was 10-1 bar, with the next three in the betting – Get Me Out Of Here, Menorah and Oscar Whisky – all British-trained.

Dunguib

7 b g; Trainer Philip Fenton
Hurdles form 1111, best RPR 156
Left-handed 1, best RPR 156
Right-handed 111, best RPR 154
Cheltenham form (bumper) 1, best RPR 151
At the festival 11 Mar 09: Took keen hold, held up well in rear, progress and still pulling 6f out, still keen when closing on leaders over 3f out, led over 2f out and quickened clear, won Champion Bumper by 10l from Some Present

Stands like a colossus over the 2m novice division and if connections resist the temptation to run him in the Champion Hurdle he'll be one of the shortest-priced favourites in the history of the festival's opening race. Looked a sensational prospect for hurdles after last season's Champion Bumper, in which he pulled like a train all the way round but still had more than enough in reserve to coast to a ten-length victory in a race that has worked out remarkably well, and nothing he has done since has changed that view. Has gone off at long odds-on for all four hurdles starts, the last two in Grade 1s, and has won unextended each time. If you wanted to be picky you could say his jumping leaves a lot to be desired and he may get found out off a faster pace on better

ground, but he has a ridiculously high cruising speed and doesn't seem to lose any ground even when paddling through a hurdle. Not surprisingly for a race in which the Irish do incredibly well (won seven of the last nine), he has impeccable credentials as far as trends are concerned and, if this is the route connections take – as they have maintained all along – and he fails, a lot of Irishmen will be heading home before the Arkle.

Menorah

5 b g; Trainer Philip Hobbs
Hurdles form 1212, best RPR 153
Left-handed 12, best RPR 137
Right-handed 12, best RPR 153

Won a bumper in August for Thomas Mullins at Naas and subsequently switched to Philip Hobbs, for whom he has developed into a smart novice. Made mistakes on his hurdling debut at Warwick but still had the class to sprint away from a Nicky Henderson hotpot, then found an extended 2m3f at Doncaster too far when put in his place by Bobby Ewing, being eased down in the final 100 yards. Proved a revelation dropped back to 2m at

Kempton over Christmas, winning what is usually an informative novice hurdle by ten lengths from Bellvano, another well-touted Henderson horse. He really stepped up the pace after the third-last that day and his hurdling was far more fluent than before. Suffered a reverse in his Ascot prep when getting sucked into going too fast too soon, tiring and being caught by Lush Life. He is better than that, but looks a short-runner if the ground is testing, so connections will be hoping for a dry start to the week.

Get Me Out Of Here
6 b g; Trainer Jonjo O'Neill
Hurdles form (all left-handed) 1111, best RPR 150

Made debut in bumper only last May, but now unbeaten in five starts, the last four over hurdles. Odds-on favourite for first two hurdles starts and scored with the minimum of fuss, even if he was a less than fluent jumper at the time. Stepped into handicap company after that, winning easily off a mark of 123 at Newbury and then being well backed for the valuable Totesport Trophy against largely much more experienced rivals off 12lb higher. It didn't make much difference, though, as he travelled well in mid-division before making his move and, despite making a hash of the last, found an excellent turn of foot to get back up and win going away. That marked him down as a high-class novice, and arguably the best in Britain, but he suffered a cut during the race and connections are far from certain to ask him to go to the well again too quickly. Deserves plenty of respect if he lines up, as he's a strong trends scorer and clearly handles a strong-run race.

Oscar Whisky
5 b g; Trainer Nicky Henderson
Hurdles form 11, best RPR 136
Left-handed 1, best RPR 130
Right-handed 1, best RPR 136

Trainer often introduces his best recruits at Newbury and this one had his first three races

there, taking two bumpers in clear-cut fashion before doing the same again over hurdles in the middle of December. Was again impressive at Sandown in his prep, but was entitled to win as he liked there (started at 4-11) and. though Henderson regularly has a strong stable of novice hurdlers, his novice record outside the Triumph Hurdle is not great in recent years – he hasn't won the Supreme since 1992 and has never won the 2m5f or the relatively new 3m novice. Indeed, Zaynar's Triumph win last season was his first novice success since Katarino in the same race ten years earlier.

Blackstairmountain
5 b g; Trainer Willie Mullins
Hurdles form (right-handed) 1, best RPR 135

Bumper winner and won a fairly valuable Flat maiden in July, after which trainer Willie Mullins said he had the potential to go to the top level over hurdles. He wasn't seen again until the end of January, winning a Punchestown maiden hurdle with any amount in hand, jumping adequately, travelling strongly and quickening up well. The competition wasn't great, but he's the type to improve considerably given better ground according to his trainer. Mullins sprang a shock three years ago with 40-1 chance Ebaziyan, who, like Blackstairmountain, did not make his debut over hurdles until the end of January.

Bellvano
6 b g; Trainer Nicky Henderson
Hurdles form 121, best RPR 145
Left-handed 11, best RPR 136
Right-handed 2, best RPR 145

Ridden by owner's son JP Magnier to win two of his three bumpers (left at the start in the other) and made fine start to hurdling career at Newbury in November in the hands of Tony McCoy, coasting ten lengths clear of Prince Buster in a race that is usually informative (won in recent years by Rhinestone Cowboy, Sizing Europe and Copper Bleu). McCoy was of the opinion he would be even better in a more

Peddlers Cross: unbeaten and well regarded

Bellvano: won good race at Newbury

strongly run race, but he couldn't live with Menorah when that one wound it up after three out at Kempton in December. Back on track after that with a fluent enough victory at Newbury, but didn't do any more than he was entitled to and arguably there are plenty of stronger contenders.

Peddlers Cross

5 b g; Trainer Donald McCain
Hurdles form (both left-handed) 11, best RPR 148

Unbeaten point and bumper winner, who cost current connections £100,000 in April. Has won both his hurdles starts by wide margins, showing a pretty decent level of form, most notably on his second start when leading all the way and thrashing Scriptwriter by 16l in the Grade 2 Rossington Main at Haydock on soft ground. He surprised his trainer that day with the speed he showed, which means this race on the agenda, though he is seen as a potential stayer in the making. Trainer has made no secret of the regard in which he holds

him, so interesting wherever he goes.

General Miller

5 b g; Trainer Nicky Henderson
Hurdles form (both at Cheltenham) 12, best RPR 143

Yet another potential contender from the Henderson yard. Dual bumper winner at the end of last term and dented the reputation of Paul Nicholls' much-touted Ghizao with a gutsy win in a Cheltenham novice hurdle in December. Upped in trip and grade at the same track next time, he was made second favourite behind another Nicholls hotpot – this time Royal Charm – but though he handled that one, he proved no match for the Robin Dickin-trained Restless Harry, who powered up the hill for an 8l win. He had cruised into contention at the penultimate flight but had no answer to the strong-galloping winner and simply may not have stayed. Worth another chance, especially back at 2m, though his trainer obviously has a few who could take this route and they won't all run in the same race.

Pepe Simo

6 b g; Trainer Paul Nicholls
Hurdles form 1115, best RPR 145
Left-handed 1, best RPR 141
Right-handed 115, best RPR 145
Cheltenham form (bumper) 9
At the festival 11 Mar 09: held up in midfield, squeezed out over 5f out and lost place, renewed effort over 3f out, outpaced over 2f out, weakened, finished 9th, 35l behind Dunguib, in Champion Bumper

Useful if slightly wayward bumper performer who has 35l to make up on Dunguib on Champion Bumper form (encountered trouble but would not have been a great deal closer). Went 3-3 in novice hurdles, showing progressive form on each occasion, but unsurprisingly put firmly in his place when 21l fifth to Go Native in the Grade 1 Christmas Hurdle at Kempton on Boxing Day. Only falls down on trends because he didn't win last time out, but seems to have plenty to find.

Ghizao: Taunton winner has a lot to find

Ghizao

6 b g; Trainer Paul Nicholls
Hurdles form 21, best RPR 138
Left-handed 2, best RPR 125
Right-handed 1, best RPR 138
Cheltenham form (including bumper) 12, best RPR 125

Beat the highly regarded Lidar 6l in a Cheltenham bumper in November, but then no match for General Miller over hurdles at the same track the following month, going down by a length. Achieved the last-time-out success that nine of the last ten Supreme winners could boast before turning up here when thrashing a poor field at Taunton at odds of 1-5, but that form is a long way behind what Dunguib has already shown and he looks just a fringe contender. Nicholls believes he'll be better on good ground and he also has the Neptune as an alternative.

Other contenders

Decent ex-Flat racers used to be well represented in this, but the first ten in the betting this year all came from bumpers. At the time of writing it's 33-1 bar (and including some of) those mentioned and the chance of that changing before race time was reduced when Alan King's **Salden Licht** proved a bitter disappointment in the Dovecote at Kempton, where he was a distant third. King has a better candidate in Sandown Grade 2 **Manyriverstocross**, though that one was a stayer on the Flat and may head for the Neptune despite a heavy defeat in the Challow at Newbury, as he looked a stayer when running on into third in the Totesport Trophy. Willie Mullins' **Morning Supreme** put up a big figure when landing a Cork mares' novice hurdle in December, but she hasn't been sighted since and is a shorter price for the Neptune, while stablemate **Flat Out** was hugely impressive on his hurdles debut at Punchestown in February and could make the line-up despite his lack of experience. David Pipe's dual bumper winner **Dan Breen** hacked up on his hurdles debut at Doncaster in February, but he beat a poor bunch and is a long way off Dunguib on the figures. ∎

SPINAL RESEARCH SUPREME NOVICES' HURDLE (GRADE 1)
Tuesday 1.30   2m¹/₂f

FORM		WINNER	AGE	& WGT	WINNING RPR	PRE-RACE RPR	SP	TRAINER	H.Runs	BEST RPR LAST 12 MONTHS (RUNS SINCE)
09	12121	Go Native D	6	11-7	152	146	12-1	Noel Meade (Ir)	5(20GS)	won Punchestown nov hdl Lstd (2m) (2)
08	1/711	Captain Cee Bee D	7	11-7	159	144	17-2	Edward P Harty (Ir)	2(22GS)	won Punchestown hdl (2m) (0)
07	21	Ebaziyan D	6	11-7	150	116	40-1	W Mullins (Ir)	2(22S)	2nd Cork mdn hdl (2m) (1)
06	-3111	Noland C, D	5	11-7	150	137	6-1	P Nicholls	4(20GS)	won Exeter class 1 nov hdl Lstd (2m1f) (0)
05	1143	Arcalis D, BF	5	11-7	146	143	20-1	Howard Johnson	4(20G)	4th Christmas Hurdle Gd1 (2m) (1)
04	1-111	Brave Inca D	6	11-7	152	145	7-2F	C Murphy (Ir)	7(19G)	won Deloitte Nov Hdl Gd2 (2m2f) (0)
03	0-211	Back In Front C, D	6	11-8	160	149	3-1F	E J O'Grady (Ir)	3(19G)	won Limerick nov hdl (2m4f) (0)
02	-1111	Like-A-Butterfly D	8	11-3	147	156	7-4F	C Roche (Ir)	4(28GS)	won Leopardstown nov hdl Gd2 (2m2f) (0)
01		Cancelled								
00	11	Sausalito Bay D	6	11-8	147	132	14-1	Noel Meade (Ir)	2(15G)	won Naas nov hdl (2m) (0)
99	111	Hors La Loi III C, D	4	11-0	159	151	9-2	M Pipe	3(20GS)	won Cheltenham class 1 nov hdl Gd2 (2m1f) (0)

WINS-RUNS: 4yo 1-13, 5yo 2-89, 6yo 5-74, 7yo 1-23, 8yo 1-6 **FAVOURITES:** +£1.25

TRAINERS IN THIS RACE (w-pl-r): Noel Meade 2-1-12, Howard Johnson 1-0-5, P Nicholls 1-1-12, W Mullins 1-0-10, A King 0-1-4, G Moore 0-1-2, M Morris 0-1-3, N J Henderson 0-4-13, P J Hobbs 0-2-6, T J Taaffe 0-1-1

FATE OF FAVOURITES: U311105325 **POSITION OF WINNER IN MARKET:** 2511102046

RECORD OF IRISH RUNNERS: 7-5-63 (+£26.75) **HORSES WEARING HEADGEAR:** 0-2-13 (-£13.00)

RECORD OF TRIAL WINNERS: Sharp Novices' Hurdle (Cheltenham, November) 070900; Royal Bond (Fairyhouse, December) **1200**
Kennel Gate (Ascot, December) 0P092; Future Champion Novice (Leopardstown, December) 235U0
Tolworth (Sandown, January) **501**; Deloitte (Leopardstown, February) **311**; Dovecote (Kempton, February) 00

Key trends
» Won at least 50 per cent of hurdle starts, 10/10
» Pre-race RPR of at least 132, 9/10
» Ran within the last 45 days, 9/10
» Won last time out, 9/10
» Rated within 12lb of RPR top-rated, 8/10
» Previously contested a Graded race, 7/10 (four won, three made the frame)

Other factors
» The Irish have won this 11 times in the past 20 years. Three winners came via the Flat, where they had earned an RPR between 91 and 110, and none of the three had won outside minor novice hurdle company. Of the other seven, six had started their careers in bumpers, where they had earned an RPR of at least 110
» Only one winner (Back In Front) had previously run at the festival, finishing third in the Bumper
» Montelado (1993) is the only winner of the Bumper to follow up here, but surprisingly only two others have tried – Cork All Star (seventh) and Cousin Vinny (fifth)
» The last horse to win this after just one hurdle outing was Flown in 1992
» For many years the shortest-priced Irish runner was often beaten by a compatriot. However, of the last six to win, four were the most fancied

Notes

2.05
Race 2

Irish Independent Arkle Trophy Chase
(Grade 1)

2m

Key stats A race for fancied runners – since Waterloo Boy scored at 20-1 in 1989, only one winner has started bigger than 9-1, though there has been just one winning favourite

Captain Cee Bee and Sizing Europe arrive at the festival with leading chances, just as they did on the same day two years ago. That day they had contrasting fortunes, with Captain Cee Bee winning the Supreme Novices' and Sizing Europe folding tamely after going off favourite for the Champion Hurdle, but on their only meeting over fences the luck was with Sizing Europe when Captain Cee Bee crashed out at the last at Leopardstown. They are the main Irish hopes, along with Willie Mullins's Sports Line, while the home challenge is led by Somersby, last year's Supreme Novices' third and unbeaten in two chase starts. Kingmaker winner Long Run would be a live chance but is likely to go for the RSA Chase, leaving Riverside Theatre to represent Nicky Henderson.

Captain Cee Bee

9 b g; Trainer Edward Harty
Chase form 1F1 (all left-handed), best RPR 163,
Cheltenham form (hurdles) 1, best RPR 159
At the festival 11 Mar 08: in touch 3rd, pushed along 4th, driven and stayed on to chase leaders 3 out, challenged after 2 out, kept on under pressure to lead final 110 yards, driven out, won Supreme Novices' Hurdle by 2l from Binocular

Pulled up at Aintree in April 2008, a month after winning the Supreme Novices' at Cheltenham, and not seen again until December this season, but proved he retained most of his ability with a battling debut chase win by a neck from Zaarito at Naas, form that has been boosted by both the runner-up and third since. He stepped up massively on that run when arguably unlucky not to land the Grade 1 Bord Na Mona With Nature Novice Chase at Leopardstown on Boxing Day, as he appeared to be travelling all over Sizing Europe approaching the last, only for his legs to give way on landing. The ultra-critical could argue it was a tired fall, but he appeared to be moving powerfully to most eyes and in any case he was showing top-class form. Showed no ill-effects from that when sauntering home 13l clear of the useful Fosters Cross at Naas in his final prep in February and looks a major

player despite his age being a trends negative (only two winners have been as old as nine).

Sizing Europe

8 b g; Trainer Henry de Bromhead
Chase form 1111, best RPR 163
Left-handed 1, best RPR 159
Right-handed 111, best RPR 163
Cheltenham form (both hurdles) 10, best RPR 154
At the festival 11 Mar 08: Chased leaders, driven to challenge 2 out, weakened quickly before last, virtually pulled up before run-in, finished 14th, beaten 101l by Katchit, in Champion Hurdle

Winner of the AIG Europe Champion Hurdle at Leopardstown in 2008, Sizing Europe appeared to go wrong in that season's Champion Hurdle – he was cantering and looking the winner approaching the second-last, but was beaten very quickly once the other side of it – and it wasn't until his final start last season, when fourth to Solwhit at Punchestown, that he looked on the way back. Since then he has been reinvented as a high-class novice chaser and is unbeaten in four. He jumped impeccably to win easily on his first three starts, earning an RPR 1lb superior to that awarded to Forpadydeplasterer for winning last season's Arkle when trouncing Harchibald on just his

Somersby (right) has taken well to fences and looks the strongest of the British challengers

second outing. Was not as fluent in better company when arguably lucky to keep his unbeaten record intact thanks to Captain Cee Bee's last-fence fall in a Grade 1 at the Leopardstown Christmas meeting. He has since been a mild drifter in the betting, with many concerned about his ability to get up the hill given his Champion Hurdle effort, but his five-and-a-half-length win over Osana (163 over hurdles and previously unbeaten in two chases) would have been given a much better reception if Captain Cee Bee hadn't been in the race. It's still top-notch form whichever way you look at it. There haven't been many winners as old as eight (just two since 1990) and that's the only major trends negative.

···

Somersby

7 b g; Trainer Henrietta Knight
Chase form 11, best RPR 157
Left-handed 1, best RPR 142
Right-handed 1, best RPR 157
Cheltenham form (hurdles) 3
At the festival 10 Mar 09: in touch on outside, lost position after 3 out, pushed along after 2 out, ridden and kept on well run-in to take 3rd last strides, but no impression on leading duo, finished third, beaten 3l, to Go Native in Supreme Novices' Hurdle
···

Always considered more of a chaser than a hurdler by his trainer, so it was highly encouraging that he managed to finish third in the Supreme Novices' at the festival last season, especially given that first and second Go Native and Medermit have gone on to prove it a particularly hot renewal. Has not disappointed so far over fences, jumping with aplomb to land a fair novice chase at Warwick and then stepping up markedly to land the Henry VIII at Sandown, beating one-time Arkle favourite (now crocked) Crack Away Jack with another fencing masterclass. The first of the market leaders to qualify on the age trend and has plenty of other ticks, so looks the strongest of the British challengers.

···

Tataniano

6 b g; Trainer Paul Nicholls
Chase form 112, best RPR 154
Left-handed 12, best RPR 154
Right-handed 1, best RPR 151
Cheltenham form (none at the festival) 411, best RPR 154
···

Didn't look anything special over hurdles until his final start at Cheltenham in April when he made all and spreadeagled a fair field, and he has carried that progression over to fences, winning his first two starts. In the first he had little to beat (sent off at 1-5) but impressed with his jumping for a 32-length success, while next time he was equally slick when winning at Cheltenham. The wheels appeared to come off in his Arkle prep, though, when he jumped stickily at Newbury and was beaten at odds of 2-11 by Suntini, who has no pretensions to Arkle class. Paul Nicholls may not have had him fully wound up for that, but it was bitterly disappointing all the same and there are now major question marks.

Long Run

5 b g; Trainer Nicky Henderson
Chase form 121111, best RPR 164
Left-handed 12111, best RPR 155
Right-handed 1, best RPR 164

Created a tremendous impression with a largely fluent round of jumping as he cruised to 13-length success from Tazbar in the Grade 1 Feltham Novices' Chase at Kempton on his British debut, recording a superb RPR of 164. Didn't put up such a big figure (155) but was still impressive dropped to 2m in February for the Kingmaker at Warwick, having no trouble going a quicker pace and storming clear. His main rivals were disappointing – Take The Breeze running below form and King Edmund not jumping fluently - and he made a couple of mistakes, but there's no doubting he has a huge engine. A danger wherever he goes, but trainer has said the RSA is the plan unless the ground is very soft, so clearly can't be seen as an ante-post proposition and anyone looking to back him should wait.

Riverside Theatre

6 b g; Trainer Nicky Henderson
Chase form 11, best RPR 156
Left-handed 1, best RPR 150
Right-handed 1, best RPR 156

His third in the Champion Novice Hurdle at Punchestown in April qualified him from a hurdles form perspective and he bags a tick pretty much everywhere else as well. Two

Osana: in with a shout on his best form

chase victories, at Newbury in November and at Kempton's Christmas meeting, were each settled with an impressive burst of speed around half a mile out and he has put up some decent figures without breaking sweat. Possibly only in the second rank of Nicky Henderson's powerful battalion, but would be a star in any other stable and would be well worth his place, though connections are reportedly considering the handicap route. Good career win record (6-10).

Sports Line

7 b g; Trainer Willie Mullins
Chase form (both left-handed) 12, best RPR 149

Put up as a potential Arkle dark horse by trainer Willie Mullins earlier in the season and has proved himself to be more than that in just two chase starts to date, winning a big-field beginners chase at Navan and then being mugged late by An Cathaoir Mor in the Grade 1 Irish Arkle at Leopardstown in January. Nine of the last ten winners were rated within 12lb of the RPR top-rated on the day, so he just falls short of that, but he was better than the bare result at Leopardstown as he helped to press a strong pace yet finished 20 lengths clear of the two who went with him. Jumps well in the main, but good ground would be a possible negative, as would the apparent need to race up with the pace in a race likely to be run at breakneck speed.

Osana

8 b g; Trainer Edward O'Grady
Chase form (all left-handed) 1123, best RPR 154
Cheltenham form (all hurdles) 02120
At the festival 16 Mar 07: led after 1st, ridden when headed and mistake last, faded run-in, finished 10th, beaten 7½l by Pedrobob, in County Hurdle

11 Mar 08: led, 5 lengths clear 4th, ridden after 4 out, narrowly headed but upsides 2 out, still challenging last, one pace under pressure when carried left final 50 yards, finished second, beaten 1l by Katchit, in Champion Hurdle

10 Mar 09: led at a strong pace, joined 4th, headed after next, did not look keen and dropped out gradually before 3 out, finished 11th, beaten 21l by Punjabi, in Champion Hurdle

Transferred from David Pipe to Edward O'Grady for a chase campaign and started well with two comfortable wins at Navan, though was clearly only third best in a Grade 1 at Leopardstown over Christmas when he finished second to Sizing Europe after the fall of Captain Cee Bee. From a trends perspective, he falls down only on his age, and the fact he acts so well at Cheltenham will be in his favour. Often a front-runner, but new trainer seems to believe he'll be better getting a lead in a fast-run race, so interesting to see what tactics are employed. Disappointing when only third to Shakervilz on soft on his final prep at Navan, but will be suited by a livelier surface and has the ability to be on the premises.

Woolcombe Folly

7 b g; Trainer Paul Nicholls
Chase form (left-handed) 1, best RPR 143

Useful hurdler who won his last four in that sphere but then spent more than 15 months on the sidelines. Returned as good as ever in February, matching his career-best hurdles RPR with a debut victory at Grade 2 level over fences at Doncaster. He only won by a nose from I'm Delilah, so that form still needs improving upon, but he's entitled to come on a ton and you certainly couldn't fault the way he travelled or jumped. That said, this is still a tough year to be running in this race on the back of one chase start.

Other contenders

At the time of writing **Mikael D'Haguenet** had yet to jump a fence, but a late debut is by no means a bar to success here as Well Chief did not make his chase debut until a few weeks before his Arkle win and, like Willie Mullins' charge, had top-class Cheltenham form. Mikael D'Haguenet was last season's top staying novice hurdler – winning the Ballymore Novices' Hurdle and following up with another Grade 1 victory at Punchestown – and a 2m-2m1f win would see him qualify on most counts, though probably not on chase RPRs. **Max Max** and **French Opera** are other strings to Nicky Henderson's bow, but the former reportedly prefers flatter tracks and disappointed at Doncaster in February, while the latter is more likely to contest a handicap at the festival. **Shakervilz**, who is in this race and the RSA, didn't look short of pace when seeing off Major Finnegan and Osana at Navan in February, but he has solid form over a lot further over hurdles. Ferdy Murphy has talked up **Bedlam Boy** as a potential outsider, but he has a handicap mark that may be too good to waste. ▶▶**Trends, overleaf**

IRISH INDEPENDENT ARKLE CHALLENGE TROPHY CHASE (GRADE 1)
Tuesday 2.05   **2m**

FORM	WINNER	AGE & WGT	WINNING RPR	PRE-RACE RPR	SP	TRAINER	Ch.Runs	BEST RPR LAST 12 MONTHS (RUNS SINCE)
09 -1222	Forpadydeplasterer D	7 11-7	162	157	8-1	T Cooper (Ir)	4(17GS)	2nd Leop nov ch Gd1 (2m5f) (0)
08 -1112	Tidal Bay C, BF	7 11-7	168	153	6-1	H Johnson	4(14GS)	won Carlisle class 3 nov ch (2m4f) (2)
07 21211	My Way De Solzen C, D	7 11-7	165	158	7-2	A King	5(13S)	won Haydock class 1 nov ch Gd2 (2m4f) (0)
06 -1111	Voy Por Ustedes D	5 11-2	162	160	15-2	A King	4(14GS)	won Wincanton class 1 nov ch Gd2 (2m) (0)
05 -2213	Contraband C, D	7 11-7	158	154	7-1	M Pipe	4(19G)	3rd Uttoxeter class 1 nov ch Gd2 (2m) (0)
04 3-151	Well Chief D	5 11-3	157	133	9-1	M Pipe	1(16G)	won Taunton class 4 nov ch (2m1/2f) (0)
03 5-111	Azertyuiop CD	6 11-8	170	165	5-4F	P Nicholls	3(9G)	won Wincanton class 3 nov ch (2m) (0)
02 F111F	Moscow Flyer D, BF	8 11-8	167	151	11-2	J Harrington (Ir)	5(12GS)	won Denny Gold Medal nov ch Gd1 (2m1f) (1)
01	Cancelled							
00 62-11	Tiutchev C, D	7 11-8	164	145	8-1	N Henderson	2(12G)	won Sandown class 3 nov ch (2m4¹/₂f) (0)
99 21211	Flagship Uberalles D	5 11-0	157	144	11-1	P Nicholls	4(14GS)	won Warwick class 1 nov ch Gd2 (2m) (0)

WINS-RUNS: 5yo 3-28, 6yo 1-23, 7yo 5-55, 8yo 1-24, 9yo 0-7, 10yo 0-2, 12yo 0-1 **FAVOURITES:** -£7.75

TRAINERS IN THIS RACE (w-pl-r): P Nicholls 2-3-16, Howard Johnson 1-0-4, Mrs J Harrington 1-0-5, N Henderson 1-2-6, Ferdy Murphy 0-1-4, Miss H Knight 0-1-3, P Hobbs 0-2-4

FATE OF FAVOURITES: 5321F0023F **POSITION OF WINNER IN MARKET:** 7441525223

RECORD OF IRISH RUNNERS: 2-1-40 (-£24.50) **HORSES WEARING HEADGEAR:** 0-2-12 (-£12.00)

RECORD OF TRIAL WINNERS: November Chase (Cheltenham, November) **U21FF26F;** Henry VII Chase (Sandown, December) **352F1729** Wayward Lad Chase (Kempton, December) **5835P;** Durkan Chase (Leopardstown, December) **51U669** Lightning Chase (Doncaster (ex Ascot), January) **5P5350;** Irish Arkle Chase (Leopardstown, January) **5F620640** Kingmaker Chase (Warwick, February) **123U126**

Key trends
▶▶SP no bigger than 11-1 (only one bigger than 16-1 at ante-post stage), 10/10
▶▶Aged five to seven, 9/10
▶▶Finished in the first two on all completed chase starts, 9/10 (exception finished third at worst)
▶▶Rated within 12lb of RPR top-rated, 9/10
▶▶Pre-race RPR of at least 144, 9/10
▶▶RPR hurdle rating of at least 143, 9/10 (five of last eight were 157-plus)
▶▶Three to five runs over fences, 8/10
▶▶Won novice chase over 2m to 2m1f, 8/10

Other factors
▶▶Six had previously won a 2m-2m1f Graded Chase, although only Warwick's Kingmaker has produced more than one winner
▶▶Seven winners had previously run at the festival, showing mixed form in a variety of hurdle races
▶▶Three French-bred horses have scored, and only twice has a French-bred not finished in the top three
▶▶Only ten German-breds have run, but they include a winner, two seconds and a third
▶▶There has been only one winning favourite in the past decade

Notes

2.40
Race 3

William Hill Trophy Handicap Chase
(Grade 3)

3m¹/₂f

Key stats None of the last ten winners carried more than 10st 12lb. Apart from 2007 winner Joes Edge (50-1) the other eight winners in the last nine runnings went off no bigger than 8-1

Gerald Delamere's view This is the top handicap chase of the meeting and has been won by subsequent Gold Cup winners Kerstin and Charter Party, as well as Grand National heroes Royal Tan, Team Spirit, West Tip, Seagram and Rough Quest. Winners are usually well fancied in the market (eight in the past decade have been no bigger than 8-1) but Wichita Lineman last year became only the second winning favourite in the past 25 years and the first since 1994. Twenty-seven of the past 35 winners had SPs ranging from 4-1 to 12-1.

Previous festival form is hugely important, as Wichita Lineman (the 2007 Albert Bartlett winner) demonstrated last year. Since 1973 former winners had finished 1451152U3213F6 over the course in the season of their success.

Over the past 35 years only three winners were outside the seven to ten age group, suggesting that horses have to be in their prime. Since 1983 no winner was rated above 150 or below 127, which should be a helpful rating band. Just three winners in the same period carried more than 11st 4lb, which demonstrates what a competitive handicap this is, and only two below 10st 2lb. The pair carrying 10st were out of the handicap.

Only four winners in the past 36 hadn't made the 1-2-3 in a well-known handicap in their past three outings. Twenty-four had made the first three last time out and, of those to finish, none was placed worse than eighth (three failed to complete).

Paul Nicholls has yet to win this event, with many of his big-race winners over-handicapped by the time they get to this meeting.

There was a long Irish drought until Youlneverwalkalone won in 2003, and he was followed by Dun Doire three years later. They carried 10st 11lb and 10st 9lb respectively and both had just won major Irish handicaps, as well as having run well in Britain that season. The three novice winners since 2003 carried between 10st 5lb and 10st 9lb.
▶▶**Trends, overleaf**

The William Hill Chase attracts a competitive field and previous festival form is important

WILLIAM HILL TROPHY HANDICAP CHASE (GRADE 3)

Tuesday 2.40   3m¹/₂f

FORM	WINNER	AGE & WGT	OR	SP	TRAINER	C.Runs	BEST RPR LAST 12 MONTHS(RUNS SINCE)
09 9-121	Wichita Lineman C, D	8 10-9	142^T	5-1F	Jonjo O'Neill	3$^{(21GS)}$	won Chepstow class 3 nov ch (3m) (0)
08 3-P61	An Accordion D	7 10-12	143^{-6}	7-1	D Pipe	6$^{(14GS)}$	won Doncaster class 1 Lstd hcap ch (3m) (0)
07 76-78	Joes Edge	10 10-6	130^{-8}	50-1	Ferdy Murphy	17$^{(23GS)}$	13th Gold Cup (3m21/2f) (4)
06 11111	Dun Doire D	7 10-9	129^{-9}	7-1	A Martin (Ir)	9$^{(21GS)}$	won Gowran Park hcap ch (3m) (0)
05 03F43	Kelami D	7 10-2	133^{-9}	8-1	F Doumen (Fr)	19$^{(20G)}$	3rd Haydock class 1 hcap ch (3m41/2f) (0)
04 31U21	Fork Lightning C, D	8 10-5	136^{-4}	7-1	A King	5$^{(11G)}$	2nd Kempton class 3 nov ch (3m) (1)
03 0-131	Youlneverwalkalone D	9 10-11	142^{-9}	7-1	C Roche (Ir)	9$^{(18G)}$	won Thurles chase (3m) (2)
02 3-133	Frenchman's Creek C	8 10-5	131^{-4}	8-1	H Morrison	11$^{(23GS)}$	3rd Doncaster class 1 Lstd hcap ch (3m) (0)
01	cancelled						
00 -PU12	Marlborough D	8 10-3	141^{-1}	11-2	N Henderson	10$^{(12G)}$	2nd Racing Post Chase Hcp Gd3 (3m) (0)
99 55/16	Betty's Boy C	10 10-2	127^{-12}	25-1	K Bailey	10$^{(18GS)}$	won Uttoxeter class 3 hcap ch (2m7f) (1)

WINS-RUNS: 6yo 0-12, 7yo 3-25, 8yo 4-45, 9yo 1-35, 10yo 2-38, 11yo 0-18, 12yo 0-5, 13yo 0-2, 14yo 0-1 **FAVOURITES:** -£8.00

FATE OF FAVOURITES: F26300P231 **POSITION OF WINNER IN MARKET:** 0343452031

OR 121-135 5-7-63, **136-151** 5-21-107, **152-166** 0-2-11

RECORD OF IRISH RUNNERS: 2-0-11 (+£5.00) **HORSES WEARING HEADGEAR:** 1-4-33 (-£25.00)

Key trends

▶▶Aged seven to ten, 10/10

▶▶Carried no more than 10st 12lb, 10/10

▶▶Officially rated 127-143, 10/10

▶▶Won over at least 3m, 9/10

▶▶Finished first, second or third in either or both last two starts, 9/10

▶▶SP between 5-1 and 10-1, 8/10

▶▶No more than 11 runs over fences, 8/10

▶▶Ran no more than four times that season, 8/10

▶▶Top-three finish last time out, 8/10

Other factors

▶▶Five winners had run at a previous festival, three recording at least one top-four finish

▶▶No winner in the past 10 years has won from out of the handicap (Maamur achieved the feat in 1996)

▶▶Five winners had run well (three placing, one falling when going well and one sixth) in a handicap at Cheltenham earlier in the season

▶▶Just two winning favourites (Antonin, 1994, and Wichita Lineman, 2009) in the last 30 years

▶▶Three of the last four winners had all won a class 1 handicap chase

▶▶Once seemingly an impossible task for novices, but three of the last six winners have been novices

Notes

3.20
Race 4

Smurfit Kappa Champion Hurdle
(Grade 1)

2m¹/₂f

Key stat Punjabi last year became only the third winner in the past 20 years to have been to the festival before without being successful. Nine of the last 11 winners had won at a previous festival

Go Native has a shot of landing the £1m WBX bonus by completing the Fighting Fifth/Christmas/Champion Hurdle hat-trick, but he has plenty of challengers in a wide-open contest. The other leading Irish hope is Solwhit, who was beaten by Go Native in a slowly run Fighting Fifth before bouncing back to win the two key Irish races. Nicky Henderson appeared to have the strongest hand in Britain but has had several setbacks, with Zaynar losing favouritism after his unbeaten record was ended at odds of 1-14 at Kelso in his Champion prep, the form of Punjabi's 2009 Champion win taking several knocks and Binocular being pulled out of the race. Khyber Kim, formerly trained by Henderson, put himself in the reckoning with two impressive wins at Cheltenham before Christmas.

Zaynar

5 gr g; Trainer Nicky Henderson
Hurdles form 111112, best RPR 169
Left-handed 1112, best RPR 162
Right-handed 11, best RPR 169
Cheltenham form 11
At the festival 13 Mar 09: midfield, niggled along briefly on bend after 2nd, headway 4th, challenging when bumped 2 out, soon led, hard pressed last, driven out and stayed on gamely towards finish, won Triumph Hurdle by ³/4l from Walkon

Zaynar: doubts raised by shock Kelso defeat

But for a neck last year, we would have been treated to back-to-back five-year-old winners of the Champion Hurdle, having waited 25 years until Katchit broke the hoodoo in 2008. Given that this age group has now finished first and third, and second, third and fourth in the last two Champion Hurdles, the 'six or older' trend is probably not one to which we should give much credence any more. That's one of only two key criteria that Zaynar falls down on, the other being experience as nine of the last ten winners had raced at least nine times over hurdles. The main worry is whether he has sufficient speed to win a Champion Hurdle, as he has been campaigned over 2m2f-2m5f since his Triumph Hurdle win, winning easily against decent opposition on his first two starts but then coming a cropper at odds of 1-14 in the Morebattle at Kelso, where he went down by a length to Quwetwo, who was receiving 8lb but was officially a 35lb inferior horse. The sticky ground and a lack of fitness were blamed for his defeat, but he still should have won to be considered a first-rate contender. Whatever price he goes off at, he'll be bigger in running at some point as stamina is his forte and it's hard to see him travelling throughout the race on the bridle.

Go Native

7 b g; Trainer Noel Meade
Hurdles form 12121141211, best RPR 167
Left-handed 21111, best RPR 167
Right-handed 121421, best RPR 163
Cheltenham form 1, best RPR 152
At the festival 10 Mar 09: held up in mid-division, steady headway on inside after 3 out, led travelling well soon after 2 out, ridden last, held on all out, won Supreme Novices' Hurdle by nk from Medermit

The only horse who will turn up boasting a clean sweep of ticks in the key trends criteria and clearly has solid claims, as he has won seven of his 11 hurdles starts, is unbeaten on ground officially good to soft or faster and in Britain, with three raids yielding three Grade 1 wins. A drifter in the Champion Hurdle market after being thumped by Voler La Vedette on bad ground at Down Royal in November, he stormed back into the picture with an effortless success in the Fighting Fifth at Newcastle (a race taken by last year's Champion Hurdle winner Punjabi), showing far too much speed for the rest off a funereal pace. Indeed, so slow was the pace at Newcastle that he still wasn't being taken seriously and it wasn't until he claimed the second leg of the WBX £1m bonus series that he took his place near the head of the Champion Hurdle market. Even so, his victory in the Christmas Hurdle posed just as many questions as answers because he idled on the run-in and was nearly caught by Starluck. That, of course, invited comparisons with his recently retired stablemate Harchibald, who famously didn't get home when looking to be cantering halfway up the run-in in Hardy Eustace's second Champion Hurdle in 2005.

Such comparisons are unfair, though, as Harchibald was already a proven short-runner up the Cheltenham hill whereas Go Native is 1-1 at the track, having won last season's Supreme Novices' Hurdle in a good time. With the exception of one novice hurdle early in his career, he's yet to lose a race he looked like winning. Indeed, it's questionable if such comparisons would have been drawn if he had been in another stable and there is a danger that he's being damned by association. In a year that sees a large chunk of contenders boasting stamina over speed, his turn of foot could prove a potent weapon if delivered at the right time, and if there is a jockey again prepared to risk the sort of stick he got for Harchibald in 2005, it is undoubtedly the super-confident Paul Carberry. Big player.

Solwhit

6 b g; Trainer Charles Byrnes
Hurdles form 15112111131, best RPR 169
Left-handed 1131, best RPR 169
Right-handed 5112111, best RPR 167

Scores well on all major trends, with the exception that he is not a previous Cheltenham Festival winner, which, remarkably, nine of the last 11 winners were. Two of the last three were not, but both (Sublimity and Punjabi) had run well at a previous festival, so we shouldn't underestimate the importance of form at the meeting. That said, Solwhit seems to act pretty much everywhere else and there is little doubt he will be well suited by the likely strong pace. His only defeat in his last six starts (all at Grade 1 level) came in the Fighting Fifth when he was swamped for speed by both Go Native and Sublimity, but he had no problem reversing form with the latter in the December Festival Hurdle on his next start when the pace, though far from strong, was more reasonable. He looked even better when landing the Irish Champion Hurdle at the end of January. Trainer Charles Byrnes believes he wants 2m4f – he won his first Grade 1 at the trip at Aintree last season – when the ground is riding good or faster, but good ground doesn't seem to be allowed on day one of the festival, so there is

The Champion has been Celestial Halo's big target and he is sure to be trained to the minute

probably nothing to worry about on that score. A tough horse, he is not devoid of pace at the business end and merits plenty of respect.

Celestial Halo

6 b g; Trainer Paul Nicholls
Hurdles form 12122120124, best RPR 169
Left-handed 12122024, best RPR 169
Right-handed 211, best RPR 169
Cheltenham form 122, best RPR 169
At the festival 14 Mar 08: led after first, joined 2 out, hard driven soon after, stayed on gamely, won Triumph Hurdle, beating Franchoek by 2¼l

10 Mar 09: with leaders, clear in leading trio 4th, led before 3 out, hard ridden and headed last, kept on well flat, just held, finished second, beaten nk by Punjabi in Champion Hurdle

As tough and game as you can get and yet another high trends scorer (though falls down on the lack of a last-time-out win). The 2008

Triumph Hurdle winner failed by only a neck to emulate Katchit by landing the Champion Hurdle the following season and whatever beats him will know it has been in a fight. Paul Nicholls' six-year-old returned to the track as good as ever this season and recorded joint career-bests on his first two starts, the first when hacking up off top weight in a Wincanton handicap to defy a big drift in the market, and the second when runner-up in the Boylesports International for the second year in a row, this time at the course's traditional home of Cheltenham. Though odds-on and therefore disappointing in the eyes of punters in the Boylesports, he was giving 4lb to Khyber Kim, who had always threatened (but until then failed to deliver) to develop into a top-class hurdler, so he still came out best at the weights. He wasn't at his best in the Irish Champion behind Solwhit, but this has been

Khyber Kim was good in his pre-Christmas wins, but his March-April form figures are 0400

his only target of the season, so he's sure to be trained to the minute. If nothing is willing to take up pacemaking duties, he will make sure there is a solid gallop. While conceding he has an excellent chance in an open race, it is hard to see him ever becoming a great hurdler and it will be disappointing for the purists if something can't do him for speed.

Khyber Kim

8 b g; Trainer Nigel Twiston-Davies
Hurdles form 14042000511, best RPR 167
Left-handed 1404200511, best RPR 167
Right-handed 0, best RPR 139
Cheltenham form 0011, best RPR 167
At the festival 11 Mar 08: soon in touch, chased leaders from 3rd, ridden 3 out, weakened next, finished 10th, beaten 23l by Captain Cee Bee in Supreme Novices' Hurdle

13 Mar 09: led after 1st and took keen hold, clear third, headed 2 out, weakened quickly bend soon after, finished 22nd, beaten 47l by American Trilogy in County Hurdle

At the start of February Nicky Henderson had

three of the first seven in the betting, but it hasn't gone according to plan since and it would be ironic if the horse that took the crown away from Seven Barrows was one he never managed to get to the bottom of. Khyber Kim has threatened to be high-class over hurdles ever since recording a hurdles debut RPR of 148 (few have been rated higher) at Newbury in December 2007, but he never came close to that in three subsequent runs for Henderson and was moved to Nigel Twiston-Davies, with whom a similar story of good first run followed by bitter disappointment ensued last season. So when Khyber Kim returned this season it wasn't the greatest surprise to see him put up a career-best to land the Greatwood Hurdle at Cheltenham. The surprise came when he followed it up by beating Celestial Halo in the Boylesports International, especially as he won a shade comfortably even if he was in receipt of 4lb from the runner-up. So has he turned the corner? If you believe so he's probably still a good price at around the 10-1 mark as he was borderline Group-class on the Flat and is a big trends scorer, but he still has to prove he is the same horse in the spring (March-April form figures of 0400) as he is in the winter (November-January figures of 142011).

Punjabi

7 b g; Trainer Nicky Henderson
Hurdles form 1142142311F312421, best RPR 167
Left-handed 42231142, best RPR 167
Right-handed 11141F321, best RPR 167
Cheltenham form 4314
At the festival 16 Mar 07: challenged going well from 3 out until slight lead before 2 out, headed before last, weakened run-in, finished fourth, beaten 17l, to Katchit in Triumph Hurdle

11 Mar 08: headway 3 out, stayed on well from 2 out and kept on run-in to take 3rd, but never going pace to reach leading duo, finished third, beaten 6l, to Katchit in Champion Hurdle

10 Mar 09: well placed behind clear leaders, progress from 5th to go close up before next, tracked leader after 3 out, ridden to lead last, all out to hold on finish, won Champion Hurdle by nk from Celestial Halo

Was the forgotten horse going into last season's race, as he'd probably have been gunning for the £1m WBX bonus but for a last-flight fall in the Christmas Hurdle at Kempton, having earlier taken the Fighting Fifth at Newcastle. He scored well on the trends before winning last year and will do so again, having put a '1' on the board in a soft conditions race at Kempton in February that was put on for him after Wincanton's Kingwell Hurdle was abandoned the week before. He'd earlier failed to live up to his Champion-winning status, running only fourth behind Khyber Kim in the Boylesports International, having travelled really well until they turned for home. A below-par run was expected from this notoriously stuffy horse on that occasion, but he fared no better when brushed aside by Medermit at Haydock in January. His victory stroll at Kempton should have put him spot on and, with his festival record, he still needs to be given some respect. Having said that, only three of the first ten in last year's Champion have subsequently won a hurdle race (two of them in soft races at odds of 1-6 and 1-7), so the form looks suspect.

Starluck

5 b g; Trainer Alan Fleming
Hurdles form 11143122, best RPR 163
Left-handed 14312, best RPR 153
Right-handed 112, best RPR 163
Cheltenham form 41
At the festival 13 Mar 09: held up, headway approaching 3 out, challenging winner after 2 out, shaken up and lost 2nd last, soon ridden, weakened inside final 100 yards, finished fourth, beaten 7l by Zaynar in Triumph Hurdle

Went into last year's Triumph on the back of three easy wins, but there were worries about his stamina up the hill and they seemed well founded when he flattened out going to the last and finished only fourth to Zaynar, having looked the biggest threat two out. Connections brought him back to Cheltenham on his return this season and he hacked up in a small-field conditions event, but the runner-up was subsequently thumped off a mark of 135 in a handicap, putting the form in perspective. Stamina again appeared to desert him when he emptied at Haydock, having looked to be running all over Mr Thriller going to the last (traded at 1-100 in-running), and though he was closing fast on Go Native in the Christmas Hurdle at Kempton, the winner was idling and that course appears to suit him a lot better than Cheltenham. Not a high scorer on trends, he looks overrated and under-priced.

Medermit

6 gr g; Trainer Alan King
Hurdles form 21125331, best RPR 166
Left-handed 25331, best RPR 166
Right-handed 211, best RPR 145
Cheltenham form 233
At the festival 10 Mar 09: soon in touch, chased leaders after 3 out, staying on strongly when hampered last, rallied gamely and finished well final 75 yards, not quite get up, finished second, beaten a neck by Go Native in Supreme Novices' Hurdle

One of the few horses to show progressive form in the first half of the season for Alan King, whose horses were largely out of sorts at the time, and he has forced his way into the reckoning by running three consecutive career-bests. He didn't look anything more than a fringe challenger when running third under top weight in the Greatwood behind Khyber Kim and then filling the same spot behind the same rival in the Boylesports.com International, but he now has a verdict over the reigning champion, having thumped Punjabi by four lengths in Haydock's Champion Hurdle Trial in January. The form looks solid enough despite that being only a four-runner race and his win means he falls down on only one major stat, having never won a Grade 1 or a Grade 3 handicap hurdle. His close second to Go Native in last season's Supreme looks even better than it did at the time given the winner's exploits, but one major worry is that he seems to get a little outpaced before staying on again. His progressive profile means he is not out of it.

Other contenders

According to Paddy Power, **Dunguib** would be favourite if he lined up, but trainer Philip Fenton has been adamant all along that he'll stick to the novice route and that looks the wise move. When a Champion Hurdle challenge was first mooted the Racing Post looked at three hurdlers who tried and succeeded as novices (Royal Gait, Make A Stand, Alderbrook) and three that failed (Ruling, Large Action, Rhinestone Cowboy). Interestingly, each trio had one thing in common. The three who were successful were all heavily raced ex-Flat horses with loads of experience in big fields, while the three failures were more lightly raced, having come from bumpers. Champion Bumper winner Dunguib is potentially as good as any of those, but he's had only a handful of starts over hurdles and, despite winning easily, still has plenty to learn about the art of jumping. **Sublimity** will be back for another crack and will almost certainly travel as well as he usually does, but he doesn't appear to get home as well as he did when he won the Champion in 2007. Noel Meade has often said there is not that much between **Muirhead**, **Donnas Palm** and **Go Native** at home, but the odds and form suggest otherwise. **Voler La Vedette** and **Quevega** were left in at the latest forfeit stage, but both are still considered more likely to contest the David Nicholson Mares' Hurdle. ■

Medermit has run three consecutive career-bests on Racing Post Ratings

SMURFIT KAPPA CHAMPION HURDLE CHALLENGE TROPHY (GRADE 1)

Tuesday 3.20 2m¹/₂f

FORM	WINNER	AGE & WGT	WINNING PRE-RACE RPR	RPR	SP	TRAINER	H.Runs	BEST RPR LAST 12 MONTHS (RUNS SINCE)
09	1-1F3	Punjabi D, BF	6	11-10	157	164	22-1	N Henderson	12(23GS)	won Punchestown Champion Hdl Gd1 (2m) **(3)**
08	-1321	Katchit CD	5	11-10	167	162	10-1	A King	12(15GS)	won Kingwell Hurdle Gd2 (2m) **(0)**
07	444-1	Sublimity D	7	11-10	170	148	16-1	John Carr (Ir)	5(10S)	4th Supreme Nov Hurdle Gd1 (2m¹/₂f) **(2)**
06	11311	Brave Inca CD	8	11-10	171	170	7-4F	C Murphy (Ir)	20(18GS)	won Punchestown Champion Hurdle Gd1 (2m) **(4)**
05	12331	Hardy Eustace CD	8	11-10	168	170	7-2JF	D Hughes (Ir)	16(14G)	won Champion Hurdle Gd1 (2m¹/₂f) **(5)**
04	-2722	Hardy Eustace C, D	7	11-10	170	156	33-1	D Hughes (Ir)	10(14G)	2nd Gowran Park Gd2 hdl (2m) **(0)**
03	-1111	Rooster Booster CD	9	12-0	173	170	9-2	P Hobbs	25(17G)	won Greatwood Hurdle Gd3 (2m¹/₂f) **(2)**
02	-2331	Hors La Loi III CD	7	12-0	166	166	10-1	J Fanshawe	18(15GS)	won Kingwell Hurdle Gd2 (2m) **(0)**
01		Cancelled								
00	-1211	Istabraq CD	8	12-0	171	181	8-15F	A O'Brien (Ir)	23(12G)	won Punchestown Champion Hdl Gd1 (2m) **(4)**
99	-1111	Istabraq CD	7	12-0	170	176	4-9F	A O'Brien (Ir)	16(14G)	won AIG Europe Hurdle Gd1 (2m) **(0)**

WINS-RUNS: 5yo 1-32, 6yo 1-37, 7yo 4-31, 8yo 3-24, 9yo 1-12, 10yo 0-6, 11yo 0-5, 12yo 0-5 **FAVOURITES:** -£0.77

TRAINERS IN THIS RACE (w-pl-r): A King 1-0-3, C A Murphy 1-2-4, N J Henderson 1-4-13, Jonjo O'Neill 0-2-7, Noel Meade 0-1-8, P F Nicholls 0-1-3

FATE OF FAVOURITES: 11P3211603 **POSITION OF WINNER IN MARKET:** 1142011659

RECORD OF IRISH RUNNERS: 6-6-54 (+£7.31) **HORSES WEARING HEADGEAR:** 2-3-27 (+£11.50)

RECORD OF TRIAL WINNERS: Boylesports International (Cheltenham, December) **S189623** Christmas Hdl (Kempton, December) **3453250;** Irish Champion Hurdle (Leopardstown, January) **110451400;** Kingwell Hurdle (Wincanton, February) **021386P10** Previous year's Champion Hurdle winner **1PR213246;** Previous year's Supreme Novices' winner **20350;** Previous year's Triumph Hurdle winner **70F612**

Key trends

▶▶Ran within the last 51 days, ten winners in ten runnings

▶▶Aged between six and nine, 9/10

▶▶Ten to 25 runs over hurdles, 9/10

▶▶Had won either a Grade 1 hurdle or a Grade 3 handicap hurdle, 9/10

▶▶Pre-race RPR of at least 156, 9/10

▶▶Previous festival winner, 8/10

▶▶Won a Grade 1 or 2 hurdle that season, 8/10

▶▶Topspeed of at least 152, 8/10

▶▶Rated within 7lb of RPR top-rated, 8/10

▶▶Won last time out, 8/10

▶▶Started no bigger than 10-1, 7/10

Other factors

▶▶Only one winner (Hardy Eustace, 2004) had an unplaced effort in their form figures for that season. In 2008 Katchit broke a long-standing trend when he became the first five-year-old to win since See You Then in 1985. In the intervening years 73 had failed

▶▶Neither Punjabi nor Sublimity had won at the festival, although the former had twice made the frame there

▶▶Make A Stand, Collier Bay, Alderbrook and Royal Gait are the only other winners in the past 20 years not to have won at Cheltenham

▶▶Only three winners in the past 30 years had not run since the turn of the year

Notes

HOW DO THE LEADING CONTENDERS CONFORM TO THE CHAMPION HURDLE TRENDS?

	Aged 6 to 9, nine winners in the last ten runnings	10 to 25 career runs over hurdles, 9/10	Won Gd1 hdl or Gd3 hcap hdl, 9/10	RPR of at least 156, 9/10	Festival winner, 8/10 (p=placed)	Won Grade1 or 2 hdl that season, 8/10	Topspeed of at least 152, 8/10	Rated within 7lb of RPR top-rated, 8/10	Won last time out, 8/10	TOTAL
Celestial Halo	✔	✔	✔	✔	✔	✔	✔	✔	✗	8
Dunguib	✔	✗	✔	✗	✔	✔	✗	✗	✔	5
Go Native	✔	✔	✔	✔	✔	✔	✔	✔	✔	**9**
Khyber Kim	✔	✔	✔	✔	✗	✔	✔	✔	✔	8
Medermit	✔	✔	✗	✔	✗p	✔	✔	✔	✔	7
Mikael D'Haguenet	✔	✗	✔	✔	✔	✗	✗	✗	✔	5
Punjabi	✔	✔	✔	✔	✔	✗	✔	✔	✗	7
Quevega	✔	✗	✗	✔	✔	✗	✔	✗	✗	4
Solwhit	✔	✔	✔	✔	✗	✔	✔	✔	✔	8
Sublimity	✗	✔	✔	✔	✔	✗	✔	✔	✗	6
Starluck	✗	✗	✗	✔	✗p	✗	✗	✔	✗	2
Voler La Vedette	✔	✗	✗	✗	✗	✗	✗	✗	✔	2
Zaynar	✗	✗	✔	✔	✔	✔	✔	✔	✔	7

▶▶Record of previous year's Champion Hurdle winner **1PR213246**
▶▶Record of previous year's Supreme Novice winner **20350**
▶▶Record of previous year's Triumph Hurdle winner **70F612**
▶▶Record of current AIG Europe Champion Hurdle winner **110451400**
▶▶Record of current Christmas Hurdle winner **3453250**
▶▶Record of current Boylesports Hurdle winner **S189623**
▶▶The last horse aged ten or more to win the Champion Hurdle was Sea Pigeon
▶▶Katchit is the only winning five-year-old in the past 25 years

Based on results up to February 1, 2010

Notes

4.00
Race 5

Glenfarclas Cross Country Handicap Chase

3m7f

Key stats All five winners had won a cross-country race at Cheltenham or Punchestown. Every winner has been trained in Ireland and the Irish have had a 1-2-3-4 three times

Gerald Delamere's view Some strong trends are apparent after only five runnings of this race. The most obvious is that Enda Bolger, a specialist in this type of race, is the dominant trainer and that Irish horses have taken most of the places. Bolger has won four of the five renewals, all ridden by amateurs, and his winners had finished 13F1 over course and distance in the equivalent handicap at the December meeting. The past three Bolger winners were ridden by Nina Carberry.

Spot Thedifference's mantle as king of the cross-country has been taken over by dual winner Garde Champetre, and they are the only horses who have been able to defy a big weight in this race. Both carried 11st 12lb to victory, with Spot Thedifference winning off a mark of 143 and Garde Champetre off 150. The other three winners carried 10st 13lb or less and were rated from 126 to 129.

Three recent winners came into the race having won the PP Hogan Memorial Chase over the banks course at Punchestown, but this season's renewal didn't look as strong as usual (won by 20-1 shot Another Jewel, with the fancied Bolger-trained runners disappointing).

The market has been a clear guide, with all the winners being first or second favourite between 5-2 and 4-1. Maturity is essential, with the five winners aged from nine to 12. ■

GLENFARCLAS CROSS COUNTRY HANDICAP CHASE

Tuesday 4.00   **3m7f**

	FORM	WINNER	AGE & WGT	OR	SP	TRAINER	C.Runs	BEST RPR LAST 12 MONTHS(RUNS SINCE)
09	1-421	Garde Champetre CD	10 11-12	150⁴	7-2	E Bolger (Ir)	15^(16GS)	won Chelt Cross-Country hcap ch (3m7f) (0)
08	9-9F1	Garde Champetre	9 10-13	129ᵀ	4-1	E Bolger (Ir)	11^(16GS)	won Punchestown Cross-Country ch (3m) (0)
07	-2341	Heads Onthe Ground	10 10-2	126⁹	5-2F	E Bolger (Ir)	14^(16S)	won Punchestown Cross-Country ch (3m) (0)
06	5P-31	Native Jack	12 10-8	126ᵀ	7-2J	P Rothwell (Ir)	16^(16GS)	won Punchestown Cross-Country ch (3m) (0)
05	10114	Spot Thedifference CD	12 11-12	143⁻¹²	4-1	E Bolger (Ir)	30^(16GS)	won Chelt Cross-Country hcap ch (3m7f) (0)

WINS-RUNS: 6yo 0-1, 7yo 0-1, 8yo 0-12, 9yo 1-15, 10yo 2-21, 11yo 0-12, 12yo 2-11, 13yo 0-5, 14yo 0-2 **FAVOURITES:** £1.75

FATE OF FAVOURITES: F1162 **POSITION OF WINNER IN MARKET:** 21122

OR 117-127 2-5-39, **128-139** 1-7-33, **140-150** 2-3-8

RECORD OF IRISH RUNNERS: 5-6-34 (-£9.50) **HORSES WEARING HEADGEAR:** 0-1-4 (-£4.00)

Key trends
▶▶Trained in Ireland, 5/5

▶▶Won one of last two starts, 5/5 (four last time out)

▶▶Winner of a cross-country race at either Cheltenham or Punchestown, 5/5

▶▶Won over at least 3m, 5/5

▶▶Officially rated 126-129, 3/5

▶▶Carried no more than 10st 13lb, 3/5 (two exceptions both topweight)

Other factors
▶▶JP McManus and Enda Bolger have teamed up for four of the winners

▶▶The previous year's winner has finished 2nd, 11th, 9th and 1st, off 11lb, 10lb, 13lb and 21lb higher marks

4.40
Race 6

David Nicholson Mares' Hurdle
(Grade 2)

RUK

2m4f

Key stat Both winners have been five-year-olds (from 30% representation for that age group) and both had won their previous outing

This has not been an easy race to weigh up, with doubts swirling around most of the principals in the ante-post market. Quevega, last year's winner, was a best-priced 11-8 even when it emerged she would be going straight to the festival without a run since May. Voler La Vedette is a high-class mare, with five wins out of six over hurdles and a 13-length victory over Go Native in November to her credit, and connections have toyed with running her in the Champion Hurdle. Whiteoak, the inaugural winner in 2008, has been running over 3m to test her credentials for the World Hurdle but could drop back in trip here. United, beaten 14 lengths into second last year, has been off since April. Of the others around the 20-1 mark in the ante-post market, Jessica Harrington has a couple of possibles in No One Tells Me and Zarinava, who is closely matched with My Petra on Grade 2 Doncaster form in February, and Candy Creek is a progressive novice for Nicky Henderson but has ground to make up on RPRs. ■

Quevega: last year's winner will be having her first run since May when she returns to defend her title

DAVID NICHOLSON MARES' HURDLE (GRADE 2)

Tuesday 4.40   **2m4f**

FORM	WINNER	AGE & WGT	WINNING RPR	PRE-RACE RPR	SP	TRAINER	H.Runs	BEST RPR LAST 12 MONTHS (RUNS SINCE)
09 19-31	Quevega D	5 11-3	155	142	2-1F	W Mullins (Ir)	5$^{(21GS)}$	won Punchestown hdl (2m4f) (0)
08 23121	Whiteoak	5 11-0	142	128	20-1	D McCain Jnr	5$^{(13GS)}$	won Ascot class 3 nov hdl (2m) (0)

WINS-RUNS: 4yo 0-2, 5yo 2-10, 6yo 0-8, 7yo 0-5, 8yo 0-5, 9yo 0-4 **FAVOURITES:** £1.00

FATE OF FAVOURITES: 31 **POSITION OF WINNER IN MARKET:** 71

RECORD OF IRISH RUNNERS: 1-1-6 (-£3.00) **HORSES WEARING HEADGEAR:** 0-1-4 (-£4.00)

Wednesday, March 17, 2010 (Old Course)

1.30
Race 1

National Hunt Chase
(Amateur Riders' Novices' Chase)

`C4/RUK`

4m

Key stat Jonjo O'Neill has won four of the last eight runnings (and five in all), with a level-stakes profit of £63 on all his runners in the last eight years

Gerald Delamere's view The penalty structure has been completely abolished this year and in the past trainers tried to avoid them, so the complexion of this race is likely to change. All runners now carry 11st 6lb, while less than ten years ago a double penalty meant that a horse carried 12st 7lb.

Some decent trends remain. Seven- and eight-year-olds have won 24 of the past 35 renewals, with Tricky Trickster last year becoming the fourth six-year-old winner. It is virtually essential to have made the first four last time out (only two winners in the past 26 years had not done that, though both had excellent handicap form on their previous outing). Every winner in the past decade had between four and eight outings in their successful season.

This is Jonjo O'Neill's best race by far at the festival, with five victories since 1995. The problem for punters is that two of them were returned at 25-1 and 33-1, while more fancied runners, including last year's 4-1 favourite Can't Buy Time, were beaten.

Irish trainers always target this race and there have been two Irish-trained winners in the past decade – Deejaydee (trained by Michael Hourigan) in 1999 and Another Rum (Ian Duncan) in 2005. In addition, there have been eight Irish-trained placed horses in the past decade.

Paul Nicholls' runners often go off very short in a race he has yet to win, but the new conditions are now much more in his favour. This also applies to the Pipe stable. Favourites have a poor record generally, with just seven successes since 1973.

Don't be put off by a jumping blemish as 11

Jonjo O'Neill: marathon specialist

of the past 35 winners had fallen in their recent runs.

The biggest problem of all for punters is judging whether a horse who looks one-paced over three miles will come into his own in this four-mile slog. ▶▶**Trends, overleaf**

140TH YEAR OF THE NATIONAL HUNT NOVICES' CHASE CHALLENGE CUP (AMATEURS)

Wednesday 1.30   4m

FORM	WINNER	AGE	& WGT	WINNING RPR	PRE-RACE RPR	SP	TRAINER	Ch.Runs	BEST RPR LAST 12 MONTHS (RUNS SINCE)
09 42212	Tricky Trickster	6	11-11	150	144	11-1	N A Twiston-Davies	3(19GS)	2nd Cheltenham class 2 nov hcp ch (2m5f) (0)
08 27322	Old Benny	7	11-7	140	128	9-1	A King	3(20GS)	2nd Newbury class 2 nov ch (3m) (0)
07 11430	Butler's Cabin C	7	12-0	142	131	33-1	Jonjo O'Neill	7(19GS)	won Aintree class 3 hcap ch (2m4f) (4)
06 15361	Hot Weld	7	11-11	132	110	33-1	Ferdy Murphy	4(22G)	3rd Wetherby class 4 nov ch (3m1f) (2)
05 -22F4	Another Rum	7	11-7	123	116	40-1	I Duncan (Ir)	4(20G)	4th Navan nov ch Gd3 (3m) (0)
04 -2212	Native Emperor C	8	11-11	147	139	5-1J	Jonjo O'Neill	4(22G)	2nd Wetherby nov ch Gd2 (3m1f) (0)
03 FF342	Sudden Shock	8	11-7	139	116	25-1	Jonjo O'Neill	4(24G)	2nd Kempton class 3 nov ch (3m) (0)
02 32212	Rith Dubh	10	11-11	135	117	10-1	Jonjo O'Neill	12(26GS)	2nd Kempton class 3 nov (3m) (0)
01	cancelled								
00 F24U2	Relaxation	8	12-0	137	124	8-1	H Daly	5(21G)	2nd Exeter class 3 nov ch (2m6^1/₂f) (3)
99 14314	Deejaydee	7	12-0	119	100	13-2	Michael Hourigan (Ir)1(21GS)		4th NH Novices' Chase (4m) (5)

WINS-RUNS: 5yo 0-2, 6yo 1-33, 7yo 5-73, 8yo 3-59, 9yo 0-30, 10yo 1-9, 11yo 0-5, 12yo 0-2, 13yo 0-1 **FAVOURITES:** -£6.00

TRAINERS IN THIS RACE (w-pl-r): Jonjo O'Neill 4-1-18, A King 1-0-3, Ferdy Murphy 1-1-6, I Duncan 1-0-1, Michael Hourigan 1-0-3, N Twiston-Davies 1-0-10, A Martin 0-1-2, D Pipe 0-1-2, D Hughes 0-1-2, J Quinn 0-1-1, Miss V Williams 0-1-2, T George 0-1-8, V Dartnall 0-1-2

FATE OF FAVOURITES: 4P02153F54 **POSITION OF WINNER IN MARKET:** 2369100045

RECORD OF IRISH RUNNERS: 2-8-46 (+£2.50) **HORSES WEARING HEADGEAR:** 3-0-36 (+£19.00)

Key trends

▶▶Ran at least three times over fences, 9/10

▶▶Finished first or second in a chase over at least 3m, 9/10

▶▶Top-four finish last time out, 9/10 (exception unplaced in a class 1 handicap chase)

▶▶Aged six to eight, 9/10

▶▶Finished first or second on either or both of last two starts, 8/10

▶▶Had won over at least 3m (hurdles or chases), 7/10

Other factors

▶▶Since the conditions of the race were changed eight years ago, all bar one winner had a hurdles RPR of at least 119. Four had yet to win over fences

▶▶Three winners had run and won in handicap company

▶▶This is the best race at the festival for horses wearing headgear

▶▶The difference between the pre-race RPR and the winning RPR for the ten winners is between 6lb and 23lb (average 11.6lb)

▶▶Four of the last seven winners started 25-1 or bigger. A poor race for favourites – the last outright favourite to win was Keep Talking in 1992 (Native Emperor was joint-favourite in 2004)

▶▶Paul Nicholls has never won this race despite strong representation (three beaten favourites in past decade)

Notes

2.05 Neptune Investment Management Novices' Hurdle C4/RUK
Race 2
(Grade 1)
2m5f

Key stats Seven of the last ten winners were in the top four in the betting. Eighteen of the last 20 winners were aged five or six

With Dunguib looking unbeatable in the Supreme on day one, several high-class horses could be diverted to this longer Grade 1 novice hurdle in search of a winning opportunity. Chief among them is Rite Of Passage, beaten favourite when third behind Dunguib in last year's Champion Bumper but who returns with good Flat form (won the Leopardstown November Handicap) and two smart wins over hurdles. Willie Mullins, going for a hat-trick in this race, has a chance with Quel Esprit, while the British hopes are led by the Nicky Henderson-trained Finian's Rainbow, who has won three out of four over hurdles but was only third behind Reve De Sivola and Restless Harry in the Challow Hurdle, one of the key form races in a fascinating contest.

Rite Of Passage

6 ch g; Trainer Dermot Weld
Hurdles form 11, best RPR 148
Left-handed 1, best RPR 142
Right-handed 1, best RPR 148
Cheltenham form (bumper) 3, best RPR 139
At the festival 11 Mar 09: held up in midfield, smooth progress to press leaders over 3f out, upsides over 2f out, soon outpaced by winner, finished third, beaten 11l by Dunguib in Champion Bumper

Rite Of Passage: smooth switch to hurdles

Finished third to Dunguib when favourite for last year's Champion Bumper and could have taken on his conqueror again in the Supreme, but sealed his position as ante-post favourite for this when he stepped up to 2m4f at Punchestown in February on only his second hurdles start and made mincemeat of the 144-rated Healys Bar, winning unextended. His jumping wasn't particularly impressive, but it was sticky ground and he has already confirmed himself a high-class horse. Has decent Flat speed as well, as he won the Leopardstown November Handicap by sprinting away from Champion Hurdle outsider Donnas Palm. If there is a negative it is his lack of experience (seven of the last ten winners had run at least three times, with the same

Reve De Sivola's win over Restless Harry and Finian's Rainbow is a key piece of form

number having won or been placed in Graded company) but he's still a big contender in a race the Irish have won in three of the last four years.

Quantitativeeasing

5 ch g; Trainer Nicky Henderson
Hurdles form 112, best RPR 134
Left-handed 11, best RPR 134
Right-handed 2, best RPR 132

Impressive winner of his first two starts in novice hurdles at Newcastle and Newbury, but his RPR of 134 for the second win is 11lb lower than all ten previous winners had taken into the festival and it can't be said that his victims have done anything for the form. Made odds-on for the step up to 2m5f in another novice at Kempton in February but failed to settle off the slow early pace, made a hash of the final hurdle and was outbattled by the front-running Phidippides (who is not even entered for Cheltenham), with The Betchworth Kid snapping at his heels in third. Gave the impression there that he'd learn a fair bit for the experience and he could certainly do with a stronger pace, but he is still a long way off having justified even his revised quotes (around 14-1).

Finian's Rainbow

7 b g; Trainer Nicky Henderson
Hurdles form (both left-handed) 131, best RPR xxx
Left-handed 13, best RPR 142
Right-handed 1, best RPR ???

Another lightly raced entrant for Nicky Henderson and he has at least run over the correct trip and in Graded company, finishing third to Reve De Sivola in the Challow Novices' Hurdle at the end of December. That form was solid enough, but it's hard to say he improved on it when an easy winner on his latest start at Ascot in February, as he was a 4-11 chance in relatively modest company (runner-up was rated just 129). Doesn't have many negatives on trends (though hasn't finished first or second on all completed starts) but his level of form is some way below some of the others (including the Challow winner) and he looks short enough for a trainer yet to win the race.

Reve De Sivola

5 b g; Trainer Nick Williams
Hurdles form (all left-handed) 63326121, best RPR 149
Cheltenham form 3262, best RPR 149
At the festival 13 Mar 09: prominent, stumbled when not much room on bend after 2 out, one pace from before last, finished sixth, beaten 11½l by Zaynar in Triumph Hurdle

Far more experienced than most runners in this race and thus has had far more defeats than a usual winner, as he was taking on all the top juveniles on a regular basis last season and did well for one without a Flat background to finish sixth to Zaynar in the Triumph Hurdle. If you take only this season's efforts into account he'd have the perfect profile and his Challow win last time out is among the best form on offer (boosted by runner-up Restless Harry). Still a bit clumsy when it comes to hurdling technique, but clearly stays well and hard to see him not being on the premises.

Peddlers Cross

5 b g; Trainer Donald McCain
Hurdles form (both left-handed) 11, best RPR 148

Shorter in the betting for this than the Supreme, though Dunguib has plenty to do with that, and seen as a potential stayer in the making by Donald McCain, who expressed surprise at the speed he showed when slaughtering a small field in the Grade 2 Rossington Main at Haydock on his second

start over hurdles. At the time of writing he has the same lack of experience and trip form that is against many of the top contenders in the market but, like the others, still has time to rectify that. Trainer rates him highly and, on RPRs, he has achieved more than three of the four above him in the betting.

Quel Esprit

6 b g; Trainer Willie Mullins
Hurdles form 112, best RPR 144
Left-handed 2, RPR 144
Right-handed 11, best RPR 144
Cheltenham form (bumper) 4, best RPR 137
At the festival 11 Mar 09: tracked leaders, close enough 3f out, soon well outpaced, edged left but kept on, finished fourth, beaten 13l by Dunguib in Champion Bumper

Fourth in last season's Champion Bumper and has the perfect profile for this after winning two of his three hurdles starts and finishing second in the other. The main worry is that stamina looks very much his forte and he is a shorter price for the Albert Bartlett over 3m. He has already won over that trip, having taken a Cork Grade 3 in good style in December, and his defeat (at odds of 30-100) came when he was dropped back to 2m4f at Leopardstown a month later. In fairness Ruby Walsh probably didn't make it enough of a test and he'll get a much stronger pace if he runs here in preference to the three-miler. One for when 'non-runner no bet' concessions kick in.

Fionnegas

6 b g; Trainer Willie Mullins
Hurdles form 1132, best RPR 143
Left-handed 32, best RPR 143
Right-handed 11, best RPR 137

Has won over 2m4f and been placed twice at Grade 1 level this season, so has plenty going for him on trends. Unbeaten in bumpers and an impressive winner of his first two novice hurdles over 2m4f, he looked a bit short of pace for the drop back to 2m when only third in the Future Champions Novice Hurdle at Leopardstown over Christmas and was again made to look pedestrian by Dunguib in the Deloitte over 2m2f (though that can't really be held against him as Dunguib has made everything he has run against look slow).

Summit Meeting

5 b g; Trainer Jessica Harrington
Hurdles form 141, best RPR 140
Left-handed 4, best RPR 0
Right-handed 11, best RPR 140

Decent bumper performer who is the Pricewise ante-post selection at 33-1. An easy winner at Punchestown on his hurdles debut, he ran no sort of race when stepped up to Grade 1 company at Navan in December, but he was beaten so far and so early that it simply could not have been his running. He was much better in February when staying on strongly to beat Arvika Ligeonniere over 2m1/2f at Fairyhouse despite reportedly being desperately in need of the run and "blowing his head off after the race" according to his trainer. Not a bad trends fit and should be all the better for the extra distance at Cheltenham.

Other contenders

The problem with previewing any of the novice hurdles at this stage is that so many potential runners have possible alternative targets. Of the horses detailed above, only the Henderson pair and Reve De Sivola do not have other festival entries, while Fionnegas could run in any of three. There are plenty of others who would be major contenders if coming here, but the market suggests **Tell Massini**, **Restless Harry** and **Shinrock Paddy** are far more likely to contest the Albert Bartlett over 3m (as is Quel Esprit, though Willie Mullins said the Neptune was the plan after his defeat by Coole River), so they are dealt with in more detail in that race guide. Mullins has other contenders like **Morning Supreme** (also in the Supreme) and **Arvika Ligeonniere**, who was beaten only half a length by Summit Meeting at Fairyhouse and is another likely to be better over this trip. Thomas Mullins' **Some Present**, though probably fed up of seeing the backside of Dunguib, did not look like he was crying out for further last time. Alan King has seven entered, with the best two looking to be **Manyriverstocross** and **The Betchworth Kid**. However, the former was well beaten upped to this trip in the Challow and may be targeted at the Supreme after his third in the Totesport Trophy in February, while The Betchworth Kid is more likely to go up in trip as he's shorter for the Albert Bartlett. ∎

Totesport Trophy third Manyriverstocross is one of seven entries for Alan King

NEPTUNE INVESTMENT MANAGEMENT NOVICES' HURDLE (GRADE 1)
Wednesday 2.05   2m5f

FORM		WINNER	AGE	& WGT	WINNING PRE-RACE RPR	RPR	SP	TRAINER	H.Runs	BEST RPR LAST 12 MONTHS (RUNS SINCE)
09	21111	Mikael D'Haguenet	5	11-7	158	158	5-2F	W Mullins (Ir)	7(14GS)	won Punchestown nov hdl Gd2 (2m) (0)
08	153-1	Fiveforthree	6	11-7	149	136	7-1	W Mullins (Ir)	1(15GS)	won Fairyhouse mdn hdl (2m) (0)
07	21U53	Massini's Maguire CD	6	11-7	149	147	20-1	P Hobbs	9(15GS)	won Cheltenham class 2 nov hdl (2m5f) (3)
06	1F221	Nicanor	5	11-7	155	146	17-2	Noel Meade (Ir)	5(17G)	won Leopardstown nov hdl Gd3 (2m4f)(0)
05	121	No Refuge D	5	11-7	148	145	17-2	Howard Johnson	3(20G)	won Warwick class 1 nov hdl Gd2 (2m5f) (0)
04	12	Fundamentalist	6	11-7	157	148	12-1	N Twiston-Davies	2(15G)	2nd Haydock class 1 nov hdl Gd2 (2m7¹/₂f) (0)
03	-1d112	Hardy Eustace	6	11-7	153	149	6-1	D Hughes (Ir)	4(19G)	2nd Deloitte & Touche Nov Hdl Gd2 (2m2f) (0)
02	1	Galileo D	6	11-7	154	142	12-1	T George	1(27GS)	won Kempton class 3 nov hdl (2m5f) (0)
01		Cancelled								
00	11111	Monsignor C, D	6	11-7	164	163	5-4F	M Pitman	5(14G)	won Warwick class 2 nov hdl (2m4¹/₂f) (0)
99	11111	Barton D	6	11-7	160	158	2-1F	T Easterby	5(18GS)	won Doncaster class 1 nov hdl Gd2 (2m4f) (0)

WINS-RUNS: 4yo 0-8, 5yo 3-52, 6yo 7-79, 7yo 0-28, 8yo 0-6, 9yo 0-1 **FAVOURITES:**-£1.75

TRAINERS IN THIS RACE (w-pl-r): W Mullins 2-1-8, D Hughes 1-0-2, Howard Johnson 1-2-5, N Twiston-Davies 1-1-11, Noel Meade 1-0-8, P Hobbs 1-1-7, T George 1-0-1, A King 0-1-4, C Swan 0-1-1, E O'Grady 0-3-4, Ian Williams 0-1-2, Jonjo O'Neill 0-1-7, M Morris 0-1-3, Nick Williams 0-1-1, P Nicholls 0-1-5

FATE OF FAVOURITES: 1142252501 **POSITION OF WINNER IN MARKET:** 1153544841

RECORD OF IRISH RUNNERS: 4-7-47 (-£19.00) **HORSES WEARING HEADGEAR:** 0-0-9 (-£9.00)

RECORD OF TRIAL WINNERS: Royal Bond (Fairyhouse, December) **71;** Winter (Sandown, December) **1S2d260**
Barry & Sandra Kelly Memorial (Navan, December) **2531;** Challow (Newbury, December) **4442d23;** Deloitte (Leopardstown, February) **77454**

Key trends
▶▶At least three runs over hurdles, 7/10
▶▶Aged five or six, 10/10
▶▶Won a Graded hurdle, 6/10 (two of the exceptions were placed)
▶▶Pre-race RPR of at least 142, 9/10

Other factors
▶▶Finished first or second on all completed starts over hurdles, 9/10
▶▶Only two winners had previously run at the festival, both contesting the Bumper – one winning, one coming fifth
▶▶Won at least 50 per cent of hurdle runs, 9/10
▶▶Scored over at least 2m4f, 9/10
▶▶Formerly a strong race for favourites, but last year Mikael D'Haguenet ended a seven-year losing run for jollies
▶▶Rated within 11lb of RPR top-rated, 8/10
▶▶Started career in either Irish point-to-points or bumpers, 7/10

Notes

2.40
Race 3

RSA Chase
(Grade 1)

3m¹/₂f

Key stats The last ten winners had run at least three times over fences. No Feltham winner has ever followed up here

Nicky Henderson holds a strong hand here with former top staying hurdler Punchestowns and high-class French import Long Run, both unbeaten in two chase starts in Britain (though Long Run has more experience, having arrived with Grade 1-winning form over the Auteuil fences). Two smaller British stables have leading chances with another pair of unbeaten chasers: the Nick Williams-trained Diamond Harry followed Punchestowns out of staying hurdles and has won both chase starts, while Ian Williams sends Weird Al back to Cheltenham, where the three-time chase winner has already scored twice. The Irish challenge is led by last year's Albert Bartlett Novices' Hurdle winner Weapon's Amnesty, a dual Grade 1 runner-up over fences.

Punchestowns

7 ch g; Trainer Nicky Henderson
Chase form 11, best RPR 164
Left-handed 1, best RPR 148
Right-handed 1, best RPR 164
Cheltenham form (all hurdles) 3122
At the festival 12 Mar 09: in touch, not fluent 5th, closed 7th, led approaching 2 out, quickened on bend between last 2, pressed last, edged left run-in, headed 150yds out, held by winner when switched right towards finish, 2nd, beaten 1³/₄l by Big Buck's in World Hurdle

As a high-class hurdler he wouldn't fit the normal pattern for this race, as eight of the last ten winners had achieved an RPR of no better than 135 over hurdles. However, the two exceptions were Denman in 2007 and Cooldine last year, so that pattern may be changing. Last year's World Hurdle runner-up also falls down on experience, unless he runs again, as he has had only two outings over fences – even so, on the trends, his extensive hurdling career means he has run slightly more times in his career than a usual winner. He couldn't have done it much easier on his debut, winning a four-runner novice at Newbury hard held by seven lengths, but he made a terrible blunder down the back straight at Sandown on his second start in the Scilly Isles Novices' Chase. That he

was able to pick himself up and still run out an easy eight-length winner from the useful Tchico Polos is testament that he's a high-class horse, but you don't often get away with that sort of mistake at the festival.

Long Run

5 b g; Trainer Nicky Henderson
Chase form 121111, best RPR 164
Left-handed 12111, best RPR 155
Right-handed 1, best RPR 164

Grade 1 winner over fences in France and Britain, having made a seriously impressive British debut in the Feltham Novices' Chase at Kempton over Christmas, destroying a decent field to win as he liked. That form was boosted by the easy win of runner-up Tazbar, but ante-post punters must have been worried when he was given an Arkle entry and his next run came over 2m in the Kingmaker at Warwick. He was just as impressive there despite a couple of minor errors, but trainer has confirmed that the 3m race is the preferred option as long as the ground isn't soft. Winners aged younger than seven are rare, but he looks top class.

Diamond Harry

7 b g; Trainer Nick Williams
Chase form (both left-handed) 11, best RPR 160
Cheltenham form (all hurdles) 113, best RPR 154
At the festival 11 Mar 09 held up in rear, steady
headway from 3 out, led, went left and mistake 2 out,
headed well before last when went left and mistake,
soon one pace, finished third, beaten 5½l by Mikael
D'Haguenet in Ballymore Novices' Hurdle

High-class novice hurdler who didn't taste
defeat in that sphere until finishing third to
Mikael D'Haguenet at last year's festival. After
destroying a field of handicappers at Haydock,
he was no match for champion staying hurdler
Big Buck's at Newbury and connections were
quick to switch to fences in the hope that he
would develop into an RSA candidate. It didn't
take long to turn that hope into reality, as he
sauntered home in a four-runner novice at
Haydock, running close to his best hurdles
figures according to Racing Post Ratings. Made
mistakes and not so impressive at Newbury in
February when landing three-runner contest by
two lengths from old rival Bensalem (fell when
challenging at Haydock) and will need to brush

Diamond Harry: high-class but inexperienced

up his jumping, especially as his one major
negative is a lack of experience over fences
(most winners had run at least three times).

Weird Al

7 b g; Trainer Ian Williams
Chase form (all left-handed) 111, best RPR 151
Cheltenham form 11, best RPR 147

Bred to jump fences and connections have not
wasted any time on him over hurdles as he ran
only once in that sphere and once in a bumper
before this season. Hard to fault over fences,
going 3-3 and jumping impeccably, something
that will stand him in good stead against some
higher-profile rivals. He is proven over the
Cheltenham fences, having won his first two
chase starts there at around 2m5f in November
and December. He beat Knockara Beau by a
neck in the first of those and stretched that to
two and a half lengths when stepped up to
3m1f at Wetherby in February (though that
margin was nowhere near the 16 lengths by
which Diamond Harry beat Knockara Beau at
Haydock). In control all the way up the straight
at Wetherby, he may be the type who does just
enough and there should be more to come. He
will have had far fewer career runs than an
average winner of this race, but otherwise
scores fairly high on trends.

Weapon's Amnesty

7 ch g; Trainer Charles Byrnes
Chase form 3F122, best RPR 150
Left-handed 122, best RPR 150
Right-handed 3F, best RPR 121
Cheltenham form (hurdles) 1, best RPR 154
At the festival 13 Mar 09: in touch, closed on leaders
after 2 out, led last, idled 100 yards out, found extra
when joined close home, won Albert Bartlett Novices'
Hurdle by ½l from Pride Of Dulcote

Well-backed winner on the day of last year's
Albert Bartlett Novices' Hurdle and promises to
be at least as good over fences if he can stop
kicking the birch out of the way and start
jumping cleanly. In fairness he's rarely had the
sort of decent ground that brought about his
hurdling improvement at Cheltenham last term

The Nightingale puts in another perfect jump on his way to victory in the Pendil at Kempton

and he jumped much better on the one occasion that he did, at Leopardstown in December when a close second to Pandorama over 3m. The 2m5f was too short for him in the Dr P J Moriarty Chase back at the same track in February and he again jumped stickily early but showed what an engine he has by getting back into contention very easily. His second place behind enterprisingly ridden winner Citizen Vic looked the perfect warm-up for Cheltenham (he was runner-up at the same track on his pre-festival warm-up last year) and, with the exception of being higher-rated over hurdles than a normal winner, he is a good scorer on trends.

The Nightingale

7 b g; Trainer Paul Nicholls
Chase form 111, best RPR 151
Left-handed 1, best RPR 147
Right-handed 1, best RPR 151
Cheltenham form (hurdles) 6, best RPR 139

At the festival 11 Mar 09: chased leaders, ridden 3 out, weakened after 2 out, beaten when hit last, finished sixth, beaten 19½ lengths by Mikael D'Haguenet in Ballymore Novices' Hurdle

Finished distressed on his final two starts over hurdles, including when beaten nearly 20 lengths by Mikael D'Haguenet in a hot Ballymore, but had a wind operation over the summer and has looked a terrific prospect in two chase starts since his return to action in January. Won as he liked in small fields both times, first over 2m2f at Fontwell and then in the Grade 2 Pendil Novices' Chase (2m4½f) at Kempton in late February, when he jumped his rivals silly. Will obviously be facing a much stiffer test if lining up at Cheltenham (Aintree is a distinct possibility instead), but his sure-footed jumping (something many of his rivals cannot boast) will be an advantage. He is more inexperienced than most winners, though, and has yet to prove himself over 3m (though that was equally true of four of the last ten winners).

Bensalem

7 b g; Trainer Alan King
Chase form 12F2, best RPR 151
Left-handed 1F2, best RPR 151
Right-handed 2, best RPR 143
Cheltenham form (hurdles) 21, best RPR 151

Looked likely to challenge Diamond Harry at Haydock in January when unsighted by that rival and coming down at the third-last and again did not have the run of things when second to his old rival at Newbury in February. This time it was jockey error, though, as his rider Robert Thornton chose to move to the right of the right-jumping Inchidaly Rock five out and the blunder Bensalem made there, which cost him more than the two lengths he was beaten, was not his fault. Still needs to brush up his jumping but looks likely to be well suited by a searching gallop.

Has always looked likely to put in a big performance in a strongly run race and was in the process of putting up his best effort when he came down three out at Haydock in January. Taken along at a fair gallop by Knockara Beau, he was making his challenge three out when partially unsighted by eventual winner Diamond Harry's slight mistake. Although he failed to complete, that form would put him in the mix. You'd like to see him get some more experience after that fall, though, especially as all of the last ten winners had finished first or second last time out, and he could be diverted to the William Hill Chase to take advantage of a good handicap mark.

Uimhiraceathair

8 b g; Trainer Willie Mullins
Chase form 11, best RPR 140
Left-handed 1, best RPR 140
Right-handed 1, best RPR 140

More like the usual fit for this as he wasn't particularly good over hurdles, yet has already looked like being much better over fences. He impressed on his Gowran Park debut with an easy success and then showed good battling qualities to get back up to dead-heat with Telenor in the Grade 2 Ten Up Novice Chase at Navan in February, proving he has the required stamina in abundance. Both those successes came on bad ground, but he put up his best hurdles run when encountering a decent surface in April last year, so that's encouraging. More inexperienced than usual and some way off the top RPR record by Long Run, but an interesting contender all the same.

Other contenders

So highly rated is last season's Ballymore Novices' Hurdle winner **Mikael D'Haguenet** that even at the end of February he had only five ahead of him in the betting for this – and he has still yet to jump a fence in public. He is an exciting horse, but even if he does turn up he will be well short of experience. Willie Mullins also has **Citizen Vic**, who burst on to the scene when given an enterprising ride by Paul Townend in the Dr PJ Moriarty Chase at Leopardstown in February, seeing off Weapon's Amnesty. His profile is just about the best fit of all and his trainer has a good record in the race (Cooldine won the RSA for the stable last year after winning the Dr PJ Moriarty) but the market suggests Citizen Vic is an unlikely runner. In a normal year Ascot's Reynoldstown Chase winner would be among the favourites but, despite maintaining his unbeaten record over fences with a four-length win over useful yardstick Knockara Beau, **Burton Port** was still among the 33-1 rags at the time of writing. His form doesn't entitle him to be so big, but trainer Nicky Henderson already has Punchestowns and Long Run for the race and is more likely to keep Burton Port for Aintree. Among the outsiders, Colin Tizzard's **Hey Big Spender** could be interesting if his trainer reckons he is weighted out of the Jewson. His novice handicap win over 2m5f on Cheltenham's Trials day in January looked decent form as, taking jockey claims into account, he carried 26lb more than established 134-rated handicapper **The Sawyer**, who was not much more than half a second faster when winning over the same course and distance half an hour later. ▶▶**Trends, overleaf**

RSA CHASE (GRADE 1)

Wednesday 2.40   3m¹/₂f

FORM		WINNER	AGE & WGT	WINNING PRE-RACE RPR	RPR	SP	TRAINER	Ch.Runs	BEST RPR LAST 12 MONTHS (RUNS SINCE)
09	-8131	Cooldine	7 11-4	170	160	9-4F	W Mullins (Ir)	3(15GS)	won Leopardstown nov ch Gd1 (2m5f) (0)
08	-1211	Albertas Run CD	7 11-4	162	154	4-1F	Jonjo O'Neill	4(11GS)	won Reynoldstown Nov Ch Gd2 (3m) (0)
07	-1111	Denman C, D	7 11-4	165	169	6-5F	P Nicholls	4(17GS)	won Newbury class 2 nov ch (3m) (0)
06	-1231	Star De Mohaison	5 10-8	153	141	14-1	P Nicholls	4(15G)	3rd Cheltenham class 1 nov ch Gd2 (2m5f) (1)
05	P-122	Trabolgan BF	7 11-4	160	155	5-1	N Henderson	3(9G)	2nd Feltham Nov Ch Gd2 (3m) (1)
04	F1332	Rule Supreme D	8 11-4	161	154	25-1	W Mullins (Ir)	8(10G)	2nd Punchestown hcap ch (3m4f) (0)
03	-1311	One Knight	7 11-4	159	151	15-2	P Hobbs	4(9G)	won Chepstow class 1 nov ch Gd2 (2m3¹/₂f) (3)
02	-21F2	Hussard Collonges BF	7 11-4	156	141	33-1	P Beaumont	4(19GS)	2nd Huntingdon class 3 nov hcap ch (3m) (0)
01		cancelled							
00	4-212	Lord Noelie D, BF	7 11-4	154	142	9-2	Miss H Knight	4(9G)	2nd Kempton class 3 nov ch (3m) (0)
99	U2511	Looks Like Trouble D	7 11-4	170	142	16-1	Noel Chance	5(14GS)	won Sandown class 3 nov hcap ch (3m¹/₂f) (0)

WINS-RUNS: 5yo 1-5, 6yo 0-21, 7yo 8-56, 8yo 1-27, 9yo 0-16, 10yo 0-2, 11yo 0-1 **FAVOURITES:** £0.45

TRAINERS IN THIS RACE (w-pl-r): P Nicholls 2-1-8, W Mullins 2-2-7, Jonjo O'Neill 1-0-3, Miss H Knight 1-1-5, N Henderson 1-0-6, A King 0-1-1, Anthony Mullins 0-1-1, Mrs J Harrington 0-1-2, Mrs S Smith 0-1-2, N Twiston-Davies 0-1-5

FATE OF FAVOURITES: F45532P111 **POSITION OF WINNER IN MARKET:** 6204840111

RECORD OF IRISH RUNNERS: 2-4-29 (+£0.25) **HORSES WEARING HEADGEAR:** 0-0-11 (-£11.00)

RECORD OF TRIAL WINNERS: Feltham Chase (Kempton, December) **262366;** Knight Frank Chase (Leopardstown, December) **FPBF5**
Towton Chase (Wetherby, February) **52;** Dr P J Moriarty Chase (Leopardstown, February) **F4U3B71;** Reynoldstown Chase (Ascot, February) **2P5314**

Key trends

▶▶Did not run on the Flat, 10/10

▶▶Finished first or second last time out, 10/10

▶▶Last run between 24 and 53 days ago, 10/10

▶▶Chase RPR of at least 141, 10/10

▶▶Ran at least three times over fences, 10/10

▶▶Rated less than 14lb off RPR top-rated, 9/10

▶▶Nine to 12 hurdles and chase runs, 9/10

▶▶Aged seven, 8/10

▶▶Contested a Graded chase (four won, three placed), 7/10 (the last seven)

▶▶Previous season's best RPR over hurdles no higher than 135, 8/10 (the two exceptions have come in the last three years)

Other factors

▶▶Four winners had won Graded races, including the last three – three over 2m4f and just one over 3m

▶▶In 2008 Albertas Run became the first Reynoldstown winner to follow up here since Killiney in 1973

▶▶No Feltham winner has ever won this race

▶▶Unplaced efforts are very rare (only one example in 36 completed starts among the last ten winners). However, only Denman was unbeaten over fences

▶▶Three winners had previously run at the festival and all three had excellent form – one second and one seventh in the Bumper, plus one second in 2m5f novice hurdle

Notes

3.20
Race 4

Seasons Holidays Queen Mother Champion Chase (Grade 1)

2m

Key stats Three of the last eight favourites failed to complete the course, but the five who did get round collected four wins and a second

Master Minded towers over this race again as he attempts to become the first chaser to complete a hat-trick in the two-mile championship since Badsworth Boy 25 years ago. All has not gone smoothly since his win here last year but, having recovered from a cracked rib, he was in better shape in his warm-up race, surviving a rare mistake at the last to score impressively in the Game Spirit. Twist Magic has had a good winter, winning the Tingle Creek and Victor Chandler, but he has never shone at Cheltenham. Big Zeb has the ability if his jumping holds up (fell last year), while the new blood is Forpadydeplasterer and Kalahari King, separated by a short head in last year's Arkle.

Master Minded

7 b g; Trainer Paul Nicholls
Chase form 1F1F2U1112111131, best RPR 187
Left-handed 1F1F21121131, best RPR 187
Right-handed U111, best RPR 181
Cheltenham form 113, best RPR 186
At the festival 13 Mar 08: soon tracking leaders, led 7th, came readily clear from 2 out, impressive, won Champion Chase by 19l from Voy Por Ustedes
11 Mar 09: held up in touch, quickened to challenge from 4 out until led soon after 2 out, driven and came clear approaching last, kept on strongly, won Champion Chase by 7l from Well Chief

Put up one of the best performances ever seen by a 2m chaser when thumping defending champion Voy Por Ustedes to land his first Champion Chase two seasons ago and won it again last term, but the crown was not resting so easily on his head when in November he was beaten into third by veteran Well Chief and Mahogany Blaze at Cheltenham. He hung badly right throughout the race and was subsequently diagnosed with a fractured rib, which required rest until the Game Spirit at Newbury in February. However, not everyone was convinced that was the only reason for his defeat, as Master Minded had been well below his imperious best for some time. That first Champion Chase win, as a five-year-old, saw Master Minded awarded a Racing Post Rating of 186, which made him (at the time) a better

horse than staying stars Kauto Star and Denman, but he's struggled to live up to that since and in his last four starts has only once managed to bust the 170 mark. He was workmanlike when beating Well Chief in the Champion last year, would almost certainly have lost at Punchestown had Big Zeb not made one of his customary howlers at the wrong time and then was beaten, albeit when giving 10lb, by Well Chief. He looked well on his way back when he returned from a three-month layoff to win the Game Spirit, giving 10lb and a 13l beating to Mahogany Blaze, despite an horrific error at the last (Ruby Walsh blamed himself). His last-time-out Graded win means he fulfils all the key trends (except the one on age, which he has already bust twice) and he is clearly still the one to beat.

Big Zeb

9 b g; Trainer Colm Murphy
Chase form F1F2211FF2141
Left-handed F21F1, best RPR 167
Right-handed 1F21F241, best RPR 167
All Cheltenham form F
At the festival 11 Mar 09: chased leaders, 4 lengths off leaders and going okay when fell 4 out in Champion Chase won by Master Minded

Considered Ireland's big hope last year and was

Kalahari King's February comeback from a layoff was packed with promise

still going well enough when coming to grief four from home, but that was his fourth fall on his ninth chase start and, though he has managed to stay on his feet in four subsequent outings, earning a trends-qualifying best RPR of 167 in the process, those jumping frailties are a long way from having been ironed out. That he has the ability is not in question because he arguably should have beaten Master Minded (below par but not miles off his Champion Chase win a month earlier and that may be all he is capable of now) at Punchestown last April, but the question that has to be answered is whether he is so far clear of the others that you can justify his price with those jumping worries ever-present and bearing in mind that his career-best was achieved in two slow-run small-field races. He was an abject failure when laughably made favourite for the Tingle Creek won by course specialist Twist Magic and, while he was back on track at Punchestown next time, what he did there was nothing he hadn't done before. Scores higher on trends than many (except for not being a course winner), but he has fallen

on three of the four occasions he has run in a chase with more than seven runners and still looks a risky proposition.

Kalahari King

9 b g; Trainer Ferdy Murphy
Chase form 11212121, best RPR 169
Left-handed 12211, best RPR 169
Right-handed 112, best RPR 163
Cheltenham form 42
At the festival 11 Mar 08: Not fluent 1st, held up in rear, smooth headway from 4 out to track leaders after 3 out, stayed on approaching last but never going pace of leading trio, finished fourth, beaten 11½l by Captain Cee Bee in Supreme Novices' Hurdle

10 Mar 09: held up in rear, still there when mistake 9th, good progress on inner from 3 out, went 2nd after last and closed on winner, just held final strides, finished 2nd, beaten short head by Forpadydeplasterer in Arkle Chase

Confirmed himself one of last season's best novices when just losing out to Forpadydeplasterer in the Arkle and, like his conqueror, he has yet to finish out of the first two over fences (has a better conversion rate with five wins to three seconds). Was just as good at Aintree following his Cheltenham second when coasting to an eight-length win in the Grade 1 novice there and, though comfortably put in his place by Twist Magic at Sandown later on, could simply have had enough for the season. There were doubts over his wellbeing for much of this season, largely because he hadn't been seen since Sandown in April, but he dispelled them when winning the hotly contested Blue Square Handicap Chase at Doncaster under 11st 12lb, recording a career-best RPR of 169 despite trainer Ferdy Murphy warning he was far from fully wound up. Is going to need to find even more to challenge Master Minded, but did it easily at Doncaster, so no reason to think he is not capable of better still.

Twist Magic

8 b g; Trainer Paul Nicholls
Chase form 12F1112614F6F1311, best RPR 172
Left-handed 1F16F, best RPR 159
Right-handed 211214F61311, best RPR 172
Cheltenham form F6F
At the festival 13 Mar 07: headway to track leaders 8th, staying on well and disputing close 3rd when fell 2 out in Arkle Chase won by My Way De Solzen

13 Mar 08: in touch until not fluent 8th, well behind when blundered 3 out, finished sixth, beaten 52l by Master Minded in Champion Chase

11 Mar 09: unruly parade, hit 7th and 8th, weakened quickly 4 out, no chance when fell 2 out in Champion Chase won by Master Minded

Twist Magic: best efforts going right-handed

Take Master Minded out of the race and stablemate Twist Magic is comfortably the best in the field on Racing Post Ratings. Indeed, his last three RPRs are all superior to the last three that Master Minded had turned in before the Game Spirit, so there are grounds for saying he is a massive price at around the 6-1 mark. He is that price for more than one reason, though, and the main ones are that he has always looked to have an unstable temperament (was unruly in the parade for this last season, having been mulish at Kempton before that) and has not carried his best form into past festivals (two falls and a submission to show for three attempts). Much depends not just on whether he is a reformed character – the signs are reasonably good as his last four runs have been the best of his life – but whether he can produce the goods going left-handed. According to RPRs Twist Magic has run to figures of 169-172 on six occasions, but all of them were right-handed, four at Sandown. Going the other way, he has a peak figure of just 159, which would do well to see him placed in even an average year. Stamina used to be considered a worry in a championship event at Cheltenham, but he looked strong enough at 2m2f in the Haldon Gold Cup under a big weight in November and again when winning the Victor Chandler easily over 2m1f in January, and it might be that he is simply a stronger horse now, as connections always said he had plenty of scope. Notwithstanding his lack of Cheltenham form, he has more ticks than crosses compared with last year and can't be written off.

Forpadydeplasterer

7 b g; Trainer Thomas Cooper
Chase form 12221222, best RPR 162
Left-handed 221, best RPR 162
Right-handed 12222, best RPR 157
Cheltenham form 41, best RPR 162
At the festival 14 Mar 08: Held up towards rear, steady headway 3 out, chasing leaders between last 2, stayed on final 100yds, finished fourth, beaten 5l by Fiveforthree in Ballymore Properties Novices' Hurdle

10 Mar 09: prominent, left 2nd at 3rd, mistake next, with leader until narrow advantage and hit 3 out, definite lead fast, hard pressed near finish, battled on well, won Arkle Chase by a short-head from Kalahari King

Last season's Arkle winner was taken out of the betting early in February after being found to be lame with a stone bruise, but was brought back into the fray a couple of weeks later when it emerged the problem wasn't so bad after all. He's still no more than a possible runner according to trainer Tom Cooper and he would have plenty to find on the form book to make an impact. In two outings this term he's been well below his Arkle-winning standard, which is some way behind what will be needed anyway, so fans will be pinning their hopes on better ground and a left-handed track. There is some hope there, as two of his three best runs have been left-handed, but he's still below the minimum RPR based on trends, hasn't won this season and his setback won't have done him any favours.

Petit Robin

7 b g; Trainer Nicky Henderson
Chase form 111223712, best RPR 164
Left-handed 11137, best RPR 164
Right-handed 2212, best RPR 164
Cheltenham form 63, best RPR 164
At the festival 11 Mar 09: chased leaders, blundered 5th, challenged 4 out, slight lead next, headed after 2

out, held when mistake last, caught for 2nd run-in, finished third, beaten 9l by Master Minded in Champion Chase

Trainer appears to see him as a 2m4f horse (won over that trip at Pau as a four-year-old) but that is no bad thing for this race as every winner for as long as you can remember had won over at least 2m2f at least once prior to landing this. Indeed, Petit Robin is going to have a good deal more going for him this year than last when he lacked experience and had not won at Graded level. He's now got the required runs under his belt and, having stayed on well to beat Well Chief in the Desert Orchid Chase in December, can tick off the Graded chase requirement. He is still not quite up to standard as far as RPRs are concerned (that goes for most of the field) but has plenty of room for improvement given his age and experience. He proved no match for Twist Magic in the Grade 1 Victor Chandler at Ascot in January, but not for the first time looked as though he'd appreciate going the other way round. He still won't score particularly highly on the trends criteria, but probably would have been second in this race but for a mistake at the final fence last season, so he has to be taken seriously for place purposes.

Barker

9 gr g; Trainer Willie Mullins
Chase form 2PF01121U, best RPR 163
Left-handed P01, best RPR 128
Right-handed 2F121U, best RPR 163

Former Pierse Hurdle winner who didn't show much over fences until being moved to Willie Mullins. After eventually getting off the mark he went on a steep upward curve, running second to Aran Concerto in the Powers Gold Cup before thumping Arkle winner Forpadydeplasterer by 15 lengths in the Grade 1 Swordlestown Cup at Punchestown in April. How much of that was down to the runner-up being past his best after Cheltenham is open to question, but Barker has been seen only once since and he unseated too far from home for any judgment to be made. He is not a high scorer on trends.

Petit Robin's Kempton victory over Well Chief added to his progressive profile

Golden Silver

8 b g; Trainer Willie Mullins
Chase form 022672411074112, best RPR 166
Left-handed 022671101, best RPR 166
Right-handed 247412, best RPR 164
Cheltenham form 0, best RPR 124
At the festival 10 Mar 09: mistake second, pressed leading pair, still right there 3 out, weakened rapidly after next, finished 14th, beaten 40l by Forpadydeplasterer in Arkle Chase

Looked to be going to Cheltenham on a roll, having won two Graded chases in a row, but then he ran into Big Zeb in the Tied Cottage at Punchestown at the end of January. Sent off favourite to make it three on the spin, he was let down by his jumping as he was slow at plenty of his fences, most notably the fourth and fifth. That leaves him with questions to answer and he can't be seen as anything more than a fringe contender, as his best form has come off a slow pace in small fields and he found the frenetic pace too much for him in last season's Arkle, dropping out quickly after the third-last. Trainer Willie Mullins put that down to him having a hard race when winning the Irish Arkle in a close-fought battle with Forpadydeplasterer, but he might just have stamina issues in a strong-run contest.

Well Chief

11 ch g; Trainer David Pipe
Chase form 11123F12211F321324, best RPR 179
Left-handed 112F1221F321, best RPR 179
Right-handed 131324, best RPR 178
Cheltenham form (chase only) 1212F21, best RPR 179
At the festival 13 Mar 03: soon led, kept narrow advantage, hard ridden last, caught final 75 yards, finished second, beaten a head by Spectroscope in Triumph Hurdle

16 Mar 04: held up in rear, not fluent 5th, steady headway from 8th, tracked leaders 3 out, slight lead next, not fluent last, driven out, won Arkle Chase by 1l from Kicking King

16 Mar 05: held up in rear but in touch, headway 5th, went 3rd 8th, tracked winner after 3 out, ridden and stayed on well approaching last but no impression on winner, finished second, beaten 2l by Moscow Flyer in Champion Chase

14 Mar 07: in touch when fell 2nd in Champion Chase won by Voy Por Ustedes

11 Mar 09: held up towards rear, headway to track leaders 4 out, outpaced 3 out, rallied from next, edged left last and run-in but stayed on well, no chance with winner, finished second, beaten 7l by Master Minded in Champion Chase

Despite his age – which, even allowing for Moscow Flyer's win as an 11-year-old in 2005, is a major negative as horses of this age are rare winners of any race at the festival – he is going to score a good deal higher on the trends than most of his rivals. At his best, he'd have kicked all these bar Master Minded out of the way and it was probably with this in mind that bookmakers cut him to as short as 8-1 for Champion Chase glory after he had beaten Paul Nicholls' superstar in the Connaught Chase in receipt of 10lb in November. Looking at it more realistically, the last time he bust the 170 mark on RPRs was in April 2005 and it is asking a lot for him to do so now. He has three times been put in his place since his emotional winning seasonal return, but those clinging to hope will argue that the 2004 Arkle winner is also a three-time Cheltenham Festival runner-up, including twice in this race, so all is not lost. As much as it would be great to see him do it, it would also be a surprise.

Sizing Europe

8 b g; Trainer Henry de Bromhead
Chase form 1111, best RPR 163
Left-handed 1, best RPR 159
Right-handed 111, best RPR 163
Cheltenham form (hurdles) 10, best RPR 154
At the festival 11 Mar 08: chased leaders, driven to challenge 2 out, weakened quickly before last, virtually pulled-up run-in, finished 14th, beaten 10l by Katchit in Champion Hurdle

Would be a fascinating contender, having joined the chasing ranks only in May. Although he would fall down on his peak RPR of just 163, that figure puts him right in the mix with most of the more established performers with the notable exception of Master Minded. Like the others, his winning chance would rest on Master Minded running below par. A former AIG Europe Champion Hurdle winner, Sizing Europe went off 2-1 favourite for the 2008 Champion Hurdle and cruised into contention two out, but then stopped very quickly and was virtually pulled up at the death. His return early last season suggested there was still a problem, but he wasn't far off his best when fourth to Solwhit at Punchestown in May and

he has since made a seamless transition to fences, winning easily three times before his Grade 1 victory over Osana at Leopardstown in December. Most observers were of the opinion that Captain Cee Bee had Sizing Europe's measure before he fell jumping the last but, even so, Sizing Europe still showed high-class novice form despite jumping with less fluency than on his previous outings. He is obviously going to have his work cut out against Master Minded, but few of the others are any more frightening than his Arkle opponents.

Other contenders

In January, when there were doubts swirling around Master Minded, Paul Nicholls put up one of his stablemates, **Free World**, as the best ante-post value for the race. That is obviously on what he has shown at home, though, because the horse has so far done nothing to warrant quotes that went as short as 16-1 before his third in the Blue Square Chase at Doncaster. He looked a seriously short runner even at 2m during his novice career and, despite a wind operation, did little to alter that perception when a 1-100 in-running loser on his return to action at Bangor. Since then he has been dropped in rather than making the running, but he still has a mountain to climb. **Tranquil Sea** is a more likely runner in the Ryanair but did not look short of pace in the Paddy Power, even if his trainer believes he could develop into a Gold Cup horse next year. He was only second to Golden Silver back at 2m over Christmas, but the slow pace there was no good to him at all and he definitely has the ability to outrun current odds if given the nod. **Oh Crick** wouldn't be the silliest outsider in the world. He was not given a hard ride on his first run since the Haldon when third in the Victor Chandler and is clearly at his best in as strong-run race, as proved by his Cheltenham and Aintree wins last season. He clearly didn't get home over 2m5f in the Betfair Chase at Ascot in February. ■

SEASONS HOLIDAYS QUEEN MOTHER CHAMPION CHASE (GRADE 1)

Wednesday 3.20   **2m**

FORM	WINNER	AGE & WGT	WINNING RPR	PRE-RACE RPR	SP	TRAINER	Ch.Runs	BEST RPR LAST 12 MONTHS (RUNS SINCE)
09	12-11	Master Minded CD	6	11-10	181	187	4-11F	P Nicholls	12(12GS)	won Champion Chase (2m) (3)
08	-2U11	Master Minded D	5	11-10	187	168	3-1	P Nicholls	8(8GS)	won Game Spirit Chase Gd2 (2m1f) (0)
07	2-21U	Voy Por Ustedes CD	6	11-10	170	174	5-1	A King	9(10GS)	won Kempton class 1 Gd2 ch (2m) (1)
06	-5431	Newmill D	8	11-10	172	155	16-1	John J Murphy (Ir)	8(12G)	won Thurles Gd2 ch (2m4f) (0)
05	-1111	Moscow Flyer CD	11	11-10	182	181	6-4F	Mrs J Harrington (Ir)	22(8G)	won Tingle Creek Chase Gd1 (2m) (1)
07	-U221	Azertyuiop CD	7	11-10	176	179	15-8	P Nicholls	8(8G)	2nd Victor Chandler Chase Hcap (2m) (1)
03	-1U11	Moscow Flyer CD	9	12-0	174	168	7-4F	Mrs J Harrington (Ir)	11(11G)	won Down Royal Gd3 ch (2m2f) (3)
02	244-1	Flagship Uberalles CD	8	12-0	170	173	7-4F	P Hobbs	18(12GS)	won Tingle Creek Chase Gd1 (2m) (0)
01		cancelled							
00	-5133	Edredon Bleu C, D	8	12-0	166	167	7-2	Miss H Knight	23(8G)	2nd Champion Chase Gd1 (2m) (4)
99	1/1-1	Call Equiname CD	9	12-0	167	157	7-2	P Nicholls	4(13GS)	won Victor Chandler Chase Hcap (2m) (0)

WINS-RUNS: 5yo 1-1, 6yo 2-10, 7yo 1-9, 8yo 3-26, 9yo 2-29, 10yo 0-17, 11yo 1-10, 12yo 0-1 **FAVOURITES:** -£0.64

TRAINERS IN THIS RACE (w-pl-r): P Nicholls 4-4-19, A King 1-1-2, John Joseph Murphy 1-0-4, P Hobbs 1-2-4, D Pipe 0-1-3, Howard Johnson 0-2-3, N Henderson 0-1-3

FATE OF FAVOURITES: 2311U1FF21 **POSITION OF WINNER IN MARKET:** 2211216321

RECORD OF IRISH RUNNERS: 3-3-23 (-£0.75) **HORSES WEARING HEADGEAR:** 0-0-5 (-£5.00)

RECORD OF TRIAL WINNERS: Tingle Creek Chase (Sandown, December) **3313U1F61;** Paddy Power Dial-A-Bet Chase (Leopardstown, December) **861U6PF**
Game Spirit Chase (Newbury, February) **53713F1**
Previous year's Champion Chase winner **45U3521;** Previous year's Arkle winner **231121**

Key trends

▶▶Won over at least 2m1½f, 10/10

▶▶Ran at least eight times over fences, 9/10

▶▶Rated within 10lb of RPR top-rated, 9/10

▶▶From the first three in the betting, 9/10

▶▶Course winner, 9/10

▶▶No older than nine, 9/10 (last three runnings have gone to five and six year-olds)

▶▶Pre-race RPR of at least 167-plus, 8/10

▶▶Won Graded chase last time out, 8/10

▶▶Previously won at the Cheltenham Festival, 7/10

▶▶Grade 1 chase winner, 7/10

Other factors

▶▶The last horse to retain the title twice was Badsworth Boy in 1985. Only Viking Flagship has tried since and he came second

▶▶The four winners aged less than eight were all French-breds. In fact, in the past ten years 32 French-breds have run, yielding five winners, three seconds and four thirds

▶▶Seven winners had contested the Tingle Creek, in which they finished 31U2121

▶▶Nine Tingle Creek winners (six of whom started favourite) have run, finishing 3313U1F61. The three to succeed were Flagship Uberalles, Moscow Flyer (2005) and Master Minded (2008)

Notes

HOW DO THE LEADING CONTENDERS CONFORM TO THE CHAMPION CHASE TRENDS?

	Won over at least 2m1½f, 10/10	At least eight chase runs, 9/10	Rated within 10lb of RPR top-rated, 9/10	Course winner, 9/10	No older than nine, 9/10	Pre-race RPR of at least 167, 8/10	Won Graded chase last time out, 8/10	Won at the Cheltenham Festival, 8/10	Grade 1 chase winner, 7/10	TOTAL
Barker	✔	✔	✗	✗	✔	✔	✗	✗	✔	5
Big Zeb	✔	✔	✗	✗	✔	✔	✔	✗	✔	6
Cornas	✔	✔	✗	✗	✔	✗	✗	✗	✗	3
Fiepes Shuffle	✔	✔	✗	✗	✗	✗	✗	✗	✗	2
Fix The Rib	✔	✗	✗	✗	✔	✗	✗	✗	✗	2
Forpadydeplasterer	✔	✔	✗	✔	✔	✗	✗	✔	✔	6
Free World	✔	✗	✗	✗	✔	✗	✗	✗	✗	2
Golden Silver	✔	✔	✗	✔	✔	✔	✗	✗	✔	6
I'msingingtheblues	✗	✔	✗	✔	✔	✗	✗	✗	✗	3
Kalahari King	✔	✗	✗	✗	✔	✔	✗	✗	✔	4
Lord Henry	✔	✔	✗	✗	✗	✗	✗	✗	✗	2
Mahogany Blaze	✗	✔	✗	✔	✔	✗	✗	✗	✗	3
Master Minded	✔	✔	✔	✔	✔	✔	✗	✔	✔	**8**
Newmill	✔	✔	✗	✔	✗	✗	✗	✔	✗	4
Oh Crick	✔	✔	✗	✔	✔	✗	✗	✔	✗	5
Petit Robin	✔	✔	✗	✔	✔	✗	✔	✗	✗	5
Santa's Son	✔	✔	✗	✗	✗	✗	✗	✗	✗	2
Sizing Europe	✔	✗	✗	✔	✔	✔	✗	✗	✗	4
Takeroc	✔	✗	✗	✗	✔	✗	✗	✗	✗	2
Tartak	✔	✔	✗	✗	✔	✗	✗	✗	✗	3
Tranquil Sea	✔	✔	✗	✔	✔	✔	✗	✗	✗	5
Twist Magic	✗	✔	✔	✗	✔	✔	✔	✗	✔	6
Voy Por Ustedes	✔	✔	✗	✔	✔	✔	✗	✔	✔	7
Well Chief	✗	✔	✗	✔	✗	✔	✗	✔	✔	5

Based on results up to February 1, 2010

4.00
Race 5

Coral Cup (Handicap Hurdle)
(Grade 3)

2m5f

Key stat Ten of the 16 winners in the race's history had SPs under 12-1

Gerald Delamere's view The last-time-out placings of Coral Cup winners read 11311563U 1161111, suggesting your choice has to be in form. Winners generally have been lightly raced, with nine coming to the festival with between one and three outings that season, and most have been prominent in the betting.

The four biggest weights carried to victory were by Irish-trained horses and, if you add in Tom Taaffe's 140-rated winner Ninetieth

Minute last year, you have an interesting trend for Irish raiders. Remember, in Britain, Irish-trained horses rated 140 and over run off the mark they have in the Irish file. Having given Mourad 10lb at Thurles, **Chicago Grey** looks interesting off 141.

By contrast, all ten British-trained winners carried less than 11st. No horse has won from out of the handicap since 1998. Only one of the 16 winners was a novice. ∎

CORAL CUP (HANDICAP HURDLE) (GRADE 3)

Wednesday 4.00   **2m5f**

	FORM	WINNER	AGE & WGT	OR	SP	TRAINER	H.Runs	BEST RPR LAST 12 MONTHS(RUNS SINCE)
09	-4511	Ninetieth Minute	6	10-3	140ᵀ	14-1	T Taaffe (Ir)	8⁽²⁷ᴳˢ⁾	won Thurles Lstd hdl (2m) (0)
08	12-71	Naiad Du Misselot D	7	10-13	130⁻⁷	7-1	Ferdy Murphy	5⁽²⁴ᴳˢ⁾	won Haydock class 3 hcap hdl (2m4f) (0)
07	23521	Burntoakboy D	9	9-12	128ᵀ	10-1	Dr R Newland	27⁽²⁸ᴳˢ⁾	won Leicester class 3 hcap hdl (2m4½2f)(0)
06	50121	Sky's The Limit	5	11-12	144⁻¹²	11-1	E O'Grady (Ir)	8⁽³⁰ᴳ⁾	won Fairyhouse hurdle (2m2f) (0)
05	-1626	Idole First	6	10-10	131⁻¹	33-1	Miss Venetia Williams	8⁽²⁹ᴳ⁾	2nd Uttoxeter class 3 hcap hdl (2m) (1)
04	34231	Monkerhostin	7	10-8	147⁻³	13-2	P Hobbs	21⁽²⁷ᴳ⁾	2nd Cheltenham class 2 hcap hdl (2m5½2f) (2)
03	21-21	Xenophon	7	11-0	130⁻⁵	4-1F	A Martin (Ir)	5⁽²⁷ᴳ⁾	won Pierse Hcap Hdl (2m) (0)
02	1-54U	Ilnamar BF	6	10-5	137	25-1	M Pipe	9⁽²⁷ᴳˢ⁾	4th Ascot class 2 hcap ch (2m4f) (0)
01		cancelled						
00	-11P3	What's Up Boys D	6	10-3	138ᵀ	33-1	P Hobbs	5⁽²⁶ᴳ⁾	won Sandown class 1 nov hdl Gd2 (2m6f) (2)
99	213-6	Khayrawani	7	11-3	144⁻¹²	16-1	C Roche (Ir)	16⁽³⁰ᴳˢ⁾	won Aintree class 2 hcap hdl (2m4f) (2)

WINS-RUNS: 5yo 1-49, 6yo 4-76, 7yo 4-64, 8yo 0-38, 9yo 1-30, 10yo 0-12, 11yo 0-3, 12yo 0-2, 13yo 0-1 **FAVOURITES:** -£5.00

FATE OF FAVOURITES: 050130F000 **POSITION OF WINNER IN MARKET:** 9001304426 **OR** 122-135 4-14-141, 136-151 6-15-128, 152-165 0-1-6

RECORD OF IRISH RUNNERS: 4-11-58 (-£9.00) **HORSES WEARING HEADGEAR:** 1-2-53 (-£41.00)

Key trends
▶▶Won between 2m2f and 2m6f over hurdles, 10/10
▶▶Top-six finish last time out, 9/10 (six won)
▶▶Scored at class 3 or higher, 9/10
▶▶Carried no more than 11st, 8/10
▶▶Aged six or seven, 8/10
▶▶No more than 16 runs over hurdles, 8/10
▶▶Not run for at least 39 days, 8/10
▶▶Won a race early in the season, 8/10

▶▶No more than four runs that season, 7/10
▶▶Officially rated 128 to 140, 7/10 (three exceptions 144-147)

Other factors
▶▶None of the last ten winners was out of the handicap. There were three such winners in the first six renewals (1993-1998), but none more than 7lb out of the handicap
▶▶Only one outright and one joint-favourite have obliged in the race's 16-year history

4.40
Race 6

Fred Winter Juvenile Handicap Hurdle
(Grade 3)

RUK

2m¹/₂f

Key stats The five winners of this race all had an official rating in the 124-133 band. David Pipe has had a first, a second and a third in three years (seven runners in all)

Gerald Delamere's view The Triumph Hurdle has been easier to solve in the five years since this race was added to the festival programme (every Triumph winner since then has started at single-figure odds) but finding the Fred Winter winner has not been so straightforward, with Gaspara (9-2 joint-favourite in 2007) the only one with a single-figure SP. As this event beds down, it should become more soluble using the ratings range and recent winning form. Horses given a considerate time for a possible handicap punt just don't get in at this meeting nowadays, so reading the form is better than guesswork.

Official ratings look a better guide than weights carried at this early stage of trends, with the five winners all rated between 124 and 133. The class of the race has risen quickly, with the rating of the bottom weight moving from 111 to 121 last year.

Four of the winners came to the festival having had three outings, with one appearing for the first time at the end of November, two in December and two in January. The four most recent winners won last time out and three had a victory at Sandown. Four of the five winners were bred on French lines.

At his three festivals to date, David Pipe has had a first, a third and a second in this race. Ashkazar's mark of 135 was just too high in 2008 to give the trainer a second successive victory when going for the Imperial Cup/Cheltenham bonus won by Gaspara the year before. ■

FRED WINTER JUVENILE HANDICAP HURDLE (GRADE 3)

Wednesday 4.40   2m¹/₂f

FORM	WINNER	AGE & WGT	OR	SP	TRAINER	H.Runs	BEST RPRLAST 12 MONTHS(RUNS SINCE)
09 52111	Silk Affair(5x)	4 10-4	125⁻¹²	11-1	M Quinlan	5⁽²²ᴳˢ⁾	won Sandown class 3 nov hcap hdl (2m4f) **(1)**
08 531	Crack Away Jack D	4 11-10	133⁻²²	14-1	Miss E Lavelle	3⁽²²ᴳˢ⁾	won Sandown class 3 nov hdl (2m1/2f) **(0)**
07 22111	Gaspara (4x) D	4 10-11	130ᵀ	9-2J	D Pipe	10⁽²⁴ᴳˢ⁾	won Sandown class 1 Lstd hcap hdl (2m1/2f) **(0)**
06 4P1	Shamayoun D	4 11-3	124⁻⁷	40-1	C Egerton	3⁽²⁴ᴳˢ⁾	won Southwell class 4 nov hdl (2m) **(0)**
05 225	Dabiroun	4 11-4	124⁻⁴	20-1	Paul Nolan (Ir)	3⁽²⁴ᴳ⁾	2nd Limerick mdn hdl (2m) **(2)**

FAVOURITES:-£0.50

FATE OF FAVOURITES: 00124 **POSITION OF WINNER IN MARKET:** 90144

OR 111-121 0-3-38, 122-134 5-8-72, 135-145 0-4-6

RECORD OF IRISH RUNNERS: 1-1-29 (-£8.00) **HORSES WEARING HEADGEAR:** 1-3-28 (+£13.00)

Key trends

▸▸Officially rated 124 to 133, 5/5

▸▸Did not win over hurdles until third start or later, 5/5

▸▸By a sire who won a Group 1 on the Flat, 5/5

▸▸Pre-race RPR of at least 112, 5/5

▸▸Won last time out, 4/5 (exception beaten in a Grade 2 hurdle)

▸▸Set to carry at least 11st 2lb, 4/5 (one was ridden by a conditional)

Other factors

▸▸Only three of the 32 horses rated 120 or less made the frame

▸▸Three winners had earned a Flat RPR of at least 85

5.15
Race 7
Weatherbys Champion Bumper
(Grade 1)

RUK

2m¹/₂f

Key stats Seven of the eight to start at 3-1 or less have been beaten. Five-year-olds have won ten of the past 13 runnings

We will know more nearer the day, especially when Willie Mullins (six wins in 17 runnings of this race) confirms plans, but once again the Irish raiders will be the ones to beat. Dermot Weld, who supplied last year's beaten favourite, Rite Of Passage, has two leading hopes with Elegant Concorde and Hidden Universe. The early Mullins-trained market movers were Day Of A Lifetime and Up Ou That, with other leading Irish fancies including Araucaria and Tavern Times. Ireland has won 14 of the 17 renewals and the main hopes of a British-trained win this year appear to rest with Al Ferof.

Elegant Concorde

5 br g; Trainer Dermot Weld
Bumper form (both left-handed) 21, best RPR 121

Quite a high scorer on trends as he falls down only on his failure to have won a bumper with 15 or more runners. Made favourite but only second on his debut at Leopardstown in January 2009, but made no mistake on his next start almost a year later, winning a much more valuable event over the same course and distance. There were only ten runners and he was an odds-on shot, but he picked up well from off a slow pace and quickened nicely at the end, while the third and fifth have given the form some substance by winning since. Has loads of potential for trainer who saddled last year's beaten favourite (third) and says this horse has "class, pace and stays". Absence not a worry as five of the last ten winners had not been seen since Christmas or earlier, but best RPR is only 121, so his price is based largely on reputation as there are one or two who have shown a good deal more.

Hidden Universe

4 gr g; Trainer Dermot Weld
Bumper form (left-handed) 1, best RPR 119

Gives Dermot Weld a strong hand, though both this one and Elegant Concorde are in the same

ownership, so it's possible one of them won't go. Hard to say what to make of his easy win as an odds-on shot in a newcomers' contest at Leopardstown in January as there were only eight runners and the early pace was funereal, but he was clearly in a different league to those he beat. Reportedly has the makings of a dual-purpose performer (half-brother to three Flat winners) and, as far as this race is concerned, falls down on the two major criteria as he's only a four-year-old (last winner for that age group was in 1995) and hasn't won a bumper with 15 or more runners.

Day Of A Lifetime

5 b g; Trainer Willie Mullins
Bumper form (right-handed) 1, best RPR 120

Not heard of until the middle of February, but became Willie Mullins' No. 1 contender according to the betting after he spreadeagled a nine-runner field at Fairyhouse. He was impressive in quickening up off a slow pace and he's one of many who falls into the 'could be anything' category for a trainer who won this race six times. Not exactly a high scorer on trends, as his pre-race RPR is not quite high enough and he hasn't done it in a big field, but merits respect given his connections.

Al Ferof

5 gr g; Trainer Paul Nicholls
Bumper form 311, best RPR 129
Left-handed 1, best RPR 129
Right-handed 31, best RPR 121

Showed decent form in Ireland for Elizabeth Doyle, winning at Fairyhouse on his second start, before being bought by John Hales and sent to Paul Nicholls. Reportedly took time to acclimatise to his new surroundings, but confirmed himself a smart performer at Newbury in February when taking a Grade 2 by five lengths from the well-touted recent JP McManus purchase Made In Time. The first three pulled well clear of the rest and a best RPR of 129 is better than most can boast, so if he travels to Cheltenham he'll have an obvious shout as he fulfils all the key trends criteria, though only two of the last ten winners were trained in Britain. Seen as a staying novice hurdler for next season but owner seems keen to go for this race first.

Up Ou That

5 b g; Trainer Willie Mullins
Bumper form (right-handed) 1, best RPR 127

This one's price is based largely on the trainer's reputation for winning this race. The five-year-old appeared only in January at Fairyhouse and, though impressive, it was a newcomers' race with only four runners and he completed the course in a time nearly 53 seconds outside standard (earned a Topspeed figure of 2, compared with an RPR of 127). A "proper bumper horse" according to his trainer, but clearly short of experience in a big field.

Tavern Times

6 ch g; Trainer Thomas Mullins
Bumper form (right-handed) 1, best RPR 118

Talking horse prior to debut at Fairyhouse in October and proved to be everything the racecourse gossip had suggested when quickening clear for a comfortable three-length win. Was set to go to Leopardstown over Christmas, but no-show raises question marks,

though a long absence is by no means a worry for this race. Clearly acts well on decent ground, as you would expect from a son of Presenting (sire of last year's winner Dunguib), and though his pre-race RPR is lower than usual for a Champion Bumper winner, he has at least done it in a big field.

Araucaria

6 b m; Trainer John Kiely
Bumper form 1212, best RPR 130
Left-handed 22, best RPR 119
Right-handed 11, best RPR 130

Won a 25-runner bumper on her debut in October and improved greatly on next two starts before being beaten by Shot From The Hip at Leopardstown at the end of February. Was given far too much to do but was virtually sprinting close home when second to the still unbeaten For Bill at Navan in November and then blew the opposition away in a valuable mares' event at Punchestown at the end of December. This time she was sent on three furlongs out and gradually pulled 24 lengths clear, after which trainer John Kiely called it an "exceptional" performance and said she could be "the best mare I have ever trained". Some might take that with a pinch of salt as it's a selling stable (got rid of last year's Aintree mares' bumper winner Candy Creek) but they haven't sold her on yet. Her best RPR is higher than most of her potential rivals even before you take into account the 7lb sex allowance. There have been only two winning mares in the race's history, but several have gone well. Has ticks in all the boxes.

Forty Foot Tom

5 b g; Trainer Daniel Miley
Bumper form (left-handed) 1, best RPR 114

Made his debut in December, springing a 25-1 shock in an 11-runner Navan bumper that he won by 24 lengths. The form has not been upheld since, but there was no denying this was an impressive debut. An RPR of 114 suggests it wasn't as good as it looked, though, and the trainer is a big unknown as he has had only eight winners over jumps in Ireland in the last five seasons and just two in bumpers. That need not be a negative if the horse is good enough, but he is not a trends pick.

Bishopsfurze

5 b g; Trainer Willie Mullins
Bumper form (right-handed) 1, best RPR 110

Yet another Willie Mullins contender. Created quite an impression on his debut at Fairyhouse in late February, coming from miles off the pace and sauntering to a five-length win. There were only 11 runners in a weak-looking race, however, and plenty of 16-1 was on offer afterwards, which is unusual for a Mullins bumper horse that has just hacked up.

Drumbaloo

6 b/br g; Trainer James Lambe
Bumper form 111, best RPR 130
Left-handed 1, best RPR 130
Right-handed 11, best RPR 128

Unbeaten in three bumpers, winning easily first time at Hereford in September and then showing markedly improved form back home in Ireland. Beat Western Leader at Down Royal and then, in a select five-runner Grade 2 at Navan in December, he saw off Tornedo Shay by a short-head. The runner-up had beaten Elegant Concorde on his debut and has shown more decent form since, so this was a good run. He's "a horse with a big future" according to his trainer and, though he hasn't won a race with 15 or more runners, he has shown a good deal more than a lot of those at the head of the betting, confirmed by a peak RPR of 130.

Made In Time

5 b/br g; Trainer Rebecca Curtis
Bumper form (both left-handed) 12, best RPR 124

Hacked up in a seven-runner bumper at Ffos Las for Rebecca Curtis in January and, though none of his victims have done anything for the form, was the subject of much hype after champion jockey Tony McCoy advised JP McManus to buy him. Has plenty of time to repay his new owner, but didn't really look like a potential winner of this race when put in his place by Al Ferof in a Newbury Grade 2 in February. In fairness, he failed to settle early and showed a good attitude late, but the last eight winners of this had won a bumper worth at least £4k (or Euros) to the winner and he hasn't, as well as having not won a race with 15 or more runners.

Sizing Mexico

5 b g; Trainer Henry de Bromhead
Bumper form (right-handed) 1, best RPR 118

Described by trainer as "only a frame and one to look forward to", he won a slow-run bumper at Fairyhouse in December, earning an RPR of 118 having been well backed beforehand. Even so, his trainer remarked that he wasn't sure he'd have the pace to win a bumper and it's clear that this son of St Leger winner Snurge is a stayer in the making as he has already won a 3m point. Qualifies on all counts except RPR, but it would be a surprise if there are not faster horses in the race.

Other contenders

The Edward O'Grady-trained **Shot From The Hip** was the last horse to shake up the market before the March 1 qualification deadline, beating Araucaria at Leopardstown. **Don't Turn Bach**, another Mullins horse, earned an RPR of 130 at Leopardstown in December but has been trading at three figures on the exchanges, which suggests he's not going. Philip Hobbs thinks highly of **Dunraven Storm**, who beat **Lush Life** at Ascot in November. He was due to go back to Ascot the following month but hasn't been seen since.
▶▶**Trends, overleaf**

WEATHERBYS CHAMPION BUMPER (GRADE 1)
Wednesday 5.15   2m¹/₂f

FORM	WINNER	AGE	& WGT	WINNING RPR	PRE-RACE RPR	SP	TRAINER	B.Runs	BEST RPR LAST 12 MONTHS (RUNS SINCE)
09 2-11	Dunguib D	6	11-5	151	146	9-2	Philip Fenton (Ir)	3⁽²⁴ᴳˢ⁾	won Navan NHF Gd2 (2m) (0)
08 1	Cousin Vinny D	5	11-5	138	109	12-1	W Mullins (Ir)	1⁽²³ᴳˢ⁾	won Punchestown NHF (2m) (0)
07 111	Cork All Star CD	5	11-5	138	136	11-2	Mrs J Harrington (Ir)	3⁽²⁴ᴳˢ⁾	won Cheltenham class 1 Lstd NHF (2m1/2f) (0)
06 2131	Hairy Molly	6	11-5	133	131	33-1	Joseph Crowley (Ir)	4⁽²³ᴳ⁾	won Naas NHF (2m3f) (0)
05 011	Missed That D	6	11-5	136	134	7-2F	W Mullins (Ir)	3⁽²⁴ᴳ⁾	won Naas NHF (2m) (0)
04 311	Total Enjoyment D	5	10-12	135	122	7-1	Thomas Cooper (Ir)	3⁽²⁴ᴳ⁾	won Leopardstown NHF (2m) (0)
03 21-12	Liberman D	5	11-6	142	127	2-1F	M Pipe	4⁽²⁵ᴳ⁾	2nd Cheltenham class 1 List NHF (2m1/2f) (0)
02 1-1	Pizarro D	5	11-6	152	127	14-1	E O'Grady (Ir)	2⁽²³ᴳˢ⁾	won Naas NHF (2m) (0)
01	cancelled								
00 1	Joe Cullen D	5	11-6	149	118	14-1	W Mullins (Ir)	1⁽¹⁷ᴳ⁾	won Tralee NHF (2m) (0)
99 134	Monsignor D	5	11-6	138	121	50-1	M Pitman	3⁽²⁵ᴳˢ⁾	3rd Warwick class 6 NHF (2m) (1)

WINS-RUNS: 4yo 0-36, 5yo 7-134, 6yo 3-62 **FAVOURITES:** -£2.50

FATE OF FAVOURITES: 0221010033 **POSITION OF WINNER IN MARKET:** 0661210252

RECORD OF IRISH RUNNERS: 8-9-95 (+£7.50) **HORSES WEARING HEADGEAR:** 0-0-2 (-£2.00)

Key trends
▶▶Won a bumper with at least 14 runners, 10/10
▶▶Aged five or six, 10/10 (seven aged five)
▶▶Bred in Ireland, 9/10
▶▶Pre-race RPR of at least 121, 8/10 (two exceptions both trained by Willie Mullins, and both had won their only bumper start)
▶▶Won a bumper worth at least 4k (pounds or euros) to the winner, 8/10 (the last eight)
▶▶Off the track for at least 32 days, 7/10 (five not seen since Christmas or earlier)

Other factors
▶▶The last winning 4yo was Dato Star in 1995
▶▶Three winners had won their only previous start, but six of the last seven winners had run at least three times

▶▶The Irish have won this eight times in the last ten years, and 14 of the 17 ever run
▶▶Willie Mullins has the best record with six successes (three in the past ten years) but is often mob-handed (35 runners in the past ten years). However, on four of the occasions he has won it, he saddled just the one runner. On the other two occasions the winner traded at a longer price than up to three stablemates
▶▶The 17 winners have been sired by 17 different stallions. Those successful so far are Montelimar, Where To Dance, Strong Gale, Accordion, Welsh Term, Florida Son, Glacial Storm, Mister Lord, River Falls, Broken Hearted, Teenoso, Flemensfirth, Overbury, Shernazar, Fasliyef, Bob Back and Presenting

Notes

Thursday, March 18, 2010 (New Course)

1.30
Race 1

Jewson Novices' Handicap Chase
(Listed)

C4/RUK

2m5f

Key stats Four of the five winners were in the first three in the market. The four most recent winners were rated either 133 or 135 and carried 10st 11lb or 10st 12lb.

Gerald Delamere's view This is an ideal race over an intermediate trip for novices not good enough to contest the Arkle or RSA Chase and who might not be ready to take on experienced handicappers in the Plate over the same trip. With the benefit of hindsight, all five winners to date – King Harald, Reveillez, L'Antartique, Finger Onthe Pulse and Chapoturgeon – looked well handicapped carrying less than 11st.

The quintet had all finished in the first two last time out, with only Finger Onthe Pulse not having won previously over fences. Four of them had fallen once in their earlier races, which shows it is often worth giving young horses another chance, as they can learn from their mistakes. Seven-year-olds won the first four renewals and all five winners went to the festival with between three and six outings that season.

The ratings and weights carried are interesting. King Harald carried bottom weight of 10st 4lb, was 2lb out of the handicap and

ran off a rating of 123, but the subsequent bottom weights have run off 126, 131, 127 and 128. The five topweights were rated 143, 146, 146, 148 and 147, while the four most recent winners were rated either 133 or 135 and carried 10st 11lb or 10st 12lb. Three of the five had run well in high-quality races where you would expect RSA Chase runners to be competing.

Jonjo O'Neill's **Sunnyhillboy** looks an ideal candidate at this early stage.

Paul Nicholls-trained runners rated 143, 144, 143, 141, 146, 137, 148, 134 and 138 have failed to trouble the judge, but Chapoturgeon got it right last year off a mark of 135, storming clear to give Nicholls his first festival handicap victory at 2m4f or beyond.

In the five renewals, victory has gone to one favourite, two second favourites and one third favourite, at odds of 9-2, 8-1 and 9-1 (twice). L'Antartique was a 20-1 winner in 2007 following a defeat at Hexham and a fall at Kelso. ▶▶**Trends, overleaf**

Notes

JEWSON NOVICES' HANDICAP CHASE (LISTED)

Thursday 1.30   **2m5f**

	FORM	WINNER	AGE & WGT	OR	SP	TRAINER	C.Runs	BEST RPR LAST 12 MONTHS(RUNS SINCE)
09	9-F21	Chapoturgeon	5 10-11	135-2	8-1	P Nicholls	3(20GS)	won Doncaster class 2 nov ch (2m1/2f)(0)
08	-3F22	Finger Onthe Pulse D	7 10-12	135-7	9-1	T Taaffe (Ir)	4(20GS)	2nd Leopardstown nov ch Gd2 (2m5f) (0)
07	221F2	L'Antartique D	7 10-11	133-16	20-1	Ferdy Murphy	6(19GS)	won Bangor class 4 nov ch (2m41/2f) (2)
06	6-221	Reveillez D	7 10-11	133-1	9-2F	J Fanshawe	3(18G)	2nd Exeter class 4 nov ch (2m31/2f) (2)
05	FF212	King Harald (2oh) D	7 10-4	123T	9-1	M Bradstock	5(19G)	2nd Wetherby class 1 nov ch Gd2 (3m1f) (0)

WINS-RUNS: 5yo 1-10, 6yo 0-15, 7yo 4-41, 8yo 0-18, 9yo 0-9, 10yo 0-2, 11yo 0-1 **FAVOURITES:** £0.50

FATE OF FAVOURITES: P10F0 **POSITION OF WINNER IN MARKET:** 21032

OR 123-130 1-4-18, **131-140** 4-9-64, **141-148** 0-2-14

RECORD OF IRISH RUNNERS: 1-2-15 (-£5.00) **HORSES WEARING HEADGEAR:** 0-2-16 (-£16.00)

Key trends

▶▶Officially rated 123-133, 5/5 (four 133-135)

▶▶Carried no more than 10st 12lb, 5/5 (four 10st 11lb-10st 12lb)

▶▶Top-two finish last time out, 5/5

▶▶Finished in the top four on all completed starts over fences, 5/5

▶▶No more than one win over fences, 5/5

▶▶Aged seven, 4/5

▶▶Won over at least 2m4f, 4/5 (three over fences)

Other factors

▶▶Two winners had been placed in Grade 2 novice chases

▶▶Two winners had hurdle RPRs in the mid-140s, three in the low 120s

▶▶Four of the five had fallen at least once over fences

▶▶Four winners have come from the first three in the betting

Notes

| 2.05 Race 2 | Pertemps Final (Handicap Hurdle) (Listed) | 3m |

Key stat Ten of the last 16 winners had won last time out, with only four finishing out of the first three

Kayf Aramis (left) was a winner last time out before landing last year's Pertemps Final

Gerald Delamere's view This is one of the lower-quality handicaps of the festival and, while still competitive, it is not the nursery for fine staying chasers it used to be. Although 27 of the past 36 winners had SPs of 16-1 and under, the race has been something of a minefield in recent years, with four of the last eight winners priced above 16-1, including two 50-1 shock winners owned by J P McManus.

Since I started collating ratings in 1983, all the winners bar one have been rated between 120 and 150. However, you often need to be on a mark of 128 to get in these days. Since 1983, only six winners carried less than 10st 7lb before claims. Seven were novices, with only one of them not having handicap experience. Five-year-olds aren't mature enough for this race, with one (not a novice) being successful in the race's history, and since 1981 every winner has been aged between six and nine.

Working out which qualifier is best is tricky.

Dozens qualified for this by being entered in the Warwick qualifier that was frozen off and the course qualifier in December has disappeared this season. The Haydock qualifier is worth checking and the Tote Handicap Hurdle at Sandown in early February is a good guide. Between 1992 and 2006 there were five Irish-trained winners, who were placed 11055 in the Leopardstown qualifier in December or in its current January date. They were returned at 33-1, 14-1, 12-1, 10-1 and 50-1.

The last-time-out performances over the past 36 renewals read 144129443416F1112743131 1110111625011, with the faller being in a novice chase. The vast majority of winners since 1993 had three or four runs beforehand.

Jonjo O'Neill had his first festival winner as a trainer in this race and, with two more victories since, his J P McManus horses should be considered, along with those from the owner's large number of Irish-trained horses. ▶▶**Trends, overleaf**

PERTEMPS FINAL (HANDICAP HURDLE) (LISTED)

Thursday 2.05　　　　　　　　　　　　　　　　　　　　　　　　　　　**3m**

FORM	WINNER	AGE & WGT	OR	SP	TRAINER	H.Runs	BEST RPRLAST 12 MONTHS(RUNS SINCE)
09 26211	Kayf Aramis D	7 10-5	129-7	16-1	Miss Venetia Williams	9(22GS)	won Warwick class 3 nov hdl (3m1f) (0)
08 -1271	Ballyfitz D	8 10-8	132-3	18-1	N Twiston-Davies	6(24GS)	won Haydock class 2 hcap hdl (3m) (0)
07 2-2F0	Oscar Park	8 10-9	140-T	14-1	D Arbuthnot	9(24GS)	2nd Newbury class 2 hcap hdl (3m1/2f) (2)
06 58505	Kadoun D	9 11-7	142-2	50-1	M P O'Brien (Ir)	25(24G)	8th Fairyhouse hcap hdl (2m) (2)
05 21102	Oulart D	6 10-2	121-11	10-1	D Hughes (Ir)	6(22G)	won Leopardstown hcap hdl (3m) (2)
04 380P6	Creon (2oh)	9 10-0	120-3	50-1	Jonjo O'Neill	25(24G)	6th Chepstow class 3 hcap hdl(2m4f) (0)
03 710-1	Inching Closer	6 11-2	130-4	6-1F	Jonjo O'Neill	7(24G)	won Haydock class 3 hcap hdl (2m4f) (0)
02 3-341	Freetown	6 11-2	138-13	20-1	L Lungo	9(24GS)	3rd M Rasen class 2 hcap hdl (2m51/2f) (0)
01	cancelled						
00 41551	Rubhahunish	9 11-2	148-6	8-1	N Twiston-Davies	15(24G)	won Sandown hcap hdl Gd3 (2m6f) (0)
99 3-250	Generosa	6 10-1	130-T	12-1	J Hassett (Ir)	9(24GS)	2nd Gowran Park hcap hdl (3m) (2)

WINS-RUNS: 5yo 0-26, 6yo 4-50, 7yo 1-63, 8yo 2-44, 9yo 3-25, 10yo 0-12, 11yo 0-11, 12yo 0-3, 13yo 0-2 **FAVOURITES:**-£3.00

FATE OF FAVOURITES: 3401000020 **POSITION OF WINNER IN MARKET:** 6401050700

OR 119-132 6-18-131, **133-146** 3-11-92, **147-160** 1-1-13

RECORD OF IRISH RUNNERS: 3-7-37 (+£38.00) **HORSES WEARING HEADGEAR:** 0-7-54 (-£54.00)

Key trends

▶▶Aged six to nine, 10/10

▶▶Won at class 3 or higher, 9/10

▶▶Off the track between 20 and 42 days, 9/10

▶▶Carried no more than 11st 2lb, 9/10

▶▶Winning form between 2m4f and 2m6f, 8/10

▶▶Six to 15 runs over hurdles, 8/10

▶▶Won over at least 3m, 7/10

▶▶Officially rated 129-142, 7/10

▶▶Won last time out, 5/10 (accounts for only 19 per cent of runners)

Other factors

▶▶Only one winner has won from out of the handicap (2lb wrong)

▶▶Four winners had run at the festival before – none with any great success, but one had recorded a top-six finish in this event the year before

▶▶The three Irish winners had all finished unplaced in the Leopardstown qualifier

▶▶Only four winners from the previous year have tried again, and all were unplaced.

▶▶Two winners were novices

Notes

2.40
Race 3

Ryanair Chase
(Grade 1)

2m5f

Key stats All five winners had won or been placed in the Paddy Power Gold Cup or the Boylesports Gold Cup, and every one was in the first three in the market

The make-up of this race, as always, will hinge on how many of the potential leading fancies go for the Gold Cup. Last year's Ryanair winner, Imperial Commander, looks likely to wait for Friday's feature, while Barbers Shop is set to go the other way, dropping back from the Gold Cup (seventh last year) to contest this shorter race. He has a leading chance, along with the winners of the Boylesports.com Gold Cup (Poquelin) and Paddy Power Gold Cup (Tranquil Sea), as those two races have been the best guide to the Ryanair since its inception in 2005. Planet Of Sound, a faller in the Ascot Chase in February, and last year's Ryanair third Schindlers Hunt are others with the ability to go well.

Poquelin

7 bl g; Trainer Paul Nicholls
Chase form 11387121, best RPR 167
Left-handed 1187121, best RPR 167
Right-handed 3, best RPR 137
Cheltenham chase form 18121, best RPR 167
At the festival 16 Mar 07: in rear and not fluent, ridden 2 out, stayed on approaching last and ran on run-in, not reach leaders, finished 6th, beaten 24l by Katchit in Triumph Hurdle

13 Mar 09: Held up, jumped slowly water, kept on under pressure run-in, never able to get on terms, finished 8th, beaten 18l by Oh Crick in Grand Annual Chase

One of the major trends for this race is that all five previous winners had either won or been placed in the Paddy Power Gold Cup or Boylesports Gold Cup, though not necessarily in the same season. Poquelin is a strong qualifier, having finished second in the former and won the latter this term. Only eighth of 18 as a novice in last season's Grand Annual, he has improved dramatically for the step up to 2m4f-plus and he jumped particularly well when slamming Razor Royale over course and distance in December. That win, from a handicap mark of 151, was all the more meritorious considering his trainer believes he doesn't like winter ground, so if there is more improvement to come on a likely faster surface he deserves his place at the head of the market even though others have higher official marks.

Poquelin: much improved over 2m4f-plus

Barbers Shop

8 b g; Trainer Nicky Henderson
Chase form 2412121743
Left-handed 221274, best RPR 160
Right-handed 4113, best RPR 160
Cheltenham form 227, best RPR 160
At the festival 13 Mar 08: ridden before last, edged left run-in, stayed on and gaining close home, finished nk second to Finger Onthe Pulse in Jewson Novices' Handicap Chase

13 Mar 09: in touch, tracked leaders 15th, hit 4 out, ridden and not fluent 3 out, weakened soon after, finished seventh, beaten 33l by Kauto Star in Gold Cup

Fine second to Imperial Commander in the 2008 Paddy Power Gold Cup and was subsequently campaigned as a Gold Cup horse. Ran like a non-stayer in last season's Gold Cup (jumped and travelled really well until four out) but that race was the target again this term. The Hennessy was the first aim and he again travelled sweetly until four out to finish fourth to Denman in receipt of 18lb, while in the King George he lasted longer but tired rapidly after three out and lost second near the finish, 37 lengths behind Kauto Star. He has run to the same level on RPRs in his last five starts at trips from 2m5f-3m2.5f, so it's hard to say he definitely doesn't stay, but that's how it looks. Hasn't won at Cheltenham, but a strong trends contender otherwise, though his official mark suggests he's short enough in the betting.

Tranquil Sea

8 b g; Trainer Edward O'Grady
Chase form 155621121, best RPR 163
Left-handed 561121, best RPR 163
Right-handed 152, best RPR 146
Cheltenham chase form 61, best RPR 163
At the festival 11 Mar 08: chased leader, led after 3rd, ridden after 3 out, headed after 2 out, weakened before last, finished eighth, beaten 20l by Captain Cee Bee in Supreme Novices' Hurdle

12 Mar 09: towards rear when blundered 10th, some progress from 3 out but never in contention, finished 6th, beaten 28l by Chapoturgeon in Jewson Novices' Handicap Chase

Fair novice hurdler who had a disappointing first season over fences, but much better this season, beating fellow improver Joncol over 2m at Naas in October before landing a hefty on-the-day gamble in the Paddy Power Gold Cup, where he cruised to victory over Poquelin (gave 2lb). No match for Golden Silver in small-field Grade 1 over 2m1f at Leopardstown in December, but the slow pace was against him that day and he'll be seen to better effect in a faster-run race. Seems much better served by soft ground and has been beaten 20-plus lengths in his two festival visits, so wouldn't want a dry spring in a year when the festival takes place slightly later than usual. Big player if the mud is flying, as he had plenty in hand over Poquelin in November.

Voy Por Ustedes

9 b g; Trainer Alan King
Chase form 11111221U122U122122432136, best RPR 178
Left-handed 11112U12214216, best RPR 178
Right-handed 121133, best RPR 176
Cheltenham form 11222, best RPR 170
At the festival 14 Mar 06: chased leader before 3 out, driven and narrow lead last, won Arkle Chase, beating Monet's Garden by 1¼l

14 Mar 07: tracked leaders, challenging when hit 2 out, rallied to lead approaching last, driven out, won Champion Chase, beating Dempsey by 1½l

13 Mar 08: tracked leaders from 5th, not fluent 7th and 8th, chased winner 4 out, effort next, outpaced by impressive winner from 2 out but kept on well for clear 2nd, finished second in Champion Chase, beaten 19l by Master Minded

12 Mar 09: in touch, chased leaders 8th, tracking leaders when blundered 4 out, rallied and every chance 3 out, not fluent 2 out and one pace, rallied gamely run-in to take 2nd close home, but no chance with winner, finished second, beaten 2l by Imperial Commander in Ryanair Chase

Remarkably tough chaser who has a deserved reputation as a Cheltenham specialist, having paid four visits to the festival and finished first or second each time, winning an Arkle and a Champion Chase. Even so, his four best runs according to RPRs have been on flatter tracks like Aintree and Ascot. Was an odds-on shot when second to Imperial Commander in last year's Ryanair and has something to prove now, having finished a tame sixth upped to 3m in the Lexus Chase at Leopardstown and then

Last year's Ryanair runner-up Voy Por Ustedes has questions to answer after below-par runs

a disappointing fourth of five behind Master Minded in the Game Spirit at Newbury in February. Will be a much better price than last year and his career-best RPR of 178 is 7lb and more better than all of his probable rivals (bar Imperial Commander, who is most likely to run in the Gold Cup) have managed.

Planet Of Sound

8 b g; Trainer Philip Hobbs
Chase form 4113312F, best RPR 168
Left-handed 1133, best RPR 158
Right-handed 412F, best RPR 168
Cheltenham form 3, best RPR 158
At the festival 10 Mar 09: mistake 1st, towards rear, mistake 8th, and dropped further to rear, ridden and progress before 3 out, tried to close on leaders after 2 out, kept on same pace flat, finished third, beaten 5l by Forpadydeplasterer in Arkle Chase

Third in last year's Arkle and again in a Grade 2 at Aintree before taking his form to a new level in his first two starts this season. Ran out a fairly comfortable winner of the Haldon Gold Cup off a mark of 152 at Exeter in November and then did well to finish a three-length second to 164-rated Albertas Run over 2m3f at Ascot in December, especially given the terrible blunder he made at the ninth (mistakes also a feature of his Arkle run). Minor problems meant he wasn't seen again until the Ascot Chase in February, in which he was an early faller, which raised fresh concerns over his jumping, though that was his first fall. Definite contender on ratings, but not a strong trends pick owing to overall lack of experience and winning/big handicap form at Cheltenham, and that Ascot fall was not the best prep.

Schindlers Hunt

10 ch g; Trainer Dessie Hughes
Chase form 51211F25534U41455513222453,
best RPR 167
Left-handed 11F3U45513253, best RPR 167
Right-handed 5122554145224, best RPR 160
Cheltenham form 43, best RPR 165
At the festival 13 Mar 08: Upsides and helped to set
strong pace, led 2nd, headed 7th, hit 4 out, soon no
chance with leading duo, lost 3rd run-in, finished
fourth, beaten 36l by Master Minded in Champion
Chase

12 Mar 09: in rear, headway to track leaders 13th,
ridden and every chance 3 out, pressed winner from 2
out until after last, no impression, weakened and lost
second close home, finished third, beaten 2¾l by
Imperial Commander in Ryanair Chase

Invariably highly tried and consistent chaser
who has always been seen to better effect
when the ground dries out in the spring. Put up
a career-best effort when third to Imperial
Commander in this event last year, finishing
only three-quarters of a length behind second-
placed Voy Por Ustedes, and narrowed that gap
to a neck against that rival next time out in the
Grade 1 Melling Chase at Aintree, where he
again raised his career-best RPR. Hasn't quite
hit the same heights since, but was a good
third on ground he doesn't like in the Irish
Hennessy in February and looks to be running
into form at the right time again. Sure to be in
the thick of things at the top of the hill, but
doesn't win often.

Schindlers Hunt: running into form

Other contenders

Most of the others of interest have alternative
preferred targets. **Imperial Commander**,
last year's Ryanair winner, would jump straight
in as favourite if connections decide to swerve
the Gold Cup, but that's unlikely at this stage,
while the novice **Punchestowns**, the best
hurdler for a long while to go chasing, also has
an entry but is more likely to contest the RSA.
His trainer, Nicky Henderson, also has **Petit
Robin** in the Ryanair, but that one is
reportedly heading for the Champion Chase
even though Henderson believes he needs
much more than 2m now. Last year's Jewson
winner **Chapoturgeon** would have been a lot
closer than fourth to Poquelin in the
Boylesports.com Gold Cup in December had he
not nearly unseated at the last, but he's often
been full of mistakes and put in a tame
performance next time. **Albertas Run** would
be of more interest than most given that he's a
dual course winner and a former King George
runner-up with a liking for decent ground.
Peterborough Chase winner **Deep Purple**
seems to prefer flat tracks and missed
Cheltenham for Aintree last season, where he
was a respectable second to his Huntingdon
victim **Tartak**. The latter would look a big
price at around the 33-1 mark if he could get
his jumping together, but he seems to have hit
one out of every two fences he's jumped this
season. ∎

RYANAIR CHASE (GRADE 1)
Thursday 2.40   **2m5f**

FORM	WINNER	AGE	& WGT	WINNING PRE-RACE RPR	RPR	SP	TRAINER	Ch.Runs	BEST RPR LAST 12 MONTHS (RUNS SINCE)
09	14-16	Imperial Commander C, D8		11-10	169	161	6-1	N Twiston-Davies 5(10GS)	won Paddy Power Gold Cup Gd3 hcap ch (2m4¹/₂f) (1)
08	23-22	Our Vic CD, BF		10	11-10	168	171	4-1	D Pipe 17(9GS)	2nd King George VI Chase Gd1 (3m) (1)
07	-1F31	Taranis CD		6	11-0	160	158	9-2	P Nicholls 7(9GS)	3rd Boylesports Gold Cup Gd3 hcap ch (2m5f) (0)
06	-4B13	Fondmort CD		10	11-0	164	165	10-3J	N Henderson 27(11G)	won Cheltenham class 1 List hcap ch (2m5f) (1)
05	2-222	Thisthatandtother C, BF		9	11-3	164	164	9-2	P Nicholls 11(12G)	2nd Paddy Power Gold Cup Gd3 hcap ch (2m4¹/₂f) (2)

WINS-RUNS: 6yo 1-4, 7yo 0-5, 8yo 1-8, 9yo 1-16, 10yo 2-10, 11yo 0-5, 12yo 0-2, 13yo 0-1 **FAVOURITES:**-£1.67

TRAINERS IN THIS RACE (w-pl-r): P Nicholls 2-1-8, D Pipe 1-1-3, N Twiston-Davies 1-0-1, N Henderson 1-1-4, A King 0-1-1, D Hughes 0-1-1, P Hobbs 0-1-1

FATE OF FAVOURITES: P1452 **POSITION OF WINNER IN MARKET:** 21322

RECORD OF IRISH RUNNERS: 0-3-11 (-£11.00) **HORSES WEARING HEADGEAR:** 1-1-7 (-£3.00)

RECORD OF TRIAL WINNERS: Paddy Power Gold Cup (Cheltenham, November) **971**; John Durkan Chase (Punchestown, December) **65**; Peterborough Chase (Huntingdon, December) **53566**; Boylesports Gold Cup (Cheltenham, December) **F**; Ascot Chase (Ascot, February) **942**

Key trends
▶▶Achieved RPR of at least 158, 5/5
▶▶Offically rated at least 152, 5/5
▶▶Course winner, 5/5
▶▶Won or placed in either the Paddy Power or Boylesports Gold Cup, 5/5
▶▶From the first three in the market, 5/5

▶▶No more than four runs since October, 5/5
▶▶Top-three finish last time out, 4/5
▶▶At least 11 runs over fences, 3/5

Other factors
▶▶The four beaten favourites had all won a Grade 1 chase last time out

Notes

3.20
Race 4

Ladbrokes World Hurdle
(Grade 1)

C4/RUK

3m

Key stats The last ten winners all had a top-two finish last time out. Three winners in the past decade returned to defend the title (two won and the other was second)

Big Buck's will be the banker of the meeting for many. He returns to defend his title still unbeaten in six starts since being switched back to hurdles and the closest any rival has got to him was the length and three-quarters by which he beat Punchestowns (now sent chasing) in this race last year. Karabak was decisively beaten by Big Buck's in the Long Walk Hurdle in December, though Alan King's stable was out of form at the time and there are hopes of a better showing this time. Tidal Bay, like Big Buck's last year, has dropped back from chasing and scored well in the Cleeve Hurdle but still has ground to make up on the hot favourite.

Big Buck's

7 b/br g; Trainer Paul Nicholls
Hurdles form (all left-handed)
536U344771612111111, best RPR 176
Cheltenham form (all) 7111, best RPR 176
At the festival 13 Mar 08: In rear, hampered 8th, blundered 10th, headway approaching 3 out, plugged on from before last, never able to trouble leaders, finished 7th, beaten 5³/4l by Finger Onthe Pulse in Jewson Novices' Handicap Chase

12 Mar 09: midfield, hit 7th, headway approaching 2 out, went 2nd between last two, upsides when mistake last, rallied to lead 150 yards out, edged left and stayed on gamely towards finish, won World Hurdle by 1³/4l from Punchestowns

Has not looked back since unseating at the last fence in the 2008 Hennessy (probably would have won), which prompted connections to send him hurdling, and is unbeaten in Britain over hurdles, having won his last six starts. Those wins include a four-length Cleeve Hurdle success over Punchestowns (who gave 8lb), which was followed by victory over the same rival in the World Hurdle, with the pair 17 lengths clear of the third. Victory at Aintree followed, plus two more at Newbury this season, and he has every right to be considered equal to, if not better than, any staying hurdler of the last 20 years. Like Inglis Drever and Baracouda before him, he tends to hit a flat spot during his races, which can fool some in-

running punters (he hit 40 on Betfair during last season's World Hurdle and 5 in the rescheduled Long Walk Hurdle at Newbury in December, having gone off at 1-2), but there can be no doubting his superiority at the end. There will be no Punchestowns to worry about this year and, with Diamond Harry also having switched to fences, plausible dangers are getting thin on the ground. He is the complete package as far as the key trends are concerned and has every right to be the festival's shortest-priced ante-post favourite.

Karabak

7 b g; Trainer Alan King
Hurdles form 2112422, best RPR 166
Left-handed 1242, best RPR 166
Right-handed 212, best RPR 162
Cheltenham form 12, best RPR 156
At the festival 11 Mar 09: in touch, jumped slowly 6th, pushed along 4 out, ridden and switched right after 2 out, came wide into straight but stayed on under pressure to take 2nd run-in, no chance with winner close home, finished second, beaten 1³/4l by Mikael D'Haguenet in Ballymore Novices' Hurdle

Top-class staying novice last term and might not have been seen at his best in the Ballymore Novices' Hurdle at the festival, as that race was far from the stamina test it usually is and he

Big Buck's (red, white and black) continues to have his rivals playing catch-up

was outpaced mid-race before staying on strongly but far too late to catch the pacier Mikael D'Haguenet. He was definitely over the top for his final run at Aintree, but has put up two more promising efforts this season, finishing runner-up to current Champion Hurdle favourite Zaynar over 2m3½f at Ascot and improving on that when running second to Big Buck's in the Long Walk Hurdle. He has plenty to find on that form, but you could argue there is more to come as he has raced only seven times over hurdles and both starts this season, though a level up from last season, came when the Alan King stable was badly out of form. From a trends standpoint he falls down only on his lack of a Graded hurdle victory, but even with that in mind he looks the biggest danger to the favourite.

Tidal Bay

9 b g; Trainer Howard Johnson
Hurdles form 1112211, best RPR 162
Left-handed 112211, best RPR 162
Right-handed 1, best RPR 121
All Cheltenham form 12211341, best RPR 162
(168 chase)

At the festival 14 Mar 07: stayed on under pressure run-in, edged left close home but kept on; finished second, beaten a neck by Massini's Maguire in Ballymore Properties Novices' Hurdle

11 Mar 08: led two out, shaken up and soon drew clear, stayed on strongly, impressive, beat Kruguyrova 13l in Arkle

12 Mar 09: chased leaders, hit 7th, ridden 10th, in rear next, well behind 3 out, still plenty to do 2 out, rallied and ran on last, finished well, 4th, beaten 7¼l by Imperial Commander in Ryanair Chase

Terrifically consistent performer whose first two festival visits resulted in a neck defeat in the Ballymore Properties Novices' Hurdle in 2007 and a 13-length romp in the Arkle Chase the following year. Unfortunately he developed into a bit of a clumsy oaf over fences and it's testament to his natural talent that he managed fourth place in last year's Ryanair and this season's Peterborough Chase given the blunders he made. Connections bit the bullet in January and sent him back over hurdles and, despite being a big market drifter, he travelled supremely well to run away with the Cleeve Hurdle, scoring by five lengths from Time For Rupert. Made third favourite for this race on the strength of that and a high trends scorer, but one of the two areas he falls down on highlights the task he faces. Eight of the last ten winners had achieved a hurdles RPR of 164, but his last-time-out best was 162 and, more importantly, that's still a stone behind Big Buck's. He's also older than usual, but he has a turn of foot and those Cheltenham form figures are impressive.

Sentry Duty

8 b g; Trainer Nicky Henderson
Hurdles form 410011081, best RPR 161
Left-handed 410081, best RPR 161
Right-handed 011, best RPR 153
Cheltenham form 001, best RPR 161
At the festival 11 Mar 08: hit 2nd, mid-division until weakened 3 out, finished 15th, beaten 83l by Captain Cee Bee in Supreme Novices' Hurdle

10 Mar 09: not fluent 1st and sometimes jumped right, never beyond midfield, no impression on leaders when hampered 3 out, finished 14th, beaten 33l by Punjabi in Champion Hurdle

All his best form has been when fresh, so it's not a worry that's he's been unsighted since January 1, when he ran a career-best to beat Katchit at Cheltenham. However, he's never won a Graded hurdle, doesn't have the qualifying RPR and must prove his stamina for 3m. He got a trip on the Flat and his New Year's Day hurdle win was over 2m5f, but that was in a three-runner race and he's been tailed off at the last two festivals. The fact he's fourth favourite in many lists reflects how weak the opposition to Big Buck's is.

Time For Rupert

6 ch g; Trainer Paul Webber
Hurdles form 71101712, best RPR 160
Left-handed 71112, best RPR 160
Right-handed 107, best RPR 133
Cheltenham form 12, best RPR 160

A low trends scorer because he hasn't won a Graded hurdle, doesn't qualify with a big enough RPR, has never run at the festival and hasn't made the first four on every start this season. However, he will go into the race having run consecutive career-bests over 3m at Cheltenham and he is due some credit for his

second to Tidal Bay in the Cleeve, as he was one of several who helped to press a fast pace and was the only one of them still pitching at the finish. Progressive and has place claims, but has a mountain to climb with the favourite.

Mourad

5 ch g; Trainer Willie Mullins
Hurdles form 13324221, best RPR 154
Left-handed 334, best RPR 153
Right-handed 12221, best RPR 154
Cheltenham form 3, best RPR 153
At the festival 13 Mar 09: held up, headway approaching 2 out, progress and chasing leaders when hit last, ran on but not pace to challenge front pair, finished third, beaten 3^1/$_2$l by Zaynar in Triumph Hurdle

The each-way Pricewise selection at 33-1, but not a trends pick by any means as he's too young, has never won a Graded hurdle and has a huge amount to find on the figures. He stayed on powerfully in what has proved to be a top-quality Triumph last season, is progressing well and promises to get the trip. Still only a fringe contender, though.

Other contenders

The **Lie Forrit** bubble burst when he was pulled up in the Cleeve Hurdle in January, though he appeared to have been over-hyped on the basis of his Newbury handicap win off 138 against a 115-rated rival. He might bounce back if his fitness was an issue last time, but still has bundles to find. **Diamond Harry** would be a rock-solid place contender if he lined up, but he has been sent chasing and is one of the favourites for the RSA. Veteran **Powerstation** is well suited by a strong pace in a big field and has been placed at three festivals, so he could muscle in on the place action, as could festival regular **Katchit** (not totally convincing at the trip) and **Fair Along** (though he seems to have lost his form for now). **War Of Attrition** seems revitalised as a hurdler, but everything else has masses to find, including **Cousin Vinny**, who would be at least 100-1 if he wasn't a previous festival winner. ∎

LADBROKES WORLD HURDLE (GRADE 1)

Thursday 3.20   **3m**

FORM	WINNER	AGE	& WGT	WINNING RPR	PRE-RACE RPR	SP	TRAINER	H.Runs	BEST RPR LAST 12 MONTHS (RUNS SINCE)
09 1-U11	Big Buck's CD	6	11-10	176	166	6-1	P Nicholls	15(14GS)	won Cleeve Hurdle Gd2 (3m) (0)
08 13-11	Inglis Drever C, D	9	11-10	172	170	11-8F	H Johnson	20(17GS)	won Newb class 1 Gd2 Hdl (3m1/2f) (1)
07 1F-12	Inglis Drever CD	8	11-10	166	167	5-1	H Johnson	16(14GS)	2nd Cleeve Hurdle Gd2 (3m) (0)
06 2-211	My Way De Solzen D	6	11-10	159	159	8-1	A King	10(20G)	won Long Walk Hurdle Gd1 (3m) (1)
05 -2211	Inglis Drever	6	11-10	167	165	5-1	H Johnson	9(12G)	won Kingwell Hurdle Gd2 (2m) (0)
04 121-2	Iris's Gift CD, BF	7	11-10	176	173	9-2	Jonjo O'Neill	8(10G)	won Sefton Nov Hdl Gd1 (3m1/2f) (1)
03 11-12	Baracouda CD, BF	8	11-10	176	176	9-4J	F Doumen (Fr)	17(11G)	won Stayers' Hurdle Gd1 (3m)(2)
02 1-111	Baracouda D	7	11-10	171	176	13-8F	F Doumen (Fr)	14(16G)	won Long Walk Hurdle Gd1 (3m11/2f) (1)
01	cancelled								
00 15-12	Bacchanal	6	11-10	168	165	11-2	N Henderson	6(10GF)	2nd Cleeve Hurdle Gd1(2m51/2f) (0)
99 2/752	Anzum	8	11-10	167	157	40-1	D Nicholson	16(12GS)	2nd Kemp class 1 Gd2 Hdl Hcap (3m1/2f) (0)

WINS-RUNS: 5yo 0-8, 6yo 4-28, 7yo 2-38, 8yo 3-26, 9yo 1-18, 10yo 0-12, 11yo 0-5, 13yo 0-1 **FAVOURITES:** -£3.37

TRAINERS IN THIS RACE (w-pl-r): Howard Johnson 3-0-5, A King 1-2-9, N Henderson 1-1-6, P Nicholls 1-0-3, H Daly 0-3-4, W Mullins 0-1-6

FATE OF FAVOURITES: 2611223F14 **POSITION OF WINNER IN MARKET:** 9311234313

RECORD OF IRISH RUNNERS: 0-8-25 (-£25.00) **HORSES WEARING HEADGEAR:** 0-2-30 (-£30.00)

RECORD OF TRIAL WINNERS: Long Distance Hurdle (Newbury, November) **22111**; Long Walk Hurdle (Ascot, December) **16221202**
Cleeve Hurdle (Cheltenham, January) (only run over 3m since 2005) **4311**; Boyne Hurdle (Navan, February) **22P23**
Rendlesham Hurdle (Haydock, February) **16P823** (run at Kempton before 2006)

Key trends

▶▶Top-two finish last time out, 10/10

▶▶Ran no more than four times since August, 10/10 (average is 2.5)

▶▶Aged six to eight, 9/10

▶▶Not out of the first two all hurdle starts that season, 9/10

▶▶Ran between 8 and 20 times over hurdles over hurdles, 9/10

▶▶Won a Graded hurdle, 9/10

▶▶RPR of at least 165, 8/10

▶▶Previously ran at the Cheltenham Festival, 8/10 (six won or placed)

Other factors

▶▶The last three winners aged nine or above (Inglis Drever, Galmoy and Crimson Embers) were previous winners of the race

▶▶A five year-old has never won this race. However, four of the nine to run in the past ten seasons have been placed

▶▶Five winners had finished first or second in this race before

▶▶All four Irish winners since the mid-1980s prepped in the Boyne Hurdle at Navan

▶▶Four winners contested the Long Walk Hurdle, where they finished 7121

▶▶It is rare for the previous year's winner to return – only Baracouda (twice) and Inglis Drever have tried in the past decade, with Inglis Drever winning and Baracouda winning once and finishing second on the other occasion

Notes

HOW DO THE LEADING CONTENDERS CONFORM TO THE WORLD HURDLE TRENDS?

	Top-two finish last time out, ten winners in the last ten runnings	No more than four runs since August, 10/10	Aged six to eight, 9/10	Not out of the first two over hurdles all season 9/10	8 to 20 hurdle runs, 9/10	Pre-race RPR of at least 164, 8/10	Won Graded hurdle, 9/10	Won or placed at previous festival, 6/10	TOTAL
Big Buck's	✔	✔	✔	✔	✔	✔	✔	✔	8
Bouggler	✗	✔	✗	✗	✗	✗	✔	✗	2
Cape Tribulation	✗	✔	✔	✗	✗	✗	✔	✗	3
Cousin Vinny	✗	✔	✔	✗	✗	✗	✗	✗	2
Diamond Harry	✔	✔	✔	✗	✗	✔	✔	✔	6
Ebadiyan	✔	✗	✗	✗	✔	✗	✔	✗	3
Fair Along	✗	✔	✔	✗	✗	✔	✔	✔	5
Golan Way	✗	✔	✔	✗	✔	✗	✔	✗	4
Jumbo Rio	✗	✗	✗	✗	✔	✗	✔	✗	2
Karabak	✔	✔	✔	✔	✗	✔	✔	✔	7
Katchit	✗	✔	✔	✗	✗	✗	✔	✔	4
Lie Forrit	✗	✔	✔	✗	✗	✗	✗	✗	2
Lough Derg	✗	✗	✗	✗	✗	✔	✔	✗	2
Mourad	✔	✗	✗	✗	✔	✗	✗	✔	3
Mr Thriller	✗	✔	✗	✗	✔	✔	✔	✔	5
Ninetieth Minute	✗	✔	✔	✗	✔	✗	✔	✔	5
Oscar Dan Dan	✗	✗	✔	✗	✔	✗	✔	✗	3
Powerstation	✔	✗	✗	✗	✗	✗	✔	✔	3
Punchestowns	✔	✔	✔	✔	✗	✔	✔	✔	7
Sentry Duty	✔	✔	✔	✔	✔	✗	✗	✗	5
Tidal Bay	✔	✔	✗	✔	✔	✔	✔	✔	7
Time For Rupert	✔	✔	✔	✗	✔	✔	✗	✗	5
War Of Attrition	✔	✗	✗	✔	✔	✗	✗	✔	4

▶▶Record of Long Distance Hurdle (Newbury, November) winners **22111**

▶▶Record of Long Walk Hurdle (Ascot, December) winners **16221202**

▶▶Record of Cleeve Hurdle (Cheltenham, January) winners (only run over 3m since 2005) **4311**

▶▶Record of Boyne Hurdle (Navan, February) winners **22P23**

▶▶Record of Rendlesham Hurdle (Haydock, February) winners **16P823** (run at Kempton before 2006)

Based on results up to February 1, 2010

4.00
Race 5

Byrne Group Plate Handicap Chase
(Grade 3)

2m5f

Key stats Twelve of the last 15 winners carried no more than 11st. French-breds have won six runnings in the past decade and had a 1-2-3 last year

Gerald Delamere's view Formerly known as the Mildmay of Flete, this is a straightforward handicap that hasn't seen either a Paddy Power or Boylesports Gold Cup winner follow up, and such a winner is even less likely now that higher-class runners head for the Grade 1 Ryanair over the same trip. Remarkably, the two January handicaps over course and distance haven't had a big influence either, with just one winner from each completing the double.

Even so, course form at those two meetings, plus Warwick, Sandown and Kempton in February, is relevant. Year after year previous festival form is found in the winner's cv, though very few took any notice of Mister McGoldrick's fine third place in the 2006 Queen Mother Champion Chase before he ran away with this race in 2008 at 66-1.

Mister McGoldrick: track form unnoticed

Twelve of the past 36 winners carried 11st or more, which equals the best for weight carrying at this meeting. Just to make matters more difficult, six winners have been out of the handicap since ratings became available in 1982. Four were ridden by 7lb claimers, and last year William Biddick claimed 5lb off 33-1 winner Something Wells. Since The Tsarevich won for the second time in 1986, no horse has been successful off a rating above 147. The best band to locate the winner is between 128 and 141 (eight of the last ten winners were in that band). With the way handicaps fill nowadays, don't be put off by a few pounds extra, especially if the rating band fits.

Alan King's **Tarotino** (who has dropped to 142) is just above that band but would be of interest on good ground.

Nicky Henderson has had four victories and several places. Venetia Williams is well worth consideration, with two of the last three winners, while David Pipe hasn't added to his father's four winners yet. From plenty of fancied runners, Paul Nicholls has still to succeed. This hasn't been a good race for Irish-trained horses, with just one victory in almost 60 years.

The last-time-out results of the winners read 46F413111235223421512421211115143452, plus one debut winner. Only eight hadn't won that season and up to seven runs beforehand is the norm.

Between 1980 and 2004 seven novices were successful and only Majadou carried more than 10st 4lb, with three out of the handicap. Majadou was also the only five-year-old to succeed. Novices now have the Jewson as an alternative.

Nine of the last 36 winners had SPs between 20-1 and 66-1. Favourites have a poor record, but 22 winners were returned between 4-1 and 14-1. ▶▶**Trends, overleaf**

BYRNE GROUP PLATE (HANDICAP CHASE) (GRADE 3)

Thursday 4.00   2m5f

FORM	WINNER	AGE & WGT	OR	SP	TRAINER	C.Runs	BEST RPRLAST 12 MONTHS(RUNS SINCE)
09 20272	Something Wells	8 10-7	139⁻¹	33-1	Miss Venetia Williams	10(23GS)	2nd Ascot class 2 hcap ch (2m51/2f)(2)
08 547U5	Mister McGoldrick D	11 11-7	145⁻⁶	66-1	Mrs S Smith	33(22GS)	4th Wetherby class 2 hcap ch (2m1/2f) (2)
07 6-134	Idole First C, D	8 10-7	136ᵀ	12-1	Miss Venetia Williams	8(23GS)	won Kempton class 3 hcap ch (2m41/2f)(2)
06 0-433	Non So	8 11-3	137ᵀ	14-1	N Henderson	10(24G)	3rd Wetherby class 2 hcap ch (2m41/2f) (0)
05 -2384	Liberthine	6 10-1	128⁻⁶	25-1	N Henderson	6(22G)	3rd Kempton class 2 hcap ch (2m41/2f) (2)
04 22141	Tikram (3oh) D	7 10-0	133⁻⁹	12-1	G Moore	5(16G)	2nd Cheltenham class 2 nov ch (2m1/2f) (3)
03 /376-	Young Spartacus C, D	10 10-9	147⁻⁹	16-1	H Daly	14(19G)	3rd Peterborough Chase (2m4f) (2)
02 13-P5	Blowing Wind C	9 10-9	138⁻²	25-1	M Pipe	15(21GS)	5th Sandown class 2 hcap ch (2m) (0)
01	cancelled						
00 -24P1	Dark Stranger D	9 10-3	128⁻⁴	14-1	M Pipe	14(18G)	won Sandown class 3 nov hcap ch (2m41/2f) (3)
99 8-111	Majadou C, D	5 11-0	141⁻³	7-4F	M Pipe	4(18GS)	won Cheltenham class 3 nov ch (2m5f) (2)

WINS-RUNS: 5yo 1-4, 6yo 1-24, 7yo 1-28, 8yo 3-57, 9yo 2-37, 10yo 1-37, 11yo 1-14, 12yo 0-3, 13yo 0-2 **FAVOURITES:** -£7.25

FATE OF FAVOURITES: 122U24F0F2 **POSITION OF WINNER IN MARKET:** 1900606500

OR 118-132 2-8-67, **133-149** 8-19-125, **150-164** 0-3-14

RECORD OF IRISH RUNNERS: 0-4-24 (-£24.00) **HORSES WEARING HEADGEAR:** 1-2-230 (-£15.00)

Key trends
▶▶Won at class 3 level or higher, 10/10

▶▶Won between 2m3f and 2m5f, 9/10

▶▶Ran within the last 40 days, 9/10

▶▶Top five last time out, 9/10

▶▶Carried no more than 11st, 8/10

▶▶Ran between four and 15 times over fences, 9/10

▶▶No older than nine, 8/10

▶▶Ran at a previous Cheltenham Festival, 8/10 (including four who had run in the County Hurdle)

▶▶Officially rated 128-139, 7/10 (three exceptions in the 140s)

Other factors
▶▶Not a single winner in the last ten years had figured prominently in any of the big two-and-a-half-mile handicaps run at Cheltenham in the autumn

▶▶The two novices to win were rated 133 and 141

▶▶The Irish have not won this since Double-U-Again in 1982

▶▶The last nine winners were sent off at double-figure odds

Notes

4.40
Race 6

Fulke Walwyn Kim Muir Handicap Chase
(Amateur Riders)

RUK

$3m1^1/_2f$

Key stats Nine of the last ten winners had run over at least 3m last time out. Eight of the last 11 winners started at 12-1 or bigger

Gerald Delamere's view Having loved this race since backing Irish Coffee more than 50 years ago, last year's result was a nightmare for me. Despite having tipped Character Building for the Hennessy (withdrawn on the day) I had gone off him big time, totally ignoring his spring festival form.

Plenty of claiming amateurs – particularly Irish – have been successful and a certain Adrian Maguire was one of nine to win when claiming the 7lb allowance in the past 35 renewals. Nina Carberry hasn't won this race and was on the beaten favourite last year. She has a mediocre record in conventional handicap chases, even though she is superb in cross-country races and bumpers. There were three Irish-trained winners in the decade from 1974 to 1983, but none since. Paul Nicholls has had more than a dozen failures.

Thirteen winners were set to carry 11st or more before claims and, at the bottom end, nine carried 10st or less. The overall ratings aren't too helpful as the race became restricted to 0-140 horses in 1999. Character Building scuppered most of the trends last year when he won off 139 and carried 11st 12lb. Until then, the biggest burden carried was 11st 7lb by Juveigneur in 2005, when the significant factor was that the topweight was rated just 132. Often it is the case that the topweight is rated relatively low in a limited rating range, giving the higher-weighted runners an advantage, but I had a blind spot where Character Building was concerned. Nothing rated lower than 126 has got in for the past two years and it is best to look for the winner up to a maximum rating of 134, something like the Charlie Longsdon-trained **Far More Serious**, who has gone from a mark of 104 to 132 after an impressive comeback this season from a near two-year layoff.

Since 1972 just four winners were outside the seven to ten age group, with only four novices having been successful. Last-time-out positions vary enormously: 13121211370UU12 1P236222511192P0P9, plus two trained by Martin Pipe making their debuts. Twenty-nine of the winners had a really decent win or placed run in their past three outings.

Besides a couple of 33-1 shocks and three 20-1 winners in the past seven years, the other 30 winners were priced between 5-2 and 16-1. This includes only four favourites, all in the past 21 years.

Since 1992 a couple of winners were found in the Forbra Gold Cup at Ludlow. Another race to consider is the Racing Post Chase, which has produced two recent winners. Surprisingly, only five of the winners since 1972 had been placed (13223) over the course earlier in their successful season.
▶▶**Trends, overleaf**

	FORM	WINNER	AGE & WGT	OR	SP	TRAINER	C.Runs	BEST RPR LAST 12 MONTHS(RUNS SINCE)
09	14339	Character Building D	9 11-12	139-10	16-1	J Quinn	10(24GS)	3rd Chel class 2 hcap ch (3m2½f) (1)
08	1-43P	High Chimes	9 10-10	127-7	14-1	Evan Williams	7(24GS)	3rd Haydock class 2 hcap ch (3m) (1)
07	36120	Cloudy Lane D, BF	7 10-11	124T	15-2F	D McCain Jnr	5(24GS)	2nd Newcastle class 3 nov ch (3m) (1)
06	3621P	You're Special C, BF	9 10-12	125-6	33-1	F Murphy	18(21G)	won Doncaster class 2 hcap ch (3m2f) (1)
05	31522	Juveigneur	8 11-7	128-6	12-1	N Henderson	19(24G)	2nd Newbury class 3 hcap ch (3m) (0)
04	-42P9	Maximize D	10 10-6	127-7	40-1	M Pipe	19(22G)	2nd Cheltenham class 4 am hcap ch (3m) (2)
03	P589-	Royal Predica	9 10-13	134-3	33-1	M Pipe	27(23G)	5th Wm Hill NH Hcp Ch Gd3 (3m½f) (2)
02	313/1	The Bushkeeper D	8 11-2	125-6	9-2F	N Henderson	4(23GS)	won Huntingdon class 3 hcap ch (3m) (0)
01		cancelled						
00	12341	Honey Mount D	9 9-12	115-4	8-1	R Alner	4(23G)	2nd Cheltenham class 3 nov ch (3m½f) (2)
99	33R-1	Celtic Giant D	9 10-0	110-3	20-1	L Lungo	11(22GS)	won Musselburgh class 4 hcap ch (2m4f) (0)

FULKE WALWYN KIM MUIR CHALLENGE CUP HANDICAP CHASE (AMATEURS)
Thursday 4.40 — 3m½f

WINS-RUNS: 5yo 0-3, 6yo 0-16, 7yo 1-42, 8yo 2-53, 9yo 6-46, 10yo 1-36, 11yo 0-19, 12yo 0-10, 13yo 0-5 **FAVOURITES:** £4.00

FATE OF FAVOURITES: 0F123001U0 **POSITION OF WINNER IN MARKET:** 0310050185

OR 107-118 2-3-39, **119-130** 6-23-129, **131-142** 2-4-62

RECORD OF IRISH RUNNERS: 0-4-32 (-£32.00) **HORSES WEARING HEADGEAR:** 0-3-46 (-£46.00)

Key trends
- Rated within 8lb of RPR top-rated, 10/10
- Aged seven to ten, 10/10
- Ran over at least 3m last time out, 9/10
- Won a handicap chase, 9/10
- Officially rated no more than 128s, 8/10 (six in the 120s)
- Finished in first three in either or both of last two starts, 8/10 (two exceptions both trained by Martin Pipe)
- Won over at least 3m, 8/10

Other factors
- The Irish have not won this since Greasepaint in 1983
- Four winners had run at a previous festival, including two who were fourth and fifth in the William Hill Handicap Chase
- Six winners had run within the last 25 days, the other four had been off for at least 61
- Five winners were ridden by claiming amateurs, but four of the last five were non-claiming amateurs

Notes

Friday March 19, 2010 (New Course)

1.30
Race 1

JCB Triumph Hurdle
(Grade 1)

C4/RUK

2m1f

Key stats Eleven of the last 12 winners had been 'first past the post' last time out. Shocks are becoming rarer – seven of the last ten winners were in the first four in the betting

The Irish don't have such a good record in this race (four winners in the past 20 years) as in the other novice hurdles, but they have a strong raiding party this time with impressive Fairyhouse scorer Alaivan, Carlito Brigante – who beat a below-par Alaivan over Christmas in the middle leg of a hat-trick – and Secant Star from the Willie Mullins stable. Mille Chief, the long-time favourite, lost that position when he was found to be lame and had to miss his intended prep in the Adonis Hurdle, casting doubt over his participation. In Mille Chief's absence, Nicky Henderson's Soldatino took the Adonis to put himself in the reckoning and other leading British hopes are Advisor for Paul Nicholls and the Charles Egerton-trained Westlin' Winds.

Alaivan

4 b g; Trainer Edward O'Grady
Hurdles form 121, best RPR 142
Left-handed 2, best RPR 131
Right-handed 11, best RPR 142

Just about Group class at middle distances on the Flat after only four runs and jumped well when making an eyecatching winning debut at Gowran Park in December, scoring in a canter by 15 lengths. Started 4-9 for a Leopardstown Grade 2 just 15 days later, but got taken on for the lead and had no answer to Carlito Brigante (rated 36lb inferior on the Flat), who won by 11 lengths. Back on song at Fairyhouse in February, winning by an easy 17 lengths, and is right up there on form. This is probably coincidental, but in a seven-race career (Flat and jumps) his form figures right-handed are 12111, while left-handed they are 52.

Edward O'Grady's Alaivan put his bad Leopardstown run behind him with an easy win at Fairyhouse last time

Carlito Brigante is part of a strong Irish team, having won three out of four over hurdles

Carlito Brigante

4 b g; Trainer Gordon Elliott
Hurdles form 0111, best RPR 142
Left-handed 01, best RPR 142
Right-handed 11, best RPR 137

Nothing special on the Flat, but at least stayed well and has bust a few reputations on his climb up the ranks. Tailed off on heavy ground on his debut, he appreciated the better surface when springing a 20-1 surprise at Musselburgh five days later, but that was a still a long way from the form he showed a month later when taking a Grade 2 at Leopardstown by 11l from early ante-post favourite Alaivan. He travelled supremely well that day, suggesting there was no fluke about the win, and he was again impressive in his final prep in the Scottish Triumph Hurdle, staying on strongly for a six-length win. Looks to be improving fast and has already shown a good deal more (16lb according to RPRs) than the current favourite.

Secant Star

4 b g; Trainer Willie Mullins
Hurdles form F1, best RPR 128
Left-handed F, best RPR 121
Right-handed 1, best RPR 128

The winner of an AQPS Flat race in the French provinces as a three-year-old, he looked set for a winning debut over hurdles at Leopardstown in December when falling at the last. Made no mistake the following month in a weak contest at Gowran Park, winning by an easy seven lengths at odds of 2-5. Not a trends pick by any means, as it would be unusual for a horse unraced under Flat rules to win this and he has less experience than most winners. He could do with more experience of hurdles, as he was not fluent on either start, while his trainer says he is a chaser in the making. Has not done enough to merit his odds, with identity of trainer (last Irishman to win Triumph, with Scolardy in 2002) to blame for that.

Mille Chief
4 b g; Trainer Alan King
Hurdles form (all right-handed) B11, best RPR 126

Ante-post favourite for much of the winter, but went lame prior to his intended prep in the Adonis Hurdle at Kempton and stable now faces a race against time to get him ready. The novice races tend to have far more trends qualifiers than most, so it's no surprise that he scores on most counts, although the fact his sire never won a Group 1 (the sires of eight of the last ten winners had) is one black mark. Hasn't done much wrong so far, as he was unlucky to be brought down on his debut and has won twice since. Had to work hard enough for the first win and a peak RPR of 126 is unusually low for one who has stood as favourite for a couple of months – at this point last year there were at least five contenders boasting an RPR at least 12lb superior to Mille Chief's.

Advisor
4 gr g; Trainer Paul Nicholls
Hurdles form 11, best RPR 124
Left-handed 1, best RPR 124
Right-handed 1, best RPR 124

Fairly useful on the Flat for Michael Bell (rated 81) and just about stayed 1m4f, though appeared a little quirky. No signs of waywardness so far in his new job, handling testing conditions really well to run away with a Newbury juvenile event in December. The form of that hasn't worked out at all well, but Advisor has at least gone in again, this time taking an Ascot contest by three lengths from the hard-pulling Barwell Bridge, who was around 10lb superior on the Flat at his peak. By process of elimination has become the No. 1 contender for the Nicholls stable, but a best RPR of 124 tells you that his form is nothing special. Could do with another run to get the required amount of experience.

Pittoni
4 b c; Trainer Charles Byrnes
Hurdles form 1113, best RPR 124
Left-handed 13, best RPR 124
Right-handed 11, best RPR 124

Earned a rating of 95 on the Flat following a wide-margin maiden win on his final start and already useful over hurdles, winning three of his four starts. It's hard to know what he achieved when winning a small-field Grade 1 on his third outing (RPRs says not a lot, with a rating of 124) and he disappointed on his final prep at Navan in February, albeit against useful older rivals. It's unusual these days for a winner of this to come into the race undefeated (only two of the last ten winners had), so he can probably be forgiven that and his trainer is of the opinion that he'll be better in a much stronger-run race. That said, he also believes soft ground is a must, which is a worry given the Triumph falls on the last day of the festival.

Westlin' Winds
4 b c; Trainer Charles Egerton
Hurdles form 112, best RPR 133
Left-handed 1, best RPR 133
Right-handed 12, best RPR 133

Lightly raced on the Flat and rated only 71, but has developed into a fairly decent juvenile hurdler, winning his first two starts by wide margins at Hereford and Plumpton before running into Mille Chief at Kempton. Led at a strong pace that day, but looked like giving the winner a much tougher battle until ploughing through the last. Came out of the race the better horse at the weights, as he was giving 7lb yet was beaten just over two lengths. The winner is entitled to improve, but so is Westlin' Winds, though he could do with another run as it's been a while since a winner of this had not raced in the year of his win. Other than that he fulfils all trends, though it has been noted that other sons of Montjeu have not exactly excelled themselves up the final hill at Cheltenham.

Pistolet Noir was beaten on his only start since being transferred to Paul Nicholls

Soldatino

4 gr g; Trainer Nicky Henderson
Hurdles form (both right-handed) 11, best RPR 132

Won a hurdle for non-thoroughbred four-year-olds at Pau in January and made his British debut at Kempton at the end of February, running out a striking winner of the Grade 2 Adonis Hurdle. That race has been won by a host of good horses in recent seasons, including Triumph winners Snow Drop and Penzance and festival novice hurdle runners-up Well Chief (also won Arkle) and Binocular. This year's running looked weak, but he did it well and clearly stays well. Having not run on the Flat, he is inexperienced for this type of test and looks more of a long-term prospect.

Notus De La Tour

4 b g; Trainer David Pipe
Hurdles form (all left-handed) 43611, best RPR 126

Showed dramatic improvement to land last of four hurdles starts at Auteuil by 20l and subsequently picked up by David Pipe, for whom he was equally impressive on his debut at Plumpton in January. He turned over long odds-on shot Ranjobaie from the Nicky Henderson stable there, making ground in taking fashion down the far side and then asserting after they had jumped the second-last. The form doesn't amount to much, but he jumped fluently and gave the impression there was plenty more to come, so he's worth keeping an eye on.

Pistolet Noir

4 b g; Trainer Paul Nicholls
Hurdles form (all left-handed) 312, best RPR 134
Cheltenham form 12, best RPR 134

Did not hit the racecourse until October, finishing a close third in a Chepstow juvenile hurdle. The form did not look particularly good, but as a product of the Nick Williams academy he was always likely to improve dramatically and only a month later was a heavily backed winner of a Grade 2 at Cheltenham, winning by nine lengths from Barizan with a further four and a half back to his Chepstow conqueror Olofi in third. That prompted a big-money transfer to the champion trainer, though all has not gone to plan as Pistolet Noir made several clumsy errors on his first start for the yard in the Grade 2 Finesse at Cheltenham in January, finishing two-lengths second to 100-1 winner Baccalaureate (since well beaten by Carlito Brigante at Musselburgh). Will not be a high scorer on trends unless he wins again before the races, as he hasn't won at least 50 per cent of his starts, didn't win last time out and is not by a Group 1-winning sire, but he's not far off the best on form despite all that.

Other contenders

Even at the start of March the Triumph looks a wide-open heat, with nothing having taken a firm grip on the market, and there are plenty who could yet make an impression. Pistolet Noir's former trainer Nick Williams has a similar type in **Me Voici**, who showed nothing on his racecourse debut in September but has made big leaps in three starts since, most notably when thrashing Nicholls talking horse Sang Bleu at Chepstow in the Finale Hurdle over Christmas. That race has been a notoriously poor guide, though, with the last horse to win both being Mysilv in 1994, and he is far from a certain runner. **Barizan** had chalked up a sequence of easy wins before Pistolet Noir took his measure in November and he's been off the track since. The Paul Nolan-trained **Politeo** put up a decent effort on his Thurles debut at the end of January, but appeared to be put well in his place by Alaivan at Fairyhouse. **Diktalina** was poor on the Flat, but she seems to love jumping and punctured a few reputations when scorching home by eight lengths from Anak (Henderson hotpot According tailed off) at Sandown in February. That form needs improving upon and she failed to do that when thumped by Me Voici at Haydock next time. Among the more lightly raced types, **Barwell Bridge** makes some appeal. He was three-lengths second to Advisor at Ascot in January, but pulled far too hard and was staying on again at the death, and it was a similar story six days later at Doncaster. When he gets a fast pace he looks sure to put up an improved performance, though his former connections thought he was better on flat tracks. Nicky Henderson's **Super Kenny** had only seven ahead of him in the betting come the beginning of March, but had still to jump a hurdle in public. ■

Notes

JCB TRIUMPH HURDLE (GRADE 1)
Friday 1.30   **2m1f**

FORM	WINNER	AGE & WGT	WINNING RPR	PRE-RACE RPR	SP	TRAINER	H.Runs	BEST RPR LAST 12 MONTHS (RUNS SINCE)
09 11	Zaynar D	4 11-0	154	141	11-2	N Henderson	2(18GS)	won Newbury class 4 nov hdl (2m¹/₂f) (1)
08 12	Celestial Halo D, BF	4 11-0	149	133	5-1	P Nicholls	2(14GS)	won Newbury class 3 nov hdl (2m¹/₂f) (1)
07 12111	Katchit CD	4 11-0	154	136	11-2	A King	6(23GS)	won Cheltenham class 1 nov hdl Gd2 (2m1f) (0)
06 811	Detroit City D	4 11-0	152	135	7-2F	P Hobbs	3(17G)	won Sandown class 3 nov hdl (2m¹/₂f) (0)
05 111	Penzance D	4 11-0	141	127	9-1	A King	3(23G)	won Kempton class 1 nov hdl Gd2 (2m) (0)
04 331	Made In Japan D	4 11-0	140	120	20-1	P Hobbs	3(23G)	won Sandown class 3 nov hdl (2m¹/₂f) (0)
03 1B41	Spectroscope	4 11-0	137	121	20-1	Jonjo O'Neill	4(27G)	won Kempton class 3 nov hdl (2m) (0)
02 71211d	Scolardy	4 11-0	144	135	16-1	W Mullins (Ir)	5(28G)	2nd Leopardstown nov hdl Gd3 (2m) (0)
01	cancelled							
00 21141	Snow Drop D	4 10-9	140	144	7-1F	F Doumen (Fr)	6(28GF)	won Adonis Nov Hdl Gd2 (2m) (0)
99 -3111	Katarino C, D	4 11-0	155	158	11-4F	N Henderson	5(23GS)	won Adonis Nov Hdl Gd2 (2m) (0)

FAVOURITES: +£6.25

TRAINERS IN THIS RACE (w-pl-r): A King 2-2-8, P Hobbs 2-2-8, F Doumen 1-0-7, N Twiston-Davies 1-0-4, N Henderson 1-1-13, P Nicholls 1-0-8, W Mullins 1-2-9, C Mann 0-1-4, C Roche 0-1-2, Howard Johnson 0-1-2, M Halford 0-1-1, Miss Venetia Williams 0-1-5

FATE OF FAVOURITES: 0411P30310 **POSITION OF WINNER IN MARKET:** 4611800412

RECORD OF IRISH RUNNERS: 1-7-58 (-£41.00) **HORSES WEARING HEADGEAR:** 2-2-27 (-£16.00)

RECORD OF TRIAL WINNERS: Juvenile Novices (Cheltenham, November) **1B042127;** Durkan Juvenile (Leopardstown, December) **002030** Finale (Chepstow, December) **0F522;** Finesse (Cheltenham, January) **00B03122;** Adonis (Kempton, February) **11P201F5**

Key trends
▶▶Last ran between 19 and 55 days ago, 10/10

▶▶Ran between two and six times over hurdles, 10/10

▶▶'First past the post' last time out, 9/10 (exception beaten in an all-aged novice event)

▶▶Won at least 50 per cent of hurdle races, 9/10

▶▶By Group 1-winning sire, 9/10

▶▶Pre-race RPR of at least 123, 8/10

Other factors
▶▶There has been no once-raced winner in the past 30 years

▶▶Only two winners had been undefeated over hurdles

▶▶Five had won Graded hurdle events (three took the Adonis), but only one before mid-January. The last winner of Chepstow's Finale Hurdle to win this was Mysilv in 1994

▶▶Of the seven who raced on the Flat in Britain and Ireland, six had recorded a RPR of at least 83

▶▶Six had won and two placed over middle distances (1m2f-1m6f)

▶▶Since the introduction of the Fred Winter Hurdle all five winners have come from the first four in the betting, suggesting the days of upsets are long gone

Notes

2.05
Race 2

Vincent O'Brien County Handicap Hurdle
(Grade 3)

2m1f

Key stats Four of the last eight winners had run in the Totesport Trophy (where they finished 2183). Seven of the last 11 winners were five-year-olds

American Trilogy: first-season novice winner

Gerald Delamere's view Paul Nicholls' novice American Trilogy ran away with this race last year, confirming it as the champion trainer's best handicap at the festival with three wins in six years (he has also had a second and a fourth in that period). Nicholls controlled the weights with Rigmarole in 2004 and 2005, winning the first of those races with Sporazene, and in 2006 it was Sporazene who kept the weights down for Desert Quest to score again for Nicholls. The latter was topweight in 2007 but Ouninpohja wouldn't put his best foot forward and finished second.

The winner has come from the five to seven age range on 29 occasions in the past 34 renewals. American Trilogy's win was only the sixth by a first-season novice and just one of those novices was aged five, which is surprising as 15 winners have come from that age group.

In the past 11 renewals 11st 7lb and 11st 8lb have been carried to victory, otherwise 11st 2lb has been the maximum since 1972. A Tote Gold Trophy winner, Neblin, won off 150 less a 7lb claim. Sporazene, rated 151, carried only 10st 13lb after Rigmarole's withdrawal in 2004 meant that the bottom weights all ran off a ridiculous mark of 138. Hopefully, with a level playing field, the best range to find the winner will be between 130 and 140.

Last-time-out performances were 111924522 114021153123141212178139, so it is best to find a horse in form. Many will feel that the Totesport Trophy is the place to find the winner, as recent winners were placed 31042173 at Newbury. Outside the Newbury feature look for a late February or an early March run, because winners often had a recent run. Doncaster form has been reliable and between 1975 and 2005 winners had been placed 12422224 there. Seven of the past ten winners had form over this course in the season of their success. Three Imperial Cup winners followed up under the 7lb penalty and Neblin, an also-ran at Sandown, also came out of that race to win.

The victory of Silver Jaro in 2008 was only the second big shock if you ignore Current Romance's victory at 20-1 in 1973. With 30 of the 34 winners at 16-1 and under, it isn't a bad festival handicap for backers, though just six

favourites have been successful.

In the past two decades Philip Hobbs has had two victories, a second, two thirds, a fourth and a fifth. After the Staplestown gamble in 1981, the next Irish-trained victory wasn't until 2003, but the Irish have won twice more since then, in 2007 and 2008. All three Irish-trained winners in the past decade had finished in the first three in the Totesport Trophy or MCR (Pierse) Hurdle that season. ■

VINCENT O'BRIEN COUNTY HANDICAP HURDLE (GRADE 3)

Friday 2.05   2m1f

FORM	WINNER	AGE & WGT	OR	SP	TRAINER	H.Runs	BEST RPR LAST 12 MONTHS(RUNS SINCE)
09 1349	American Trilogy D	5 11-0	135-7	20-1	P Nicholls	4(27GS)	3rd Cheltenham nov hdl Gd2 (2m1/2f) (2)
08 22233	Silver Jaro BF	5 10-13	132-1	50-1	T Hogan (Ir)	10(22GS)	3rd Pierse Hcap Hdl (2m) (1)
07 -1713	Pedrobob	9 10-0	135-10	12-1	Anthony Mullins (Ir)	7(28GS)	3rd Totesport Trophy Hcap Hdl Gd3 (2m1/2f) (0)
06 U1131	Desert Quest (4x) D	6 10-10	131-4	4-1J	P Nicholls	8(29G)	won Newbury class 3 hcap hdl (2m1/2f) (0)
05 60048	Fontanesi (5oh) D	5 10-0	128-2	16-1	M Pipe	16(30G)	2nd Aintree class 3 hcap hdl (2m1/2f) (9)
04 -1238	Sporazene	5 10-13	151-6	7-1J	P Nicholls	7(23G)	2nd Newbury class 1 Lstd hcap hdl (2m1/2f) (2)
03 23151	Spirit Leader D	7 11-7	140-19	10-1	Mrs J Harrington (Ir)	14(28G)	won Totesport Trophy Hcap Hdl Gd3 (2m1/2f)(0)
02 55422	Rooster Booster D	8 11-1	144-2	8-1	P Hobbs	19(21G)	2nd Totesport Trophy Hcap Hdl Gd3 (2m1/2f)(0)
01	cancelled						
00 04811	Master Tern (7x) CD	5 10-3	130T	9-2F	Jonjo O'Neill	8(21GF)	won Kelso class 2 hdl (2m2f) (0)
99 2-152	Sir Talbot (1oh) D	5 10-0	135-8	10-1	J Old	5(28GS)	won Chepstow class 3 hdl (2m1/2f) (2)

WINS-RUNS: 5yo 6-55, 6yo 1-77, 7yo 1-56, 8yo 1-38, 9yo 1-18, 10yo 0-7, 11yo 0-4, 12yo 0-2 **FAVOURITES:** +£2.00

FATE OF FAVOURITES: 210P101026 **POSITION OF WINNER IN MARKET:** 4134181407 **OR** 122-134 4-17-114, 135-148 5-11-132, 149-161 1-2-11

RECORD OF IRISH RUNNERS: 3-6-54 (+£21.00) **HORSES WEARING HEADGEAR:** 1-1-39 (-£18.00)

Key trends

▶▶Ran between 4 and 16 times over hurdles, 9/10

▶▶Achieved career-best RPR of at least 129 on a left-handed track, 10/10

▶▶Officially rated 128 to 144, 9/10 (six in the 130s)

▶▶Carried no more than 11st 1lb, 9/10

▶▶Ran in the last 35 days, 9/10

▶▶No previous festival form, 9/10

▶▶Started no bigger than 20-1, 9/10

▶▶Aged five or six, 7/10

▶▶Top-four finish last time out, 7/10

▶▶Finished first or second in at least 40 per cent of starts that season, 7/10

Other factors

▶▶No winner was more than 5lb out of the handicap

▶▶There have been three winning novices (since 1996), all three of whom were rated no higher than 135

▶▶Seventeen of the 30 placed horses started 25-1 or bigger

▶▶Four winners ran in the Totesport Trophy, where they finished 2183; two ran in the Pierse (now MCR), where they came 53

▶▶Paul Nicholls has had three winners, a second and a fourth in the past six years

2.40
Race 3

Albert Bartlett Novices' Hurdle
(Grade 1)

`C4/RUK`

3m

Key stats All five winners had finished first or second last time out. Alan King (one winner, one third) has a good record

Running plans will become clearer near the day, with several of the principals having the alternative option of going for the shorter Neptune Novices' Hurdle two days earlier, but this is shaping up into a competitive contest. Tell Massini, who has won all three hurdles starts and has a course-and-distance success to his credit, is a leading chance for Tom George and another smaller stable with high hopes is Robin Dickin's Warwickshire yard, which houses Restless Harry, a course winner last time over 2m5f. Among the big-name trainers, Willie Mullins can choose from Quel Esprit, Enterprise Park and Fionnegas, Alan King has The Betchworth Kid and Paul Nicholls could send French Grade 1 winner Najaf. Paul Nolan's Shinrock Paddy is another leading chance.

Tell Massini

6 b g; Trainer Tom George
Hurdles form (all left-handed) 111, best RPR 150
Cheltenham form 11, best RPR 150

This is only the sixth running of the 3m novice at the festival, but already some strong trends have developed and he fulfils all of them. Weapon's Amnesty last season became only the second winner not to have won previously around Cheltenham, but all three British-trained winners had and Tell Massini has done so twice. He caused a minor upset when making all and staying on far too strongly for Reve De Sivola over 2m5f at the course in November and then made it a Grade 2 double upped to 3m the following month, when again in the front rank throughout and having more in hand than the official 2½l margin over Kennel Hill (Grand National winner Mon Mome 8l back in third) suggested. Looks a strong candidate on the strength of those successes, with the only possible negative being that he has never raced on anything other than soft ground. He clearly handles cut very well and it remains to be seen what he can do on livelier ground.

Shinrock Paddy

6 b g; Trainer Paul Nolan
Hurdles form 11, best RPR 151
Left-handed 1, best RPR 151
Right-handed 1, best RPR 125
Cheltenham form (bumpers) 18, best RPR 131
At the festival 11 Mar 09: mostly chased leader to 4f out, lost place 3f out, no danger after, weakened final 2f, finished eighth, beaten 32l by Dunguib in Champion Bumper

Useful bumper horse ridden by owner Barry Connell to respectable eighth in last season's Champion Bumper. Professionally handled since, first having to battle hard to win a 2m novice hurdle at Punchestown and then leaving that form way behind with a 15-length Grade 1 win over 2m4f at Navan in December. It probably makes sense to be cautious of big figures earned in small fields (only four ran) on bad ground, but he was impressive and the third and fourth have won good novice hurdles since and are possibly Cheltenham-bound. He falls down on trends because he hasn't won over at least 2m5f (though he looked a proper stayer at Navan) and hasn't had three or more runs over hurdles, but he is a course winner,

Restless Harry is a major player following his commanding win in a Grade 2 at Cheltenham

having taken a bumper in impressive fashion last season. Also entered in the Neptune, but a good deal shorter in the betting for this and worthy of respect for a trainer whose horses invariably perform well when sent to Cheltenham.

Restless Harry
6 b g; Trainer Robin Dickin
Hurdles form 27121, best RPR 149
Left-handed 21, best RPR 149
Right-handed 271, best RPR 131

Trainer is not used to success at the highest level, but he has done nothing wrong with this one, who has improved from defeat in a Towcester maiden hurdle in May to a commanding Grade 2 Cheltenham winner in January. His first experience of really bad ground came when he hosed up at Towcester in November and he went on to bely odds of 40-1 when running a half-length second to Reve De Sivola in the Challow at Newbury, rallying gamely close home. Proved that was

no fluke when making all and puncturing a few reputations at Cheltenham after that, winning going away from Nicky Henderson's General Miller, with the Paul Nicholls-trained hot favourite Royal Charm a distant third. There didn't seem to be any element of fluke about the win and he satisfies all the key trends criteria, though whether he will be quite so effective on faster ground is a worry (beaten first two starts on good).

Quel Esprit
6 b g; Trainer Willie Mullins
Hurdles form 112, best RPR 144
Left-handed 2, best RPR 144
Right-handed 11, best RPR 144
Cheltenham form (bumper) 4, best RPR 137
At the festival 11 Mar 09: tracked leaders, close enough 3f out, soon well outpaced, edged left but kept on, finished fourth, beaten 13l by Dunguib in Champion Bumper

Worthy of inclusion here because he is shorter in the betting for this race than the Neptune, although his trainer said the shorter race was still very much the target after his Leopardstown defeat in January. He is not short of pace, as last year's fourth in the Champion Bumper suggests, but he clearly has stamina in abundance as he has already won over 3m on bad ground. On trends, he's bang on the money apart from the lack of a course win, but we shouldn't hold that against him given that he's trained in Ireland.

Enterprise Park

6 b g; Trainer Willie Mullins
Hurdles form (both right-handed) 11, best RPR 139

Slightly short on experience after only two starts over hurdles, but otherwise fulfils the key criteria for an Irish-trained horse. Another from the powerful Willie Mullins stable, he's also in the Neptune, but looked very much a stayer when supplementing his maiden hurdle win (2m) with victory in a Limerick Grade 3 over 2m6f, staying on well and winning comfortably by a shade under six lengths from Quito De La Roque, who won a Listed hurdle next time. The third also went in on his next start, so the form looks solid enough, although he has not always been the most fluent and may be best served by getting some more experience.

The Betchworth Kid

5 b g; Trainer Alan King
Hurdles form 123, best RPR 132
Left-handed 1, best RPR 118
Right-handed 23, best RPR 132

This race has yet to be won by an ex-Flat racer, while only one of the five winners has been as young as five and, as it stands, The Betchworth Kid falls down on many key trends. For a start, he has not won over 2m5f, his best pre-race RPR is a fair way off the usual standard, he hasn't managed a top-two in a Graded hurdle and probably doesn't even know where Cheltenham is. He was backed for this at long odds before an intended step up in trip to 3m at Doncaster was aborted in January because of frost and he showed his best form last time at Kempton stepped up to 2m5f when, though

only third, he was running on strongly at the death, giving the impression that a really stiff test of stamina will suit. Still has a fair amount to prove.

Najaf

5 b g; Trainer Paul Nicholls
Hurdles form 431231, best RPR 145
Left-handed 43123, best RPR 145
Right-handed 1, best RPR 127

Paul Nicholls nearly won this with Pride Of Dulcote last season, but this one is as yet a relative unknown, having raced only once in Britain, when taking a relatively weak Listed event at Exeter in February in workmanlike fashion from Gifted Leader (rated 124). His French form was better, as he stayed on strongly for third on his final start there in a 2m4f Grade 1 on heavy ground at Auteuil, giving every indication that he wants a decent test. He was less than two lengths behind Jumbo Rio, who returned to Ireland to run third behind Solwhit in the December Festival Hurdle, so the form is fairly useful. Not a strong trends scorer as yet, but he represents a powerful combination of owners and is not to be discounted if he turns up.

The Betchworth Kid: falls down on key trends

Premier Victory

6 b m; Trainer Tom Hogan
Hurdles form (all right-handed) 1152112,
best RPR 142

Slow learner in bumpers, getting off the mark at the fourth attempt, but much better over hurdles, winning four of her six starts. She had allergy problems at the end of the summer but returned in November in fine heart, first taking a 2m Grade 3 at Down Royal by an easy nine lengths and then winning by 11 lengths in another Grade 3, this time over 3m at Cork. Those were not the strongest of Graded events, but you can't do more than beat what is put in front of you and she has done it well. Beaten into second in a Grade 2 at Thurles in February, but trainer said she needed it. Fulfils all the key trends other than a course win at Cheltenham, but the main worry is that in ten career starts she has never set foot on a left-handed track.

Silver Kate

7 gr m; Trainer David Richards
Hurdles form 511231, best RPR 142
Left-handed 51121, best RPR 142
Right-handed 3, best RPR 137

Useful mare in bumpers and, though she doesn't have a top-two Graded finish last time and has never been to Cheltenham, she has a progressive profile, having improved her hurdles RPR with every start. Having won a couple of novices, her big improvement started when stepped up to 3m and out of novice company for a Grade 2 mares' event at Ascot, where she belied her inexperience to finish a close third. She followed that with an easy win over a couple of well-touted rivals at Bangor, so she's worth her place in the betting, if having a bit to find even on that form.

The Hurl

7 b g; Trainer Mouse Morris
Hurdles form 4640P212131, best RPR 142
Left-handed 44213, best RPR 134
Right-handed 60P211, best RPR 142

This is his third season as a novice and, though he was nothing special in the first two, the penny seems to have dropped this term, as he hasn't finished out of the first three in six starts since October. He doesn't have a last-time-out top two in a Graded hurdle, but scores on most other trends and seems progressive enough. Though a fair way behind when third to Shinrock Paddy in a Navan Grade 1 in December, he upped his level when tackling 3m for the first time at Fairyhouse in January, proving that stamina is his strong suit. Less obvious than most, but looks tough.

Other contenders

Willie Mullins has his usual strong hand and, as well as Quel Esprit and Enterprise Park, his **Fionnegas** is well up in the betting for this, but has been dealt with in the Neptune preview and also has an entry in the Supreme Novices'. There are some fascinating entries for some of the more established stars of the winter game, including last season's Hennessy winner **Madison Du Berlais** (has never handled Cheltenham particularly well), Grand National entry **Possol** (shown good form in novice hurdles this winter) and 2009 Foxhunter winner **Cappa Bleu** (hasn't shown much at all).

Among the more lightly raced types, Emma Lavelle introduced a potentially high-class hurdling recruit at Exeter in February in **Court In Motion**, who certainly looked the part when well on his way to hacking up only to fall at the last. He is going to need some more experience quickly and show that he is over that bad episode, but he is a horse of some potential. Paul Nicholls' **Vico** is as low as 20-1 with some firms, but that is surely down to the stable he comes from rather than anything he has done on the course, as the evidence of his racecourse debut suggests he's got the best part of 3st to find. Cesarewitch third **Sereth** has an entry for Barney Curley, but needs to improve markedly on what he has done in three starts over hurdles, though that is possible given he was once rated 105 on the Flat and should be a lot better at this game when going up in trip. ∎

ALBERT BARTLETT NOVICES' HURDLE (GRADE 1)

Friday 2.40   **3m**

FORM	WINNER	AGE	& WGT	WINNING RPR	PRE-RACE RPR	SP	TRAINER	H.Runs	BEST RPR LAST 12 MONTHS (RUNS SINCE)
09 -5112	Weapon's Amnesty D, BF	6	11-7	154	145	8-1	C Byrnes (Ir)	4(17GS)	2nd Leopardstown nov hdl Gd2 (2m4f) (0)
08 1-212	Nenuphar Collonges CD	7	11-7	147	139	9-1	A King	4(18GS)	2nd Warwick class 1 nov hdl Gd2 (2m5f) (0)
07 -1211	Wichita Lineman C	6	11-7	155	154	11-8F	Jonjo O'Neill	4(20GS)	won Challow Hurdle Gd1 (2m5f) (1)
06 1-111	Black Jack Ketchum CD	7	11-7	159	154	EvensF	Jonjo O'Neill	3(19G)	won Cheltenham class 1 nov hdl Gd2 (3m) (0)
05 62162	Moulin Riche	5	11-7	146	146	9-1	F Doumen (Fr)	8(18G)	2nd Haydock class 1 nov hdl Gd2 (2m7¹/₂f) (0)

WINS-RUNS: 5yo 1-16, 6yo 2-35, 7yo 2-29, 8yo 0-11, 9yo 0-1 **FAVOURITES:**-£0.63

TRAINERS IN THIS RACE (w-pl-r): A King 1-1-6, C J Mann 0-1-1, Ian Williams 0-1-1, P Nicholls 0-2-4, W Mullins 0-1-3

FATE OF FAVOURITES: 31132 **POSITION OF WINNER IN MARKET:** 51154

RECORD OF IRISH RUNNERS: 1-4-24 (-£15.00) **HORSES WEARING HEADGEAR:** 1-0-8 (+£2.00)

RECORD OF TRIAL WINNERS: Bristol Hurdle (Cheltenham, December) **3141;** Barry & Sandra Kelly Memorial Hurdle (Navan, December) **3**
Challow Hurdle (Newbury, December) **31;** River Don Hurdle (Doncaster, January) **F85**

Key trends

▶▶Pre-race RPR of at least 139, 5/5

▶▶Won over 2m5f or further, 5/5

▶▶At least three runs over hurdles, 5/5

▶▶Top-two finish in a Graded hurdle last time out, 5/5 (two won, three placed)

▶▶Aged six or seven, 4/5

▶▶Course winner, 3/5

Other factors

▶▶The four British and Irish-trained winners had all won a Graded hurdle, while the French-trained victor had won a Listed handicap hurdle

▶▶Four winners had raced around Cheltenham at least twice

Notes

The fastest way to bet

Bet directly through **RACINGPOST.com**
by using your existing bookmaker account

Click the **red odds**
to strike a bet

HORSE	RPR	BEST ODDS	William HILL	Paddy Power	bet365	bluesq
KAUTO STAR	196	4/5	4/6	8/11	4/6	8/11
DENMAN	188	7/2	7/2	7/2	10/3	7/2
COOLDINE	167			12	12	12
TARANIS	168			25	25	20

3.20
Race 4
Totesport Cheltenham Gold Cup Chase
(Grade 1)

C4/RUK

$3m2^1/_2f$

Key stats Kauto Star last year became the first winner to improve on a placed run from the previous year since Bregawn in 1983. Nine of the last ten winners had achieved a chase RPR of at least 172

This was shaping up as the definitive clash between top-class stablemates Kauto Star and Denman, who have shared the Gold Cup between them for the past three years, but then Denman crashed out in spectacular fashion in his warm-up race – the Aon Chase at Newbury in February – and the balance tilted firmly in the defending champion's favour. Kauto Star was given a tough battle by Imperial Commander on his reappearance at Haydock but was unstoppable in the King George as he became the first chaser to win the mid-season championship four years in a row. With doubts over Denman, there is more hope for the others – principally Imperial Commander and Cooldine, last year's RSA Chase winner – but Kauto Star will be hard to stop in his bid for a third Gold Cup.

Kauto Star

10 b g; Trainer Paul Nicholls
Chase form 1221F1111112111221U1111
Left-handed 1F11112122U11, best RPR 185
Right-handed 2211111111, best RPR 192
Cheltenham form F121, best RPR 185
At the festival 15 Mar 2006: tracking leaders when fell 3rd in Champion Chase won by Newmill

16 Mar 2007: led two out in Gold Cup to beat Exotic Dancer by $2^1/2$ lengths

14 Mar 2008: not fluent throughout and well held last in Gold Cup, finished second to Denman, beaten 7l

13 Mar 2009: tracked leaders, disputed close 2nd 4 out, quickened to challenge 3 out and led soon after, came clear before last, impressive, won Gold Cup by 13l from Denman

Had already proved himself the outstanding chaser of the last 20 years prior to last season's Gold Cup, but has taken career to a new level over the past 12 months. Became the first horse to regain the Gold Cup with an emphatic 13-length success over below-par stablemate Denman, thus making the score 1-1 in meetings between them and recording a career-best RPR of 185 in the process. Was made to battle by Imperial Commander on seasonal return on heavy ground in the Betfair Chase at

Haydock in November – a race that doesn't always bring out the best in him despite three wins in it – but was simply awesome back on decent ground in the King George at Kempton. Drew comparisons with Arkle when becoming the first horse to win the race four years in a row with a truly sensational 36-length victory that earned him a new RPR best of 192 and an official handicap mark of 195. Though some clock-watchers subsequently cast some doubt on the overall merit of the form (and the handicapper had a rethink by dropping him 2lb), he was the only one who could live with the pace set by the trail-blazing Nacarat and his superiority over the field was clear with a mile to run. Trends-wise, he's had far more chase runs than a normal Gold Cup winner, though that was also the case last year, and ten-year-old winners are a rarity these days (only six in the last 40 years and none since 1998). It goes without saying, though, that none of the ten-year-old runners was anywhere near as good as Kauto Star. Paul Nicholls has stuck to the same three-run plan as last season, with the trainer reporting that Kauto Star is "lethal" when very fit and very fresh. Obviously goes into the race as the outstanding candidate for a third Gold Cup and was odds-against only because he had such a high-quality opponent in Denman. However, with Denman so lacklustre at Newbury on his prep in the Aon, he was rightly made odds-on.

Denman

10 ch g; Trainer Paul Nicholls
Chase form 11111111122F1U
Left-handed 111111112F1U, best RPR 184
Right-handed 12, best RPR 158
Cheltenham form 121112, best RPR 184
At the festival 15 Mar 06: headed after last, stayed on one pace, second to Nicanor in Ballymore Properties Hurdle, beaten 2^1/2l

14 Mar 07: Led and left clear three out, stormed home, beat Snowy Morning 10l in RSA Chase

14 Mar 08: led 12th, kicked clear after four out, driven out, beat Kauto Star 7l in Gold Cup

13 Mar 09: chased leaders, disputed close 2nd 4 out, challenged next, soon outpaced by winner but stayed on gamely under pressure, finished second to Kauto Star in Gold Cup, beaten 13l

Heart problems were much publicised before last season's truncated campaign, which saw him finish a below-par distant second to Madison Du Berlais at Kempton, a more meritorious but still well-held second to Kauto Star in defence of his Gold Cup and then fall heavily two out when challenging Madison Du Berlais in the Totesport Bowl at Aintree. The form he showed on his final two starts of last season was still better than most horses manage, but the question of whether he would ever return to his best had by no means been answered when he turned up at Newbury in November in a bid to win a second Hennessy under top weight, this time off a handicap mark 13lb higher than in 2007. With trainer Paul Nicholls making bullish noises about him for the first time in more than a year, Denman was a public gamble and he didn't let his adoring fans down as he took apart some high-class rivals with a superb display of bold jumping and relentless galloping despite conceding 13lb or more all round. Stablemate and runner-up What A Friend won the Grade 1 Lexus Chase on his next start and, while that may not have been the best field ever

assembled at Leopardstown, the fact that Denman had given him 22lb and a three-and-a-half-length beating puts his achievement into perspective. The 'glorified racecourse gallop' that Nicholls was hoping for in the Aon at Newbury in February did not work out as planned, with Denman making an horrific mistake at the fourth-last before unseating new jockey Tony McCoy at the next. Much was made about McCoy's suitability for the horse, but Denman looked to many as if he was struggling to see off Niche Market anyway, and this was against a horse to whom he had given 2st and a beating in the Hennessy. That run prompted Nicholls to consider fitting Denman with a sheepskin noseband – which he has before with Kauto Star and Master Minded. Like Kauto Star, Denman has now had more runs and is older than the average winner, but also like his illustrious stablemate he has never been out of the first two when completing over fences. Clearly a massive player as he scores highly on all the other trends, and while the softer the ground the better his chance in relation to Kauto Star, he is by no means a plodder and deserves respect whatever the surface.

Cooldine

8 b g; Trainer Willie Mullins
Chase form 13114P2
Left-handed 311P2, best RPR 170
Right-handed 14, best RPR 149
Cheltenham form 71
At the festival 14 Mar 07: Tracked leaders, ridden over 2f out, no impression over 1f out, faded, finished 7th, beaten 5^3/4l by Cork All Star in Champion Bumper

11 Mar 09: always well in touch and going well, progress to track leader 12th, mistake 15th, led 2 out, shaken up and 8 lengths clear last, stayed on strongly, won RSA Chase by 16l from Horner Woods

Beat subsequent Arkle winner Forpadyde-plasterer in a Grade 1 novice over 2m5f in his warm-up for last season's RSA Chase and there was little doubt he was going to improve for 3m if his fencing held up, which it did exceptionally well. Indeed, while the jumping of several rivals went to pieces under the pressure of the fierce pace set by Carruthers in

Kauto Star has a strong chance of joining the select band of triple Gold Cup winners

the RSA, Cooldine travelled and jumped supremely well throughout and was ready to take command when the leader made a massive howler three out, eventually strolling home by 16 lengths from Horner Woods. The finishing order behind him might have been slightly different in an error-free contest, but the right horse won and Cooldine was awarded an RPR of 170, which made him the joint-best RSA winner of the last 15 years alongside Looks Like Trouble, who won the RSA in 1999

and the Gold Cup a year later. It has been anything but plain sailing since, with a below-par fourth at the Punchestown festival put down to an infection, and a delayed return to action not seeming to have helped connections get to the bottom of things. Though well backed in the Grade 1 Lexus Chase at Leopardstown over Christmas, Cooldine was always struggling and was pulled up before the last. He reportedly coughed and 'scoped wrong', and certainly did much better next time when runner-up to Joncol in the Irish Hennessy, having been able to set his own modest gallop. His failure to win a race this season is a major black mark and he won't have Ruby Walsh on board at Cheltenham.

What A Friend

7 b g; Trainer Paul Nicholls
Chase form 116121 (all left-handed), best RPR 163
Cheltenham form 3P16
At the festival 14 Mar 08: In touch, headway to chase leaders 5th, lost place and blundered 9th, behind when pulled up before last in Albert Bartlett Novices' Hurdle won by Nenuphar Collonges

11 Mar 09: mostly in midfield, urged along from 11th, never any real impression on leaders, left behind from 16th, plugged on to finish sixth in RSA Chase, beaten 30l by Cooldine

Paul Nicholls' third string scores relatively highly on trends, being a young, lightly raced chaser with a recent Grade 1 win to his name. However, he is no certainty to run with Nicholls holding such a strong hand and he does have his share of negatives. The biggest of them, though not from a trends point of view, is a failure to carry his form through to the spring in each of the last two seasons, with his two appearances at the festival (pulled up in the Albert Bartlett, distant sixth in the RSA last season) being among the worst runs of his life. It's not that he doesn't like Cheltenham, as prior to this season his best form over both hurdles and fences was at the track, so it is tempting to put it down to being a horse who doesn't stand a lot of racing. His only win after the month of December came in April last season when he was 1-3 in a four-runner race in which his only serious market rival broke down. As well as failing to have won or been placed at a previous festival (which eight of the last ten winners had achieved), he also falls short of the benchmark 170 RPR that has been achieved going into the race by nine of the last ten winners. RPR awarded a mark of just 163 for What A Friend's hard-fought Lexus victory over Joncol at Leopardstown in December and his previous run, when beaten in receipt of 22lb from Denman in the Hennessy, was an indication of just how much he has to find.

Take his spring form into account and he'd be a long way from first on the list in betting without the big two, let alone with them in it.

Imperial Commander

9 b g; Trainer Nigel Twiston-Davies
Chase form 114161P25, best RPR 177
Left-handed 114112, best RPR 177
Right-handed 6P5, best RPR 144
Cheltenham form 146711411, best RPR 169
At the festival 14 Mar 07: not fluent 3rd, soon weakened two out, finished seventh, beaten 14l by Massini's Maguire in Ballymore Properties Novices' Hurdle

12 Mar 09: tracked leaders, led 9th, ridden 3 out, stayed on gamely run-in, won Ryanair Chase by 2l from Voy Por Ustedes

Most people's idea of the biggest danger to Kauto Star and Denman and a real course specialist, having won four of his five chase starts at Cheltenham (only defeat coming when having a back problem and not jumping well from the start). Falls down on a couple of key trends as he has not won a Graded chase this season and has yet to win over 3m. This time last year the trip was a major doubt and connections sidestepped the Gold Cup to run him in the Ryanair, which he won in commanding fashion from Voy Por Ustedes, and that race would offer by far his easiest chance of more festival glory. Trainer Nigel Twiston-Davies is not one to shirk a challenge, however, and is sticking to the Gold Cup plan despite another poor show in the King George. His run in the Betfair Chase will have done enough to assuage most punters' doubts about his stamina and, had the verdict gone the other way, he would fulfil more major trends criteria than any other horse. The photo finish showed he'd lost out by a nose to Kauto Star at level weights, but he was in front both before and after the line and there aren't many down the years that have been able to serve it up to the defending champion. The King George proved a major disappointment for the second year running, with a hefty mistake at the second effectively ending his hopes of being competitive, but an equally woeful run in that contest the previous season did not stop him from landing the Ryanair and it has long been apparent that this is a horse who goes exceptionally well fresh. If there is a horse likely to be in with a shout against the big two three from home, he is probably the one, though many have been 'broken' trying, so a place is by no means guaranteed.

Carruthers

7 b g; Trainer Mark Bradstock
Chase form 2114512, best RPR 165
Left-handed 21412, best RPR 165
Right-handed 15, best RPR 158
Cheltenham form 042

At the festival 14 Mar 08: led, headed approaching 2 out, mistake and soon weakened, finished 11th, beaten 57l by Nenuphar Collonges in Albert Bartlett Novices' Hurdle

11 Mar 09: made most at strong pace, pressed when terrible blunder 3 out, headed next, very tired after and lost 2 places, finished fourth, beaten 29l by Cooldine in RSA Chase

Definite improver, but likely to come into the race with fairly weak trends claims despite being a lightly raced chaser with a victory to his name this season. He has yet to taste success at Grade 1 level, falls well short of being within 8lb of the RPR top-rated (though

so does everything other than Denman), doesn't have a pre-race rating of 170 and has not been placed at the festival. On the plus side, he nearly was placed there last year when leading the field a merry dance in the RSA until a bone-crunching mistake at the third-last meant it was just a matter of how many places he would lose before crossing the line. In fairness, he had broken most of the field and would have finished second at worst behind Cooldine without that error. He proved a disappointment when only fifth on his return off top weight in the Badger Ales at Wincanton, but he was reportedly badly in need of the run, which was due to be a prep for the Hennessy. He missed that race after a minor setback and was much better when turned out at the end of December to win a competitive little conditions race with any amount in hand from Big Fella Thanks. That run suggests he'd have at least gone close in receipt of 24lb from Denman in the Hennessy, but it has to be pointed out that all his chase victories have come when being able to dominate in small fields, largely on softish ground. When taken on in the Argento Chase at Cheltenham in January, he had no answer to the finishing burst of Taranis. No more than an outside place hope at best.

Carruthers is best when able to dominate in small fields and is no more than an outside hope

Notre Pere

9 b g; Trainer Jim Dreaper
Chase form 211F63P41121F544U, best RPR 173
Left-handed 1F6112544, best RPR 173
Right-handed 213P41FU, best RPR 173

Became the first Irish-trained winner of the Welsh National last season and continued his upward progression when second to Neptune Collonges in the Irish Hennessy and then running out an easy winner of the Guinness Gold Cup at Punchestown in April. That was enough to suggest he could improve to challenge the very best with another season on his back, but the 2009-10 campaign has been little short of disastrous. He was still travelling okay when falling behind The Listener in the JNwine.com Champion Chase at Down Royal on his return, but subsequently trailed in 50-lengths fifth of seven behind Kauto Star in the Betfair Chase at Haydock and then 16-lengths fourth to What A Friend in the Lexus. He was fourth again in the Irish Hennessy and, though he gave the impression he would have done better in a stronger-run race, he was well cooked when unseating two out dropped in grade at Fairyhouse. Needs soft ground to show up and has stacks of negatives against him.

Other contenders

There are no other serious win prospects, but there is a market without Kauto Star and Denman, so there are others worth talking about. If you are surprised not to see **Madison Du Berlais** among the main contenders, don't be. All his best form has been on flat tracks and he has yet to run within a stone of his best form at Cheltenham, so it would be a surprise if he could bustle up the best of the rest here, let alone the big two. **Taranis** burst to prominence when he beat Carruthers in the Argento in January but, though he is entitled to improve again after such a long layoff, he could be overrated by the win. **Albertas Run** is a former RSA winner who has run second to Kauto Star in a King George, so he is worthy of consideration if he gets the go-ahead (has also been put in the Ryanair and proved he had the speed for 2m5f when winning over a tad shorter at Ascot in November). **My Will** was fifth last term and is a spring horse who could well use this as a stepping stone for the Grand National again, as could 2009 National winner **Mon Mome**, who travelled well for a long way behind Our Vic at Haydock in January and has plenty of decent Cheltenham handicap form. **Money Trix** would need very soft ground to get the go-ahead. ■

Taranis (far side) could be overrated by his Argento win, though he is entitled to improve

TOTESPORT CHELTENHAM GOLD CUP CHASE (GRADE 1)

Friday 3.20   3m2¹/₂f

FORM		WINNER	AGE	& WGT	WINNING RPR	PRE-RACE RPR	SP	TRAINER	Ch.Runs	BEST RPR LAST 12 MONTHS (RUNS SINCE)
09	2-1U1	Kauto Star CD	9	11-10	184	184	7-4F	P Nicholls	20(16GS)	won King George VI Chase Gd1 (3m) (0)
08	1-111	Denman C, D	8	11-10	185	180	9-4	P Nicholls	8(12GS)	won Hennessy Gold Cup Gd3 (3m2¹/₂f) (2)
07	11111	Kauto Star	7	11-10	175	184	5-4F	P Nicholls	10(18GS)	won Betfair Chase Gd1 (3m) (3)
06	11152	War Of Attrition	7	11-10	173	167	15-2	M Morris (Ir)	9(22G)	2nd Lexus Chase Gd1 (3m) (0)
05	B1211	Kicking King	7	11-10	177	177	4-1F	T Taaffe (Ir)	11(15G)	won King George VI Chase Gd1 (3m) (0)
04	11-21	Best Mate CD	9	11-10	174	178	8-11F	Miss H Knight	12(10G)	won Ericsson Chase Gd1 (3m) (0)
03	21-11	Best Mate CD	8	12-0	178	176	13-8F	Miss H Knight	9(15G)	won Gold Cup Gd1 (3m2¹/₂f) (2)
02	2-122	Best Mate C	7	12-0	176	172	7-1	Miss H Knight	6(18G)	2nd King George VI Chase Gd1 (3m) (0)
01		Cancelled								
00	-31P1	Looks Like Trouble C	8	12-0	173	173	9-2	Noel T Chance	10(12GF)	won Cotswold Chase Gd2 (3m1¹/₂f) (0)
99	-41P3	See More Business C	9	12-0	172	172	16-1	P Nicholls	13(12GS)	won Rehearsal Chase Gd2 Ch (3m) (2)

WINS-RUNS: 6yo 0-3, 7yo 4-21, 8yo 3-42, 9yo 3-35, 10yo 0-31, 11yo 0-13, 12yo+ 0-5 **FAVOURITES:** £4.35

TRAINERS IN THIS RACE (w-pl-r): P Nicholls 4-4-22, Miss H Knight 3-0-6, J J O'Neill 0-2-6, N Richards 0-1-1, N Meade 0-2-3, W Mullins 0-3-6

FATE OF FAVOURITES: 3401110121 **POSITION OF WINNER IN MARKET:** 8231113121

RECORD OF IRISH RUNNERS: 2-7-29 (-£15.50) **HORSES WEARING HEADGEAR:** 1-6-29 (-£12.00)

RECORD OF TRIAL WINNERS: Hennessy Cognac Gold Cup (Newbury, November) **PP57618**; King George VI Chase (Kempton, December) **P4011121**
Lexus Chase (Leopardstown, December) **U9F1P0013**; Cotswold Chase (Cheltenham, January) **15526**
Irish Hennessy Chase (Leopardstown, February) **326F004**; Aon Chase (Newbury, February) **404118**
Previous year's Gold Cup winner **401122**; Previous year's RSA Chase winner **10P19**

Key trends

▶▶Two to five runs that season, 10/10
▶▶Aged between seven and nine, 10/10
▶▶Previous Grade 1 chase winner, 10/10
▶▶Rated within 8lb of RPR top-rated, 10/10
▶▶Won Graded chase that season, 10/10
▶▶Ran between six and 14 times over fences, 9/10
▶▶Finished first or second in any race at Cheltenham, 9/10
▶▶Achieved pre-race chase RPR of at least 170, 9/10
▶▶Won or placed previously at the festival, 8/10
▶▶Won over at least 3m, 8/10

Other factors

▶▶Last year Kauto Star overcame two long-standing hoodoos. He became the first horse to regain his crown and, secondly, he was the first winner to improve on a placed effort from 12 months earlier since Bregawn in 1983
▶▶In the last ten years horses starting 16-1 or bigger have finished in the top three 13 times (one win, six runners-up and six thirds)
▶▶Denman, War Of Attrition, Kicking King and Best Mate all had made the frame in championship novice hurdles here at the festival suggesting an ability to travel and hold a position is a key attribute

Notes

HOW DO THE LEADING CONTENDERS CONFORM TO THE GOLD CUP TRENDS?

	2 to 5 runs that season, 10/10	Aged seven to nine, 10/10	Previous Grade 1 chase winner, 10/10	Rated within 8lb of RPR top-rated, 10/10	Won Graded chase that season, 10/10	6 to 13 runs over fences, 9/10	Pre-race RPR of at least 170, 9/10	Won or placed at the festival, 8/10	Won over at least 3m, 8/10	TOTAL
Albertas Run	✔	✔	✔	✗	✔	✗	✔	✔	✔	7
Carruthers	✔	✔	✗	✗	✗	✔	✗	✗	✔	4
Cooldine	✔	✔	✔	✗	✗	✔	✔	✔	✔	7
Denman	✗	✗	✔	✔	✔	✗	✔	✔	✔	6
Imperial Commander	✔	✔	✔	✗	✗	✔	✔	✔	✗	6
Kauto Star	✔	✗	✔	✔	✔	✗	✔	✔	✔	7
Madison Du Berlais	✔	✗	✔	✗	✗	✗	✔	✗	✔	4
Money Trix	✔	✔	✗	✗	✗	✔	✗	✗	✔	4
Notre Pere	✔	✔	✔	✗	✗	✗	✔	✗	✔	5
Rare Bob	✗	✔	✔	✗	✗	✔	✗	✗	✔	4
Taranis	✗	✔	✗	✗	✗	✗	✗	✔	✔	3
Tricky Trickster	✗	✔	✔	✗	✔	✔	✔	✔	✔	7
What A Friend	✔	✔	✔	✗	✔	✔	✗	✗	✔	6

Based on results up to February 1, 2010

Notes

4.00
Race 5
Christie's Foxhunter Chase

C4/RUK

3m2¹/₂f

Key stats Fourteen of the last 19 winners were aged between seven and nine, and three of the five exceptions were previous winners of the race. Six of the last nine winners have started at 14-1 or above

Gerald Delamere's view Before 1978 this event was run over four miles and well-known horses such as Spartan Missile, Grittar, Venture To Cognac, Observe, Rushing Wild, Earthmover and Kingscliff have been successful in the 31 renewals since.

With many winners coming from traditional pointing yards – roughly 66% over that period – this is not the strongest event for trends. Twenty-three winners came from the hunter chase field and, of the eight that came direct from pointing, six have been since 1995, including the past three. All the pointers had recently finished first or second. The last-time-out record of the hunter chasers reads 111111211111111111113111, so it's hard to make excuses for anything but winning form.

The age range in this event isn't hugely helpful, being from six to 13, with nine in double digits. Six favourites and six second favourites have won. In the 31 renewals there was hardly a real shock until 2002, but since then three 20-1 chances and a 33-1 have won.

Richard Barber is the top trainer with four wins, his last in 1998. Since then Paul Nicholls, who is closely connected with Barber, has had two successes, including Earthmover (2004), who had won for Barber six years earlier.

The first Irish-trained winner was in 1983 and there have been just four since. The key Irish trial is the hunter chase at Leopardstown in early February (won this year by Kilty Storm from Dusty Doolan and Agus A Vic).

Various reliable hunter chases at courses such as Newbury, Warwick, Lingfield and

CHRISTIE'S FOXHUNTER CHASE CHALLENGE CUP

Friday 4.00　　　　　　　　　　　　　　　　　　　　　　　　　　　　　　3m2¹/₂f

FORM	WINNER	AGE	& WGT	WINNING PRE-RACE RPR	RPR	SP	TRAINER	Ch.Runs	BEST RPR LAST 12 MONTHS (RUNS SINCE)
09 1-111	Cappa Bleu	7	12-0	147	130	11-2	Mrs Edward Crow	6(24GS)	won Chaddersley Corbett open (3m) (0)
08 -P211	Amicelli	9	12-0	137	137	33-1	Mrs C Coward	8(23GS)	won Brocklesby Park open (3m) (1)
07 19F0-	Drombeag	9	12-0	134	134	20-1	Jonjo O'Neill	8(24G)	9th Christie's Foxhunter Ch (3m21/2f) (2)
06 1-34U	Whyso Mayo	9	12-0	126	117	20-1	Raymond Hurley (Ir)	5(24G)	3rd Punchestown hunt ch (3m1f) (2)
05 5-1U1	Sleeping Night	9	12-0	153	156	7-2F	P Nicholls	12(24G)	won Wetherby class 6 hunt ch (3m1f) (2)
04 -11P2	Earthmover CD, BF	13	12-0	140	152	14-1	P Nicholls	36(24G)	won Cheltenham class 6 hunt ch (3m21/2f) (3)
03 11-11	Kingscliff	6	12-0	140	152	11-4F	Mrs S Alner	1(24G)	won Wincanton class 6 hunt ch (3m1f) (0)
02 P4-43	Last Option CD	10	12-0	131	132	20-1	R Tate	20(20G)	4th Scottish National Gd3 (4m1f) (2)
01	cancelled								
00 P-221	Cavalero C	11	12-0	137	139	16-1	H Manners	19(24GF)	2nd Haydock class 6 hunt ch (3m) (1)
99 1-111	Castle Mane D	7	12-0	146	128	9-2	Mrs Caroline Bailey	1(24GS)	won Warwick class 6 hunt ch (3m2f) (0)

WINS-RUNS: 6yo 1-2, 7yo 2-22, 8yo 0-35, 9yo 4-41, 10yo 1-43, 11yo 1-48, 12yo 0-27, 13yo 1-12, 14yo 0-5 **FAVOURITES:** -£1.75

FATE OF FAVOURITES: 25P1P1P2P0 **POSITION OF WINNER IN MARKET:** 2001519802

RECORD OF IRISH RUNNERS: 1-7-44 (-£23.00) **HORSES WEARING HEADGEAR:** 1-2-34 (-£13.00)

Sandown have vanished, so putting forward a noteworthy British race is difficult. Many more horses now qualify between the flags.

Last year's runner-up, **Turthen**, won in much the fastest time of the day at the mid-February meeting at Milborne St Andrew, where 2003 winner Kingscliff completed his preparation. ■

Key trends
▶▶Won over at least 3m, 10/10
▶▶Recorded a pre-race RPR of at least 128, 9/10
▶▶Ran between 12 and 33 days ago, 9/10
▶▶Aged ten or younger, 8/10
▶▶Rated within 11lb of RPR top-rated, 7/10
▶▶Won last time out, 6/10

Other factors
▶▶Record of previous year's winner is P36204, but Double Silk did achieve the double in 1994
▶▶Three winners had competed at the festival before, and all three had achieved a top-four finish
▶▶Five winners were former handicap chasers

and five had progressed through the point-to-point scene
▶▶In recent times Fantus (twice), Rushing Wild (1992), Amicelli (2008) and Cappa Bleu (last year) came here direct from a prep in a point-to-point
▶▶Five of the last nine winners started between 16-1 and 33-1
▶▶Five of the beaten favourites were trained in Ireland
▶▶In the last ten years seven horses aged eight or less have won or made the frame (59 have tried)
▶▶At the other end of the age range, 12-year-olds-plus have yielded just one win and one place (44 have run)

4.40 Race 6
Martin Pipe Conditional Jockeys' Handicap Hurdle
RUK
2m4¹/₂f

This is the newest race at the festival and last year's inaugural running produced a shock result as 25-1 shot Andytown scored in the hands of Felix de Giles, followed home by 100-1 chance Midnight Chase. The David Pipe-trained favourite Big Eared Fran was third and the desire to win a race named in honour of his father is likely to see Pipe have a big representation again (last year he had seven of the 23 runners).

MARTIN PIPE CONDITIONAL JOCKEYS' HANDICAP HURDLE

Friday 4.40 2m4¹/₂f

FORM	WINNER	AGE & WGT	OR	SP	TRAINER	H.Runs	BEST RPR LAST 12 MONTHS (RUNS SINCE)
09 -4134	Andytown C, D	6 11-2	133⁶	25-1	N Henderson	7⁽²³GS⁾	won Chelt class 3 cond hcp hdl (2m5f) (1)

WINS-RUNS: 5yo 0-3, 6yo 1-11, 7yo 0-3, 8yo 0-3, 9yo 0-2, 12yo 0-1 **FAVOURITES:** -£1.00

FATE OF FAVOURITES: 3 POSITION OF WINNER IN MARKET: 0

OR 128-131 0-2-11, 132-136 1-1-9, 137-140 0-0-3

5.15
Race 7

Johnny Henderson Grand Annual Chase
(Grade 3 Handicap)

RUK

2m¹/₂f

Key stats Eleven of the last 14 winners have been sent off no bigger than 8-1. The last ten winners carried no more than 10st 11lb

Oh Crick: won from key 130-134 ratings band

Gerald Delamere's view An in-form horse is essential for this race, which recently assumed the mantle of the festival's 'getting out stakes'. The past 35 winners were placed 2132211342124F1122422P2413111F25362 last time out, with the pulled-up placing being in the Arkle Trophy and the fifth and sixth places in handicap hurdles.

Twenty-eight of the winners were aged seven to nine. Up to 1998, 12 winners carried more than 11st, but the recent trend has been in favour of lower weights (10st to 10st 11lb), with the top weight often being controlled. Three of the four to carry 10st were up to 4lb out of the handicap. Since 1982 all the winners have been rated 147 and under, while one was subsequently raised to 153. You need to be rated 128 to get in these days and something in the 130s looks right unless the weights are seriously compressed (eight of the last nine winners have been rated between 130 and 134).

Some smart horses have won this event over the years, including subsequent dual Champion Chase winner Pearlyman, who was one of nine novices to score since 1983. Two other young chasers, Katabatic and Edredon Bleu, won this race before taking the two-mile crown. That trio were rated only 135, 137 and 139 respectively when winning this race. Another novice, the 130-rated Oh Crick, saved my bacon last year.

A novice can come from anywhere and the early February meeting at Sandown has been significant over the years. Three of the past four winners had run in the race previously. With the exception of a 33-1 winner and a pair at 20-1, all the other winners were between 9-4 and 14-1, which makes this the best long-standing festival handicap for leading fancies. Eleven favourites have won, with SPs between 9-4 and 9-2, and eight second favourites have been successful.

Paul Nicholls won this for the first time with St Pirran under 10st 1lb in 2004 and since then he has had the topweight each year except for 2006. That year Nicky Henderson (whose father is commemorated by the race) foiled him with Greenhope, who carried 10st 11lb

while one of his stablemates, Tysou, was topweight. Besides Henderson and Nicholls (who has had four beaten favourites), Venetia Williams is the type of trainer whose runners should be thoroughly checked out.

There have been four Irish-trained winners in the past ten runnings, with three of them prepared in a handicap hurdle and the other, Fota Island, being a novice. ■

JOHNNY HENDERSON GRAND ANNUAL CHASE CHALLENGE CUP (HANDICAP) (GRADE 3)

Friday 5.15 — 2m½f

	FORM	WINNER	AGE & WGT	OR	SP	TRAINER	C.Runs	BEST RPRLAST 12 MONTHS(RUNS SINCE)
09	423F2	Oh Crick (1oh) C, D	6 10-0	130⁻¹³	7-1	A King	6(18GS)	2nd Hereford class 3 nov ch (2m3f) (0)
08	4P-36	Tiger Cry D	10 10-6	134⁻¹	15-2	A Moore (Ir)	12(17GS)	3rd Ascot class 2 hcap ch (2m1f) (0)
07	3-333	Andreas CD, BF	7 10-11	143⁻¹	12-1	P Nicholls	11(23GS)	3rd Sandown class 2 Gd3 hcap ch (2m) (0)
06	163-5	Greenhope C, D	8 10-11	132⁻⁹	20-1	N Henderson	5(23G)	6th Grand Annual Hcap Ch (2m1/2f) (1)
05	33212	Fota Island (2oh) D, BF	9 10-0	130⁻⁶	7-1	M Morris (Ir)	7(24G)	2nd Navan ch (2m1f) (2)
04	4/61F	St Pirran C, D, BF	9 10-1	130ᵀ	4-1F	P Nicholls	10(21G)	won Sandown class 2 hcap ch (2m) (1)
03	-2231	Palarshan (4oh) C, D	5 10-0	134⁻¹⁰	8-1	H Daly	4(21G)	won Leicester class 4 nov ch (2m) (0)
02	5-321	Fadoudal Du Cochet D	9 10-0	131⁻⁶	6-1	A Moore (Ir)	11(18G)	3rd Fairyhouse hcap ch (2m1/2f) (1)
01		cancelled						
00	7-111	Samakaan D	7 10-11	132ᵀ	9-2F	Miss Venetia Williams	3(16GF)	won Newbury class 3 nov ch (2m2½f) (0)
99	76-F3	Space Trucker C, D	8 10-1	123ᵀ	7-2F	Mrs J Harrington (Ir)	6(15GS)	fell Punchestown ch (2m) (0)

WINS-RUNS: 5yo 1-6, 6yo 1-24, 7yo 2-35, 8yo 2-51, 9yo 3-39, 10yo 1-27, 11yo 0-13, 13yo 0-1 **FAVOURITES:**£5.00

FATE OF FAVOURITES: 112510F620 **POSITION OF WINNER IN MARKET:** 1125130422

OR 121-132 7-12-89, **133-146** 3-17-95, **147-158** 0-1-12

RECORD OF IRISH RUNNERS: 4-4-36 (-£8.00) **HORSES WEARING HEADGEAR:** 0-2-28 (-£28.00)

Key trends

▶▶Distance winner, 10/10

▶▶Officially rated 130 to 143, 9/10 (eight between 130 and 134)

▶▶No more than 12 runs over fences, 10/10

▶▶Carried no more than 10st 11lb, 10/10

▶▶Aged nine or under, 9/10

▶▶No more than four runs since August, 8/10

▶▶Started no bigger than 8-1, 8/10

Other factors

▶▶There have been four winning novices, and all were rated between 130 and 134

▶▶From a combined total of 34 outings prior

to this race in the current season, the winners finished out of the frame on only seven occasions

▶▶Four winners prepped for this with a run over hurdles

▶▶Six winners had previous festival form, including the last three who all ran in the race previously

▶▶Since 2005 when the race was renamed in honour of his father, Nicky Henderson's runners have finished 346, 180P, 80, 20, 3P

▶▶The record of the previous year's winner is 0045

Get a head start on the Flat!

RACING POST

GUIDE TO THE FLAT 2010
incorporating Racing Post Horses to Follow

A new combined book drawing on all the strengths of the two titles to give you double the insight into flat prospects for 2010

RACING POST
GUIDE to the FLAT

➤ **Exclusive, extended trainer interviews**
➤ **Specialist selections for horses to follow in 2010**
➤ **Expert guidance and pen-portraits for the Racing Post ten-to-follow competition**
➤ **Dark horses set to shine in 2010**
➤ **Quiet Achievers**
➤ **Topspeed, Racing Post Ratings, the best of Ireland**

Out on 20th March. Available in leading newsagents or direct from the
Racing Post **telephone hotline 01933 304858**
Online at www.racingpost.com/shop; or post this coupon below today:

I wish to order ...... copy(ies) of the Racing Post Guide To the Flat 2010 (incorporating Horses To Follow) at £7.50. I enclose my cheque or wish to pay by credit / debit card.

Card Number: .... / .... / .... / .... Start date: ...../........

Expiry Date: .... /............ Security Number (last 3 digits on back of card) ....

Name: ....

Address: ....

....

Postcode: .... Tel Number: ....

Email: ....

Return to: Raceform Ltd, Sanders Road, Wellingborough, NN8 4BX